RURAL VERSUS URBAN

Rural Versus Urban

THE GROWING DIVIDE
THAT THREATENS DEMOCRACY

SUZANNE METTLER

TREVOR E. BROWN

PRINCETON UNIVERSITY PRESS

PRINCETON & OXFORD

Published by Princeton University Press
41 William Street, Princeton, New Jersey 08540
99 Banbury Road, Oxford OX2 6JX

press.princeton.edu

GPSR Authorized Representative: Easy Access System Europe - Mustamäe tee 50, 10621 Tallinn, Estonia, gpsr.requests@easproject.com

All Rights Reserved

Library of Congress Control Number: 2025937105

ISBN 9780691264387
ISBN (e-book) 9780691264363

British Library Cataloging-in-Publication Data is available

Editorial: Alena Chekanov
Production Editorial: Elizabeth Byrd
Jacket: Katie Osborne
Production: Erin Suydam
Publicity: James Schneider
Copyeditor: Kelley Blewster

Printed in the United States of America

10 9 8 7 6 5 4 3 2 1

For Patrick, Jeannie, Meg, and Sally,
and in loving memory of Jody,
and for Donnelsville, Ohio

CONTENTS

LIST OF ILLUSTRATIONS

RURAL VERSUS URBAN

PART I

The Emergence
of a New Divide

Introduction

RURAL AND URBAN BECOMES
"US" VERSUS "THEM"

PATRICE HAWKINS, a Black woman in her forties, serves as the Democratic Party chairperson in a poor rural county in eastern North Carolina's coastal plains.[1] Both the Democratic and Republican Parties aim to have such leaders in place in counties nationwide, because they are responsible for organizing the party at the grassroots level, and recruiting local candidates and mobilizing support for them. Some years ago, Hawkins—wanting to make a positive difference in her community—started attending the meetings of the local Democratic Party. The mostly older members welcomed her, and within a few months they selected her to be an officer; soon after, when the county chairperson resigned, she found herself catapulted into their job.

It's hard work because, as in most rural counties, in recent decades local support for Democratic candidates has declined precipitously and the party's membership has sharply diminished. Hawkins says wistfully, "We used to be a swing county that made or broke an election in the state." But no longer. And a Democratic congressman, Bill Hefner, had represented the county from 1975 to 1999; he was one of the few Southerners to vote against the Reagan tax cuts in order to protect existing programs, and he also channeled resources to the area through his role on the Appropriations Committee. In the twenty-first century, by contrast, Republicans have held the seat in most years, and they have made strong gains in down-ticket races as well. Now, typically, when Hawkins calls a local party meeting, just twenty people will show up, and although white people make up more than half of county residents, only three now attend.

As if these challenges weren't enough, the growing vitriol and extremism on the part of local Republicans can make things feel personal and threatening. Though Trump supporters feel free to "ride around with signs on their cars," Hawkins says, "I had my Biden–Harris bumper sticker on my car, and somebody told me, 'I should run your ass right off the road.'" After that, her son grew nervous and said to her, "Mama, take that sticker off the car."

Beginning in the late 1990s, a vast gulf emerged across the political landscape, dividing white rural Americans—those living in the countryside and small towns—from urban Americans, in both cities and suburbs. It did not merely divide "coastal elites" from the heartland, or "red states" from "blue states"; rather, it runs throughout the nation, fracturing nearly every state and permeating even down-ballot elections. Republican candidates have come to seem unbeatable in most rural places, and Democrats—who have dominated the largest cities since the New Deal—bolstered their support in metro areas and gained an advantage in the suburbs that surround them. This fault line changed politics on either side, so that many people not only vote differently but also view one another as political opponents, or even as members of hostile tribes or sects. In short, the United States has become profoundly polarized by place. We have yet to fully understand, however, why this divide emerged nationwide or how it is affecting the nation's politics.

We began our research by exploring these questions from afar. We collected and analyzed data spanning roughly five decades, examining thousands of counties, the individuals who live in them, and the elected officials who represent them. We wanted to learn more about rural places in particular, because that is where politics has changed most dramatically. We hit the road and drove thousands of miles to visit rural counties. We visited primarily counties where the winning margin of Republican presidential candidates has increased the most since the late 1990s, most of which have large white majorities. We also investigated some rural counties where Black residents or Latinos make up a majority or substantial minority. Our travels took us to the wilds of northern Michigan's Lower Peninsula. In Georgia, we drove from the winding mountain roads of the north to the verdant, rich, red farmland of the south. In North Carolina, we explored eastern counties that take their livelihood from chicken production and processing, coastal ones such as those of the "inner Outer Banks," and several further inland—like those where Hawkins lives—where the departure of manufacturing industries has decimated the labor market, leaving few jobs aside from those in the fast-food restaurants that serve passersby from the nearby highways. In Ohio, we visited fertile farming areas in the north central region as well as the hilly southeastern Appalachian region. In addition, we conducted some interviews remotely with party leaders and others in rural Missouri and Texas.

These interviews revealed that rural dwellers in each state we visited face similar obstacles, including the growing feeling of partisan politics as "us" versus "them." Many Democratic county chairs told us about local supporters of the party who've become afraid to put political signs in their yard or sign a petition, for fear of losing friends, the services of repairmen, or even their job. Local businesspeople worry they'll lose customers if they reveal their political preferences. A few even mentioned receiving death threats. Nevertheless, these leaders themselves typically added that they refused to be intimidated.

By contrast, Republican Party county chairs in rural places have more often experienced growing opportunities. These trends have generally been decades in the making. They have also been accentuated since the rise of the Tea Party starting in 2010, and later the emergence of Donald Trump as a presidential candidate. In Michigan's Lower Peninsula, chairperson Kent Wilson told us that when Trump ran for office in 2016, "that was probably the biggest following that I had seen of banners, flags, and signs that were out for any presidential candidate in my lifetime." This enthusiasm among the rural electorate—predominantly white, as were its local leaders—helped Trump flip the state. In Wilson's county, where a dozen people might have attended monthly party meetings in the past, now hundreds do.

These rural Republicans despaired about place-based divisions, but from a different vantage point than Democrats. Rick Swenson, another county chair in northern Michigan, explained, "You've got [fifty-eight rural] counties that are ruled by [twenty-five urban ones]." His view reflects the sense of injustice perceived by rural Republicans when a candidate who wins in the large rural swaths of the state—or the nation—loses to a candidate favored in smaller, densely populated areas. He and his fellow partisans chafed at policy changes enacted by Democrats in power in their state, whom they perceive as urbanites imposing their will on them. Wilson said simply, "We live in a rural area, so cities don't represent us."

For all the differences in their experiences, both rural Democrats and Republicans told us that they despise the rural-urban divide and the polarization it fosters. And one person after another, in each party, said that they worry about the future of democracy.

———

Why have so many rural dwellers—particularly those who identify as white, as we will see—become such strident supporters of the Republican Party in the course of thirty years or less? What could have led to such a broad and sweeping transformation that affects people living in disparate parts of the United States, so that they shifted in unison? And now that it has occurred, how is it affecting American politics?

In broad strokes, we find that the rural-urban divide began when the rural economy faltered, starting in the 1990s. Owing in large part to public policy changes, jobs diminished in agriculture, extractive industries, manufacturing, and local businesses that were supported by employees of those industries. Rural white people whose parents and grandparents had supported the Democratic Party, whether steadily or at least intermittently, came to believe that it had abandoned them, and they turned away from it. Meanwhile, many urban areas grew to be the core of the new American economy, and they became even greater bastions of support for the Democratic Party than they had been previously. *Place-based economic inequality* spurred the beginnings of this deep rift.

Next, especially after 2008, rural dwellers came to view Democrats as people who were better off than themselves and who had a penchant for telling them how to live their lives, through a wide variety of policies. Ironically, it's not that rural Americans disagreed so much with the policies on their merits; rather, what turned them further against the Democrats was the sense that they were imposing something on them—without listening, acknowledging their communities, or treating them with respect. Place-based economic inequality also activated anti-Black racism, encouraging white rural dwellers to view the Democratic Party as catering to Black people, a group stereotyped as urban. This second set of reactions involved rural people's perception of *elite overreach* on the part of Democrats, further provoking them to distance themselves from the party.

Organizational changes helped to cement the rural-urban divide. The Democratic Party, like many civic organizations, has been relatively weak at the local level, with only small groups of seniors volunteering to keep it afloat. Meanwhile, the Republican Party gained electoral assistance from conservative grassroots organizations on the rise in recent decades, which happen to be highly concentrated in rural places. Evangelical churches, antiabortion organizations, and gun groups conveyed messages about the changing circumstances in rural places and put the blame squarely on Democrats. They also provided the foot soldiers and social connectivity that helped to mobilize voters and channel them toward the Republican Party.

———

For democracy to function well, citizens need to have a sense that they constitute a political community.[2] In part, this requires something they share that transcends differences among them, such as, in the United States, the ideals inscribed in the Declaration of Independence and the Constitution. In addition, it necessitates a degree of fluidity among groups, so that social differences do not harden into rigid political divisions that turn groups against one another, threatening their common life. American society is characterized by all sorts of social and economic diversity—such as income group, age, race, ethnicity, gender, religion, and status regarding health, homeownership, and parenthood. Only some of these differences are salient in politics, and fewer still map onto political divisions associated with the party system. Maintaining fluidity among groups is crucial for preserving social peace and the capacity of people to work together to solve problems.

The most immediate effect of the rural-urban divide is the transformation of politics into an epic battle of "us" versus "them," or social polarization. Within many rural areas, Democrats face intimidation or marginalization. Nationwide, this political chasm is dividing American society, undermining the cross-cutting social connections that hold people together and soften tensions. While the rural-urban split is by no means the only source of such divisions today, its geographic nature makes it particularly pernicious.

In addition, in rural places, this divide fosters one-party government. Representative democracy cannot thrive under such circumstances, because without a meaningful choice in elections, citizens cannot hold their representatives accountable. In places with one-party government, people are more likely to get elected not because they have good ideas or a proven record, but simply because they belong to the lone viable party, and do not face competition. At a minimum, this can lead to ineffective governance; worse yet, it can foster corruption and extremism. To be sure, many of the nation's large cities have long been subject to one-party rule. Our concerns apply there as well.

Even more, the rural-urban divide combines with several long-existing U.S. political institutions in ways that further threaten democracy. These arrangements have always given extra political leverage to people living in less populated places, yet those advantages have never before been consolidated into a single party. Now that an increasingly extreme Republican Party overwhelmingly wins in rural areas nationwide, it can exploit these small yet important advantages to gain more political power.

The rural-urban divide now gives the GOP outsized opportunities to control each of the three branches of national government. Already in the twenty-first century, two presidential elections yielded winners who lost the popular vote but triumphed in the Electoral College in part because of its rural bias. Meanwhile, the even more skewed nature of the Senate—two senators per state regardless of the now huge disparities in population—grants additional power to rural Republicans that can be used to influence legislation or judicial nominations. In fact, when Republicans held majority power in the Senate in recent decades, they were typically elected by states containing less than a majority of Americans.

Since presidents nominate federal judges and the Senate must approve them, these factors can permit stacking of the judicial branch by the party that dominates smaller, less densely populated states. Remarkably, in the current Supreme Court, most members of the conservative majority, five justices, were confirmed by senators who in combination represent less than half the U.S. population. Three of those justices were nominated by President Donald Trump after he won the 2016 election with a minority of the popular vote. Those justices have proven pivotal in undermining basic pillars of democracy, such as by declaring presidential immunity from criminal prosecution for crimes committed while in office, as well as overturning long-standing and popular precedents such as access to reproductive rights. In each of these ways, when rural voters are consolidated in one party, it can permit minority rule.

The combination of contemporary place-based polarization with U.S. institutional arrangements is threatening democracy itself. Together, these features can permit the party benefiting from them to further "stack the deck" in its favor. In time, leaders in that party may be able to change the rules to lock down their power, undermining representative government.

But it is not too late to repair the American polity. It will not be easy, and "quick fixes"—such as messaging tweaks—will not work. Neither will strategies that focus only on public policy. New policies in rural communities might improve the day-to-day lives of residents, but they are unlikely to reduce polarization by themselves. Repairing our broken polity requires rebuilding relationships. The Democratic Party needs to reestablish its presence in rural places, doing so through a long-term, full-time commitment, and by actively listening to residents. Rural dwellers deserve to have options at the voting booth, and restoring a vibrant two-party system in rural places is key to ensuring that and revitalizing American politics nationwide.

1

The Puzzle

WHY DID A RURAL-URBAN DIVIDE EMERGE?

DEBORAH EVANS, a white woman in her sixties, stepped up recently to lead the Democratic Party in a mountainous county in northwest Georgia. She grew up there, left to go to college, then lived in Los Angeles before returning some years ago to care for an aging parent. Her county, like many rural counties, is economically depressed and has seen its population decline in recent years. "People don't tend to stay here unless they just can't leave," she says.

Chairing the local party is a challenging job. Back in the 1990s, the county elected Bill Clinton to the presidency twice, but from 2000 onward it has thrown its support to Republican presidential candidates. In fact, the Republican vote share grew from 40 percent in 1996 to 80 percent in 2020. The shift began even earlier at the congressional level, when a long-serving Democratic congressman, a moderate, lost his seat in 1994; Republicans have held it ever since, and more extreme ones have been elected over time.[1] In 2020, the district elected Marjorie Taylor Greene, a conspiracy-embracing, white-supremacist, hard-right public official who quickly became a leading voice in Congress for the "Make America Great Again" base within the Republican Party. In 2022 and again in 2024, she won reelection by a landslide.

"There's a pervading sense of hopelessness in this county," Evans explains. "People are insecure about their future. That gave rise to the Tea

Party. Then Trump made racism and hatred legitimized. . . . People here are angry, and the Republicans embrace that anger and show them where to direct it. . . . There's always a different group they are targeting—now it's trans people and drag queens; in the last election it was immigrants."

The local Democratic Party is currently "running on fumes," Evans says. "I've been chairman for five years, and nobody wants the job. One of my officers is ninety-five. I can't find anyone who will step up." The weakness of the party leads to a downward spiral, as it has become all but impossible to recruit candidates to run for office.

Evans shared pages from a local newspaper that had printed, verbatim, the minutes of the recent county Republican convention. It reported that the organization aimed "to verbalize our opposition to all WOKE, LAWLESS and CRIMINAL acts being pursued by Democrats and all liberal politicians." One resolution cited "strong and credible evidence that. . . . Covid 19 injections are biological and technological weapons," and called for vaccines in the state to be seized. Another rejected the results of the 2020 presidential election, claiming irrefutable proof of election fraud.[2] Evans notes that such an article, by "saying that we are criminals," had a chilling effect on local Democratic organizing, specifically on the group's public presence at events. As she says, "Why would we put ourselves out there?"

Variants of this story are repeated in rural areas across the United States; since the late 1990s and in some instances more recently, Democrats have faced tougher and tougher odds of winning elective office at any level, while Republicans have been on the rise. Even in rural counties that boast a growing potential Democratic constituency— such as those featuring recreational amenities that attract new retirees and remote workers—electoral victories are rare. The most stellar of candidates who are willing to run for office with the party's endorsement face daunting challenges, and the party's slate nets diminishing portions of the vote with each passing election year, making it harder to recruit candidates at all. Increasingly, rural areas are dominated by one-party GOP rule, and hostility to Democrats runs deep.

Why have most rural counties across the United States rural areas become bastions of Republican support? In particular, why did politics change in these places during the late twentieth and early twenty-first centuries? How, in turn, has this seismic shift affected U.S. governing institutions and reshaped the distribution of political power? These are the questions we seek to answer in this book. To commence our journey, in this chapter we will show how rural and urban voting patterns have changed over time, creating place-based partisan polarization. Then we probe the character of contemporary polarization, to understand whether it emanates from differences in views about public policies or something else. Finally, we consider how a political divide that did not exist in the past can come into being.

Dividing Rural and Urban Nationwide

Before we go any further, we need to ask what is meant by the term "rural," and which places and their residents are included within its scope. There are many ways to define and measure it, depending on which geographic units are used (typically census tracts or counties) and whether one accounts only for population density or takes a more complex approach. Most measures suggest that as of 2020, between 14 and 20 percent of the U.S. population lived in a rural place. Throughout the book, we take a practical approach, using the best measure available for the particular question at hand, depending on constraints such as data availability. But for the most part, we rely on a county-level measure developed by the U.S. Office of Management and Budget (OMB). This measure captures population density as well as the extent to which rural areas are—or are not—incorporated into major cities, socially and economically.[3] According to the measure, as of 2020, 86 percent of Americans lived in the 1,185 counties classified as metro or "urban," while the remaining 14 percent lived in any of the 1,958 nonmetro or "rural" counties.[4] The urban or metropolitan counties include cities, suburbs, and some less densely populated areas close to major cities. Rural areas include a wide range of locales, from the most sparsely populated ones that are far from any city to ones in a closer proximity; they may include small towns and villages.[5] Geographically, of course, the nation's rural counties occupy a much greater land mass than its urban counties, despite the population disparity. Still, as of 2020, roughly forty-six million people lived in counties designated as rural. Among the states, the biggest rural population lives in Texas followed by North Carolina, Pennsylvania, Ohio, Georgia, Michigan, New York, and Tennessee, each with over one million rural residents.[6]

Historically, Americans have not been politically divided between rural and urban places nationwide. Throughout the United States' first two centuries, each of the two major political parties routinely managed to score some victories among both rural and urban dwellers in different parts of the country. Certainly the nation featured a divide organized by geography, one that literally tore the nation apart and spurred a bloody civil war. But that division was between the South and the rest of the nation rather than being rural versus urban, and it had far less to do with place than with the freedom of Black people. Social and economic tensions have also brewed between rural and urban Americans from time to time, joined by political antagonisms on occasion, and yet the catch-all character of U.S. political parties and federal public policies that addressed rural needs prevented those divisions from spreading across the nation.

In presidential elections as recent as those in the 1970s, 1980s, and early 1990s, rural and urban counties tended to shift in tandem, each voting for the winning candidate at very similar rates, with rural ones just barely more likely than urban ones to support Republicans (figure 1.1). Both rural and urban counties offered strong support for Republican candidates Nixon and Reagan, and both threw their weight behind Democrat Bill Clinton in 1992. But from 2000 onward, a stark divide emerged as rural white people increasingly supported the Republican candidate in each election. The gulf between rural dwellers and urbanites grew from just 2 percentage points as recently as 1992 to 20 percentage points by 2024.

The rural-urban political divide has widened in all regions of the nation (figure 1.2). Certainly, it is well known that dramatic political change occurred in the South, where counties transitioned from overwhelmingly supporting Democrats in the 1960s to favoring Republicans increasingly since then. Less well known is that as the South changed, particularly since 1996, it acquired a striking divide between rural and

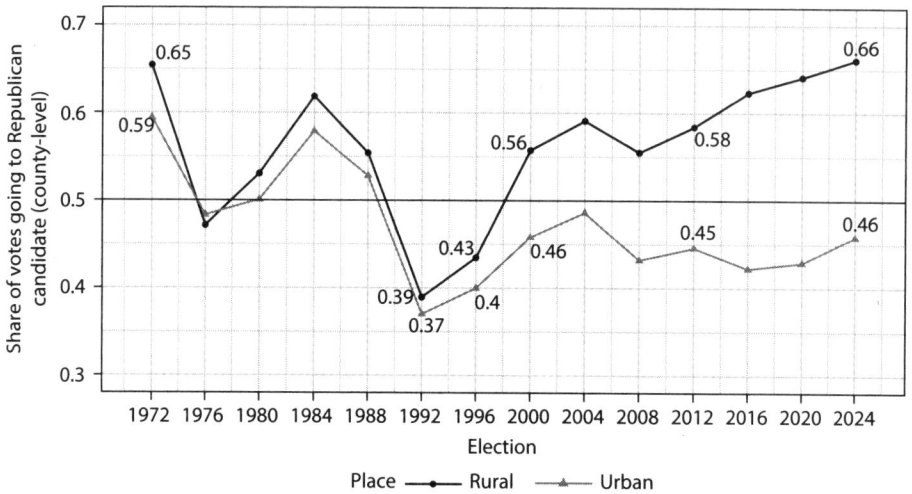

FIGURE 1.1. The emergence of the rural-urban divide in presidential voting, 1972–2024
Source: Vote returns from David Leip's Atlas of U.S. Presidential Elections; measure of rural from U.S. Office of Management and Budget (hereafter, OMB). We note that these trends are consistent with individual-level survey data.

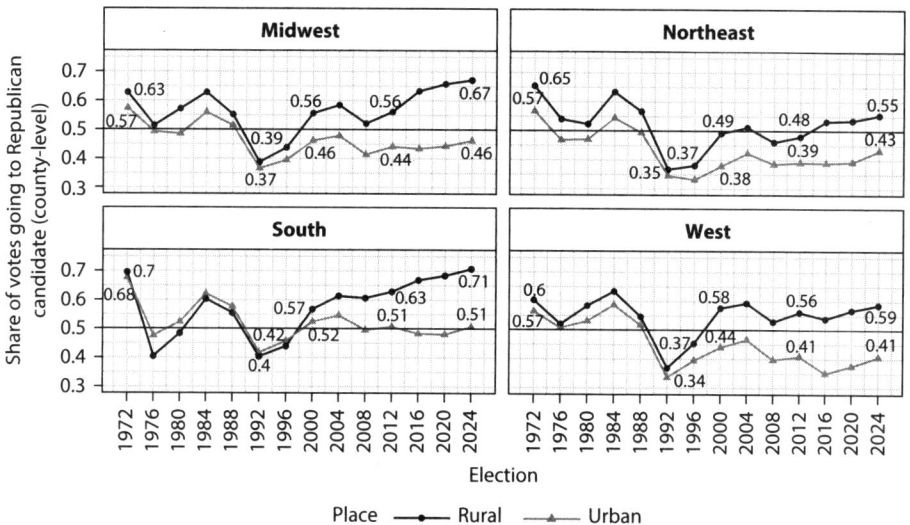

FIGURE 1.2. The rural-urban divide in presidential voting, by region, 1972–2024
Source: Vote returns from David Leip's Atlas of U.S. Presidential Elections; measure of rural from OMB

urban counties, a gap that reached 20 percentage points in the 2024 presidential election.[7] The Midwest and West, furthermore, acquired similar-sized gaps—21 and 18 percentage points, respectively, as of 2024. The divide in the Northeast has grown less than the others, though it is still 11 points.

This new geographic rift does not merely separate blue states from red states or "coastal elites" from "fly-over" territory. It permeates nearly every state. It has surpassed 20 points in states ranging from Texas to Nebraska and Missouri, as well as in several key battleground states, namely Ohio, Pennsylvania, and Georgia (figure 1.3).

The rural-urban split is now transforming down-ticket elections as well. The U.S. House of Representatives has become divided by place, with Democrats representing not only the largest cities, but also most districts containing smaller cities and suburbs, while Republicans represent the geographically larger, less densely populated districts.[8] As late as 2008, rural areas elected many individuals to Congress who helped to mitigate polarization and to forge deals across party lines. Now, by contrast, these places send to Congress some of its most conservative and uncompromising members. U.S. Senate seats in more rural states have become all but out of reach to Democrats. In sum, since the 1990s the United States has developed entrenched partisan polarization that is profoundly organized by place.

While most rural people and places have shifted to the Republican Party, not all rural dwellers have been swept up in this political tidal wave, and people of color remain for the most part unmoved by it. Rural and urban Black Americans continue to vote similarly to one another, and this is also the case among Latinos. This is significant, because even though media images of rural areas tend to focus on white people, those who do not identify as white now comprise one in four rural dwellers nationwide. They include, for example, many Black Americans in rural North Carolina and Georgia; Latinos, particularly in Texas and the Southwest, but also in many other rural places nationwide; and American Indians in several states. Certainly some have been drawn to the Republicans, or particularly to President Donald Trump: the Lumbee tribe in southeastern North Carolina warmed to him, for example, as

Share of votes going to Republican Party candidate (county-level)

Election

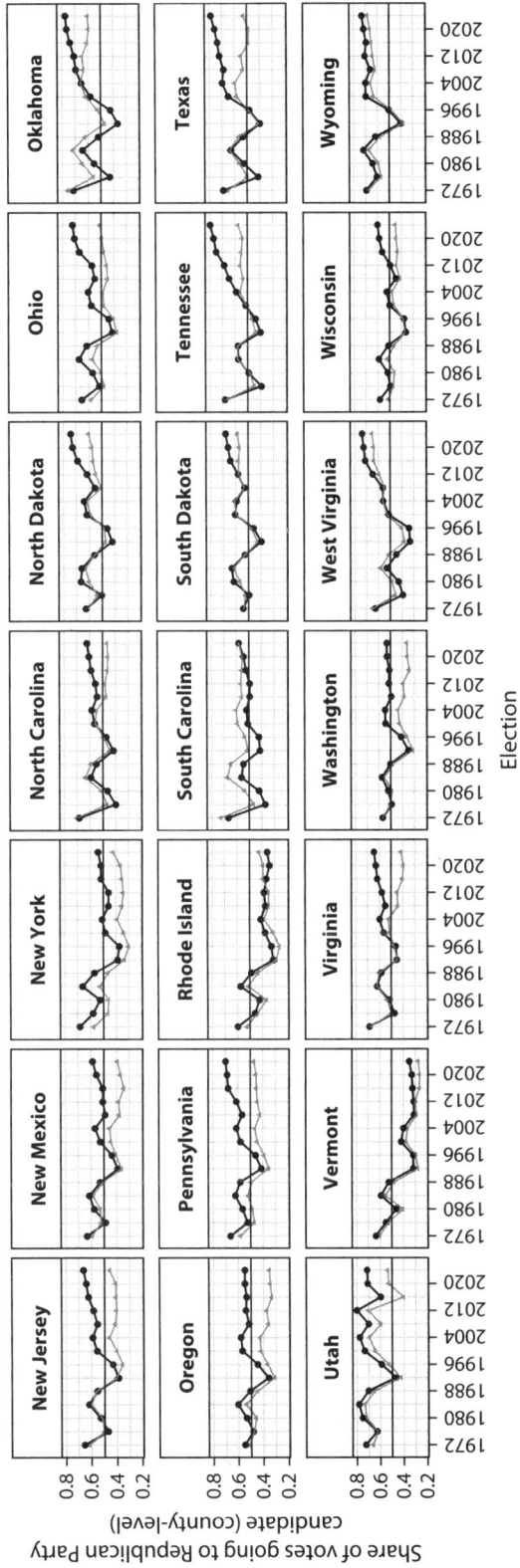

FIGURE 1.3. The rural-urban divide in presidential voting, by state, 1972–2024
Source: Vote returns from David Leip's Atlas of U.S. Presidential Elections; measure of rural from OMB

did some young Latinos in counties near the Texas border. Neverthe-less, according to our analysis, overall rural people of color have not shifted away from urban people of color; rather, they continue to vote very similarly to one another.[9]

In sum, starting in the late 1990s, a deep, insidious gulf emerged be-tween white Americans who live in rural counties and those who live in urban and suburban ones. It cuts across every region and nearly every state, with more steadfast Republican voters on the rural side and Democratic voters on the urban side.

Studying Rural Politics and Change over Time

Why did polarization in the United States take the form it did, pitting rural areas against urban ones? What explains the largest change under-lying these developments, namely, the transformation of rural places na-tionwide into Republican Party strongholds? Prominent explanations of polarization give little heed to either the timing of its development or how it varies by place. Most focus instead on individuals, stressing intrinsic aspects of human nature: individuals' psychological propensity to identify with those they perceive as their in-group and to differentiate themselves from others whom they seek to compete with and dominate.[10] This ap-proach leaves uninvestigated why people's predispositions would operate so differently today than they did thirty years ago. Presumably something changed, and that in turn altered human behavior, but what?

To the extent that scholars pay attention to historical developments to explain polarization, several highlight the relationship between race and politics, arguing that the enactment of civil rights legislation in the 1960s led to the demise of Democratic Party domination in the South and spurred conservatives to identify as Republicans and liberals as Democrats.[11] While important, these accounts cannot explain why sweeping political transformation in rural Americans' partisan behavior occurred throughout the nation, not just the South, and took place a full thirty years *after* the civil rights achievements.[12]

Others have focused on the realignment of white voters of lower so-cioeconomic status. Kicked off by journalist Thomas Frank's 2004 book,

What's the Matter with Kansas? How Conservatives Won the Heart of America, scholars have more recently—and more carefully—documented how many white working-class voters have gradually shifted to the Republican Party in the past few decades.[13] But these accounts also overlook the place-based nature of contemporary politics. If we compare two white people with similar characteristics—such as income, education, age, and religiosity—but one lives in an urban area and the other in a rural one, the rural dweller is more likely to vote for Republican candidates.[14] Put another way, focusing just on income and/or education without considering place cannot fully explain why polarization has become so pervasive throughout the polity.

In short, scholars have largely overlooked the question of why polarization takes the form that it does—dividing Americans by *place*—and why it has developed over the past three decades. To be sure, a small but growing group of researchers has begun to examine the rural-urban political divide. Katherine Cramer conducted a pathbreaking study of rural dwellers in Wisconsin, uncovering a distinct "rural consciousness" underpinned by a sense of distributive injustice, that fostered resentment of those considered urban elites.[15] Several scholars have built on her work, describing the tight link between population density and partisanship nationwide, and the various characteristics of rural identity.[16] While helping to place the rural-urban divide on social scientists' radar, this research tends to focus on the present, leaving the *causes* of the rural-urban divide largely unexplained.[17] Similarly, scholars have examined almost exclusively individuals and their attitudes, with little attention to how the place-based divide interacts with the nation's political institutions. Jonathan Rodden offers an important exception, exploring how the United States' way of electing members of the House and state legislatures privileges rural areas.[18] Yet the divide's impact on other political institutions remains underexamined, leaving its full *consequences* yet to be known.

We take a different approach.[19] We ask why this profound place-based divide ruptured when it did, and why it has intensified and spread since then. We study shifting circumstances in places throughout the United States and how they have affected Americans' lives. That includes transformation of the economy, civil society, and the relationship between government and citizens. We take a macrohistorical perspective, meaning we trace the evolution of the rural-urban divide over a longer time period, across roughly five decades.[20] First, though, we consider an alternative explanation.

Considering the Role of Policy Views and the Culture Wars

Many people assume that political polarization reflects a divide among Americans in their fundamental values, ideology, or positions on public policy issues. If that's the case, we would expect the rural-urban divide to reflect place-based differences in Americans' views about public policy, and we would expect those differences to be fairly large. If such differences exist, furthermore, it would suggest that democracy is actually functioning well, with people simply acting on their divergent views by electing public officials of different parties to represent them accordingly.[21]

Yet our fairly exhaustive analysis of public opinion surveys suggests that individuals' positions on particular policy issues cannot fully explain the rural-urban political divide in how Americans vote.[22] We first look at questions related to spending and taxation, to see if rural and urban white people actually disagree about the size of government. Both rural and urban non-Hispanic white Americans answer very similarly when they are asked about whether state legislatures should increase, decrease, or maintain spending for each of several types of state-level programs (figure 1.4). Both groups are generally supportive of spending on four of the program types—education, health care, police, and infrastructure—with only a few percentage points (1 to 3) separating them. When asked about "welfare," a descriptor of social assistance that political scientists have shown tends to elicit especially negative responses, again rural and urban white residents offer very similar answers.[23]

Some scholars have argued that the rise of social issues, or the so-called culture wars—issues such as abortion, LGBTQ rights, and gun control—is the source of polarization broadly and the rural-urban divide in

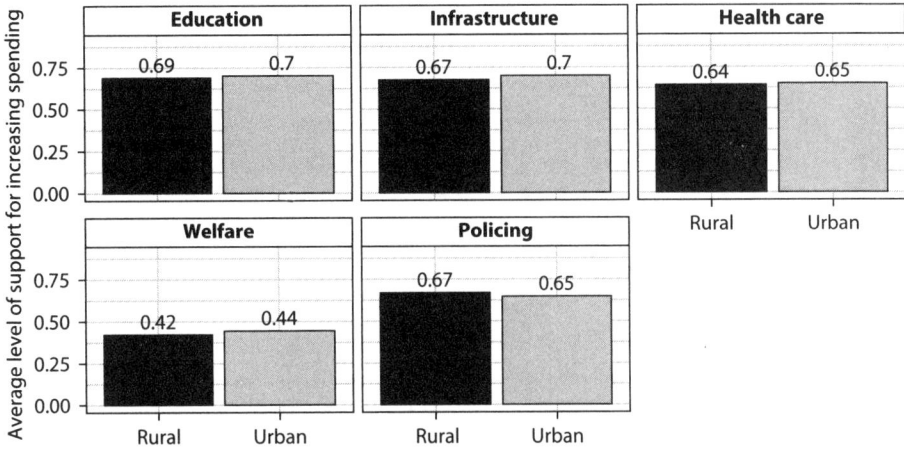

FIGURE 1.4. Non-Hispanic white Americans' views on spending, by rural and urban residence
Source: Responses from Cooperative Election Study (CES), rescaled to indicate support for spending, and pooled from years 2014, 2016, 2018, and 2020; measure of rural from OMB
Note: Error bars indistinguishable from estimates.

particular.[24] Likewise, a former senator, a Democrat who hails from a state where it now seems inconceivable to him that a member of his party could ever win again, told us, "The Democratic Party has largely been disqualified in the minds of many voters . . . due to the opening up of a cultural chasm. . . . If you go back, the Democratic Party was identified as the party of working people, farmers, people who were looking for economic opportunity, and the Democrats were seen as pretty mainstream on other cultural issues, [such as] on religion, guns, or gay rights."

To assess this claim that differences over social issues explain the rural-urban divide, first we considered views about gun control and the Second Amendment. Certainly some lawmakers and rural people we interviewed told us that guns, both for hunting and recreational shooting, are of importance to rural people.[25] But in examining several survey questions—including requiring background checks, banning assault rifles, and making it easier to conceal carry—we found that rural white people, on average, are just 8 percentage points less in favor of regulating gun use than their urban peers (figure 1.5, top left panel). While rural

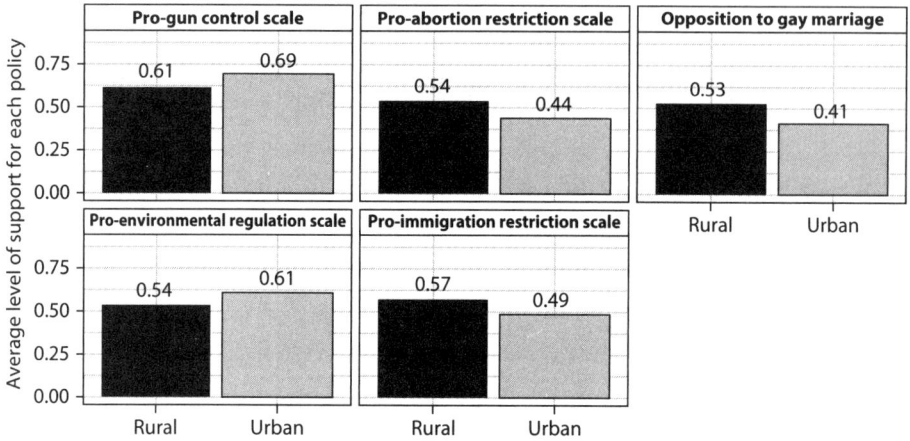

FIGURE 1.5. Non-Hispanic white Americans' views on social issues, by rural and urban residence
Source: Responses from CES, pooled for several years; measure of rural from OMB
Note: Error bars indistinguishable from estimates.

dwellers are somewhat less likely to support gun regulations, what is arguably more striking is that rural and urban dwellers overlap considerably in their views on this issue.

Next we consider abortion, an issue that has riven American politics ever since the 1971 decision that legalized it, *Roe v. Wade*, and has done so anew in the wake of the 2021 decision overturning it, *Dobbs v. Jackson Women's Health*.[26] Overall, we find that rural and urban white people differ by just 10 percentage points (figure 1.5, top middle panel).[27] This modest gap does not surprise us, given what we heard in interviews. When we asked county party leaders which issues energized voters to support them, a few Republicans mentioned abortion—and specifically a prolife position—but others did not. One county chair in Michigan, Rick Swenson, told us, "There's a huge part of the Republican Party that's just prolife, period; there's also a huge part of the Republican Party that feels the issue was decided in 1971 in *Roe v. Wade*, and that was close enough." Swenson considers himself a "constitutional conservative," and his personal stance is that abortion is "none of the government's business," but rather "between a woman, a doctor, and God." "The Constitution is clear on the separation of church and state," he added.

On gay marriage, we find that rural white people are roughly 12 percentage points less supportive than urban white people (figure 1.5, upper right panel). More remarkable is the fact that both groups have moved in parallel over time, shifting to become more accepting of gay marriage.[28] Examining several other high-profile policy issues as well, we found differences that are typically only in the single digits (see appendixes). White non-Hispanic rural dwellers hold somewhat more conservative views on some issues than urban dwellers; environmental regulation and immigration offer examples (figure 1.5, bottom row).[29]

Overall, when it comes to opinions on policies, on most issues we find few discernable differences in the views of rural and urban Americans, and on the issues where disagreement exists, the gaps are not large. When we adjust for other factors that could play a role—such as age, gender, and education—the gaps between rural and urban dwellers are reduced even further. We do not deny that attitudinal differences contribute to the rural-urban divide, and the role of such differences are likely exacerbated as elites reframe and exploit issues for political gain. But on their own, we regard the differences in views as insufficient to account for the large and growing partisan voting gap between rural and urban dwellers nationwide.[30]

More broadly, American history suggests that it doesn't make sense to consider rural people as innately more conservative than urban people. The populist movement of the late nineteenth century tried to join farmers and industrial workers together in pursuit of economic justice and a larger, more regulatory state, and it eventually led to several progressive policy achievements.[31] This same spirit infused the mobilization of farmers in the Great Plains states during the farm crisis of the 1980s, during the Reagan presidency.[32] Conversely, from the 1950s through the 1970s, white reactionary movements against the integration of Black Americans in public schools and busing were often based in cities and suburbs—hardly distinguishing them as centers of progressivism. Furthermore, as recently as the early 1990s, rural dwellers voted similarly to urban dwellers nationwide in presidential elections.

In short, although rural and urban Americans have grown deeply divided in terms of how they vote—this is the *partisan* polarization to which we refer—they are not *ideologically* polarized. In order to more fully understand this growing political gulf, we need to look elsewhere.[33]

Barely Disagreeing, but Bitterly Divided

That citizens' views on issues don't shed much light on the rural-urban political divide would come as little surprise to many scholars of political behavior, who have long shown that issue preferences are a poor explanation for contemporary polarization. As political scientists Christopher Achen and Larry Bartels explain, "Voters, even the most informed voters, typically make choices not on the basis of policy preferences or ideology, but on the basis of who they are—their social identities."[34] When it comes to politics, each of us observes what "people like us" do—which party is supported by our family, friends, or the social group with which we identify strongly. Our group attachments shape our partisanship and political behavior prior to and more routinely than our carefully discerned positions on particular issues.[35]

What can prove pivotal in shaping voting behavior, furthermore, is people's attitudes toward those in the other party. Political scientists Donald Kinder and Cindy Kam explain that human beings have a propensity to divide the world into groups—those with whom we feel solidarity and those toward whom we feel hostility. If we exaggerate both our similarity to the "in-group" and our differences from the "out-group," society may start to seem like a struggle of "us" versus "them."[36] Such hostile feelings underlie all sorts of prejudices toward groups, and in the contemporary United States, they also characterize many Americans' views toward those in the other political party.[37] "Negative partisanship," as Alan Abramowitz calls it, has grown dramatically in recent decades; Americans now see those in the other party as "very different from themselves in values and social characteristics as well as personal beliefs."[38]

Political scientist Lilliana Mason uses the term "social polarization" to define such antipathy and the political activism it engenders. She describes the psychological processes through which it arises, remarking that paradoxically, the "electorate . . . may agree on many things" when it comes to issue positions, "but nonetheless cannot get along." Rather than making dispassionate, rational assessments of candidates' issue positions and then evaluating which party to support in a given election, a partisan "behaves more like a sports fan" and evaluates their own "team" more positively than the opposing one. They support it because it "is their team," and when it wins an election, they feel a sense of personal triumph, and when it loses, it spurs negative emotions and anger at their opponents.[39] Increasingly, in a very polarized United States, politics elicits such feelings from many people.

When it comes to the rural-urban divide, although non-Hispanic white rural and urban Americans do not differ dramatically in their views of most policy issues, we find that they do diverge sharply in their attitudes about those in the other political party. In 2020, when white rural Republicans were asked to rate Democrats on a feeling thermometer from 0 to 100, they offered, on average, a dismal 14 points; white urban Democrats, similarly, put Republicans at 17 points. These low assessments of fellow citizens in the opposing party were far lower than nearly all the rankings given to other groups. For instance, white rural dwellers put Black Americans at 70, Hispanic Americans at 67, gay men and lesbians at 57, and "illegal" immigrants at 39.[40] In sum, the rural-urban partisan divide today is characterized less by differences in policy views than by a general antipathy to the political party that dominates places different from where one lives.

Creating a National Political Cleavage

This raises a basic puzzle for us. If just over three decades ago, rural and urban Americans voted more or less in tandem in presidential elections, clearly they then lacked the hostility to the other party that so many hold today. So why and how did that change? Theories about political party identity and polarization, as we have seen, offer rich descriptions of how these phenomena operate at a moment in time, solidifying and maintaining party affiliations. They do not, however, enable us to understand how a vast transformation might occur over time, such that society becomes reorganized politically. Neither do they provide conceptual tools for understanding how a seemingly innocuous form of social difference—the place where one resides—might become transformed into a gaping political divide.

The question we are investigating is, in the broadest terms, how and why a political division that did not exist previously in the United States came into being and grew—in just over a quarter century—into a major rift that is now the source of increasing dysfunction. Imagine a nation where diverse ethnic groups live together peacefully, until suddenly one group turns against another and years of bloody violence ensue. This occurred in the breakup of the former Yugoslavia with the rise of Serbian nationalism. Or picture a multicultural society in which people of different religious groups long coexist, but then at some historical juncture one group mobilizes against and seeks to dominate the other. Increasingly, this has been the fate of Muslims relative to Hindus in India, stoked by Prime Minister Narendra Modi.

Many nations experienced disruptive rural-urban political divides in the past, but the United States was not among them. When tensions emerged between rural and urban areas, they were neither national in scope nor enduring. The most prominent example, the late-nineteenth-century farmers' movement that fueled the Populist Party, gained ample supporters in the West and South, but it was resisted by many rural dwellers, even in those regions, and it did not manage to attract much support elsewhere.[41]

To analyze why the contemporary rural-urban division emerged, we draw on a classic theory developed over a half century ago by two scholars, Seymour Martin Lipset and Stein Rokkan. They reasoned that a large, diverse society may be organized politically in many different ways—for example, voters may coalesce on the basis of class, or religion, or region, or ethnicity—and the way in which they do affects the extent of political conflict in that society, and whether or not polarization occurs. In their view, political parties play a crucial role because by attracting particular alignments of voters, they have the potential to integrate local communities into the nation or, conversely, to crystallize conflicts between groups, stoking division.[42]

Some political party developments may actually lessen conflict, whereas others may heighten it. Societies are more peaceful when the inhabitants share what are known as "cross-cutting cleavages" or "cross-cutting affiliations." For example, a person's family might be mostly affiliated with one political party, but they may encounter and associate with those in the other party in their workplace, neighborhood, church, or civic association, or even in several of those. These cross-cutting cleavages help members of opposing parties understand each other and establish some degree of mutual respect, trust, and tolerance. Americans experienced such ties fairly commonly in the post–World War II period and through the 1980s. By contrast, when individuals or groups with the same political disposition associate only with others who share their own party identity, it can make people become more intolerant of others' views and more supportive of extremists in their own ranks.[43] As Paul Pierson and Eric Schickler put it, today Americans find that their social identities do not engage them in cross-cutting affiliations, but rather they are "stacked" on top of each other, lining up by partisanship.[44] In other words, Americans now associate mostly with others who vote the same way they do, whether in their neighborhoods, workplaces, or associations.[45] As this has occurred, people who live in different places also regard each other with growing disdain, as we saw earlier.

We find Lipset and Rokkan's theories helpful for thinking about the processes through which politics can become divided by place. They were interested in how some form of difference in society—a social cleavage—may become mapped onto politics and acquire political meaning and significance, such that a political divide or cleavage emerges where it did not exist previously. They understood two fundamental processes of change to drive partisan divisions: one involving *political-economic transformation* and the other involving the *territorial relationship* between more centralized and populated places versus those peripheral to them. Although they were focused on Europe in the late nineteenth and early twentieth centuries, considering how industrialization and the spread of global trade affected partisan divisions in various nations, we update their theory to address our current period. We understand them to have been advancing a two-step theory, to which we also add a third, *organizational* dimension. We call this process, involving all three dimensions, "sequential polarization."

Growing Place-Based Inequality Spurs a Nationwide Divide

Sweeping economic changes and the policies accompanying them may produce conflict over resources, products, or benefits, which can in turn fuel changes in party politics.[46] In the 1990s and early 2000s, economic changes roiled the landscape, causing rural areas in general to stagnate in terms of economic and population growth, and many to hemorrhage jobs and people. Historically, rural areas have disproportionately relied on farming and extractive industries. Throughout the 1980s, many family farms went under, replaced by agribusiness. By the 1990s, technological advances meant that fewer workers were required in gas, coal, and other forms of mining. For a time, jobs in manufacturing, which had migrated out of urban areas, helped soften the blow. But those vanished as the North American Free Trade Agreement (NAFTA) and other trade policies prompted companies to shutter their plants. Meanwhile, many urban areas have grown to become the epicenter of economic growth in the United States, buoyed by policies promoted by a bipartisan coalition of lawmakers, including several prominent urban Democrats. The confluence of these trends fostered place-based economic inequality.

These circumstances often became apparent as we interviewed rural county chairs. In Hawkins's North Carolina county, few public places exist where people can have a quiet conversation, so instead we met up for coffee in a fast-food restaurant on a busy strip just off the highway. She explained that the good-paying manufacturing jobs of the past are gone, unemployment runs high, and more than one in four local residents live in poverty. Hawkins is among the one in six over age twenty-five with a four-year college degree. "I was born here—I never left, unfortunately," she added with a laugh. "There's nothing here," she said, gesturing to the big-box chain stores lining the street—Walmart, Dollar General, and others. "They're trying to build up all this shopping stuff. No, we gotta have opportunity! You can shop anywhere, but if I ain't making enough money to buy nothing, what's the point of having all that?" She noted, "The only lucrative jobs I've had are jobs that are outside of the county." She worked for years at a local social service agency that paid her only $33,000 a year, despite her degree and years of experience. She finally sought a job in a neighboring county and gained a $15,000 raise by doing so, but it requires a long commute, as is common among many rural dwellers.

We argue that such changes in the rural economy nationwide spurred political change. They left many residents disillusioned with the Democratic Party, which many of their parents and grandparents had long viewed as the advocate of their interests. In fact, Republicans initiated most of the policy shifts that ushered in key changes, but several came to fruition when Bill Clinton served as president, and some Democrats in Congress played leading roles in their passage. The Democratic Party therefore seemed responsible. Rural dwellers began to abandon the party, commencing the rural-urban divide.

Meanwhile, as conditions worsened in rural areas nationwide, many urban economies boomed, owing to the development of the "knowledge economy"—meaning high-end services involving technology, business services, and finance.[47] These places increasingly attracted highly educated Americans—including those from rural locales—as their position at the center of the nation's economic growth was bolstered by policies supported by many Democrats. With it, a distinct politics emerged, and it would foster the second dynamic, one that deepened the growing rural-urban divide.

Elite Overreach Deepens a Growing Divide

The second dimension involves how people living in more remote places may resist what they perceive as the encroachment of dominant national elites seeking to impose their will on the populace through public policies and administrative development.[48] Some policies that rural dwellers may experience this way involve the incorporation of Americans as equal citizens, such as those that require states and localities to guarantee rights to all regardless of race, ethnicity, gender, or sexuality.[49] Others use state power to address noneconomic issues ranging from environmental concerns to gun control or liberalizing immigration.

As the 2000s continued, rural white people—aware of the growing economic inequality between the places where they lived and thriving urban areas—began to perceive the Democratic Party as prioritizing the concerns of urban elites. These urbanites were not only materially better off than rural dwellers, but now they also sought to impose their preferences nationwide, through the power of government. Characterizing Democrats, Matthew Novak, a Republican county chair in northern Michigan, remarked, "They seem completely detached from how people live here." It was not so much that rural people disagreed with urbanites all that much on the substance of the issues; rather, they felt they were subject to policies that were foisted upon them by affluent outsiders, and they resisted. This dimension acquired its force by occurring second in a process that had begun with place-based economic inequality.

The second process involves various developments that deepened the divide, including the potential role of racism or xenophobia. Some have argued that the rural-urban political divide is reducible to such attitudes on the part of white rural dwellers.[50] To be sure, these prejudices have been and remain key organizing features of American politics and are central threats to democracy in the United States.[51] Cities, moreover, have long been coded by the media and political elites as Black, leading many to suspect that rural resentment of urbanites is simply an artifact of racist attitudes.[52]

We find, however, that anti-Black attitudes have existed among both urban and rural dwellers at quite similar rates. This is not all that surprising: Consider, for example, the extensive efforts by white people in cities and suburbs to use local land regulation to hoard educational and financial opportunities in their neighborhoods.[53] As the rural-urban divide emerged in the 1990s, neither whites' attitudes about Black Americans nor an increase in immigrants in their counties appeared to be related to the growth of the divide. In more recent years, however, rural white people began to view the Democratic Party's policy agenda as catering particularly to people of color while overlooking their own needs. At this stage, racism did play a role in widening the gap, yet we find it has less explanatory power than many might assume. Similarly, in numerous other issue areas, rural people felt that overbearing Democratic elites—who knew little about them or their values or concerns—made them subject to policies in which they had little or no voice.

Conservative Mobilization Through Organization

To these forces, we add a third dimension, an organizational component, which helped cement the rural-urban cleavage by mobilizing rural voters or failing to do so.[54] Party leaders and civic organizations associated with them may help "connect the dots" for citizens, making meaning of events for political purposes. They may also promote and channel political participation. Through such activities, organizations can facilitate and reinforce a new divide among voters.

Certainly both the Republican and Democratic party organizations at the local level—like other civic organizations—have deteriorated for decades, at least since the 1960s. Yet in recent times, the Republican Party has formed enduring and powerful allegiances with groups that stepped up to interpret developments for citizens, construct shared social and political identities, and mobilize voters. Evangelical churches and local rod and gun clubs, hunting groups, or shooting ranges affiliated with the National Rifle Association, for example, made connections for rural dwellers between issues they cared about and the party that stood on what they deemed to be the right side of those issues.

Alternatively, some organizations that in the past played a mitigating role have withdrawn or grown weaker, thereby inadvertently strengthening new cleavages. The Democratic Party in earlier times benefited from a supportive relationship with organized labor, but to the extent that unions previously existed in some rural places, their presence has now subsided. State and national organizations of the

Democratic Party have failed to provide needed support for rural county chairs, many of whom feel that they have been largely abandoned. As a result, the party has been hobbled as a countervailing force to conservative organizations.

We explore how both kinds of organizational dynamics—those that operate through commission and those that involve omission—may foster deep and enduring political divides. Combined with the other two dimensions, they helped to forge a deep and consequential gulf in American politics.

Many pundits assume that the rural-urban divide only emerged once Donald Trump became a presidential candidate in 2015. To the contrary, we show that it results from long-running processes that have unfolded over time and have interacted with one another through sequential polarization. Now, because of the United States' political institutions that are biased toward rural areas, this place-based cleavage has reverberated through the nation's politics and pushed American democracy to the brink.

Methodological Approach and Sources of Evidence

Here we describe how we did our research, though readers who are eager to jump into the investigation should feel free to skip right on to the next chapter. In undertaking our study, we followed what social scientists refer to as a multi- or mixed-methods approach. In recent decades, researchers in the social sciences have tended to prize research designs that allow scholars to draw supposedly clean causal relationships between one variable and another. In these frameworks, identifying and isolating the particular effect of one phenomenon on another, while controlling for other important factors, is often the singular goal. Yet such designs are not especially well suited to study some of democracy's biggest and most important questions. For the questions at hand, we adopted what many refer to as a developmental type of analysis. This involved both lengthening our time horizon, looking back farther than most other scholars have to find the source of the rural-urban divide, and broadening our scope of analysis, examining how various forces interact across different levels of American life and governance in complicated ways. This, we argue, offers a fuller understanding of how politics has unfolded in recent decades.

To advance and test our argument, we sought out numerous forms of evidence, aiming to examine the rural-urban divide at the county, individual, and institutional levels. Most of our analysis in this book focuses squarely on places, particularly counties, and considers how they have changed over time and how that has influenced voting patterns within them. To do this, we assembled a large national dataset that includes all counties in the United States, rural and urban. We collected numerous indicators about their economic, social, and political life in all years from 1970 to 2024. We use those to conduct statistical analysis of the determinants of voting outcomes in presidential elections. Chapters 3, 4, and 5 showcase our analyses of this dataset. For readers interested in learning more about our data and methods of analysis, we refer them to the appendixes, which describe these and all others in the book in detail, chapter by chapter.

In a few instances in those same chapters, we also analyze individuals (as opposed to counties) and their political behavior. We do so in instances where we are studying political attitudes, such as those pertaining to anti-Black racism, xenophobia, or "culture war" issues (see above). To do this, we collected various public opinion surveys with protected information about individuals' places of residence that helped us to examine systematically how people living in rural and urban areas respond to shifting economic and social trends.

Beginning in chapter 6, we move to studying how the rural-urban divide is filtered through American political institutions. Here we examine the U.S. House of Representatives. We collected data on all members of Congress back to 1980, including their partisanship, voting records, and estimates of how conservative or liberal they were; we examined how these phenomena related to the characteristics and rurality of their districts. In addition, we considered cases of lawmaking to illustrate how the rural-urban divide is shaping policymaking in Congress. In chapter 7, we study how the rural-urban divide has grown to bolster the clout of the Republican Party in state and national political institutions, using decades' worth of data on congressional elections, U.S. senators, and Supreme Court nominees.

While each of these components of the project allows us to analyze all parts of the United States, both rural and urban, in other respects we focused particularly on rural places, because they have changed the most dramatically over recent decades. We also wanted to gain insight into how rural politics was changing on the ground in particular places, and so we chose a handful of states for case studies: Georgia, Michigan, North Carolina, and Ohio. Each of them includes a rural population that is either larger than or close to the national average, and features a prominent place-based political divide. We also studied Missouri and Texas, the latter particularly to conduct interviews in some Latino-majority counties. We conducted such interviews with thirty-nine county-level party chairs, both Democrats and Republicans. We also interviewed twenty-one former elected officials from rural states and districts, particularly Democrats who lost their seats as the rural-urban divide widened, as well as party leaders and a few others with knowledge of these political developments.[55] In combination, these interviews allow us to understand economic, social, and political dynamics as they are happening on the ground, particularly in places that have changed the most. We draw on the interviews throughout the entire book to illustrate points. In addition, chapter 6 highlights what we've learned from many former elected officials about developments in Congress, and chapter 9 showcases the work and insights of the county party chairs about organizing locally.

This project involves a journey—literally and figuratively—across time and across the American landscape to trace how our politics have evolved to where they are now. We invite readers to embark with us on this quest to understand how politics became polarized by place, and how it matters.

2

Averting "Revolution in the Countryside"

THE HISTORIC INTEGRATION OF RURAL PLACES IN THE AMERICAN POLITICAL ECONOMY

THE UNITED STATES was born rural. In the early republic, the vast majority of Americans lived in rural places, whether in the countryside or in small towns, and fully 75 percent of those in the workforce in 1800 were employed in agriculture.[1] Public policies put rural people front and center in the nation's commitments. Urbanization began like a faint rumbling in the distance, then, as industrialization intensified, like a speeding train tumbling down through the decades of the nineteenth century. With each passing year, more Americans took up residence in cities, and rural places grew more marginal to the nation's economy.

Rural Americans, seeking to navigate changing conditions, sought a political party that would represent them. Some in the West and South found it in the late-nineteenth-century Populist movement, but it failed to gain national power and by the early twentieth century had dissipated. Once urbanites surpassed them in the population, by 1920, rural dwellers found themselves even less integrated into the nation's development. A farm crisis in that decade devastated rural areas, and the onset of the Great Depression only made things worse. In January 1933, Edward A. O'Neal, president of the Farm Bureau, predicted at a Senate committee hearing, "Unless something is done for the American farmer we will have revolution in the countryside within twelve months." Farmers banded together to prevent foreclosures and impede the delivery of goods to market. The Farmers' Holiday Association, a militant group of Midwestern farmers, threatened a strike if Congress did not enact a relief measure promptly.[2] The nation appeared to be on the cusp of developing a searing rural-urban political cleavage.

And yet, no national rural-urban political division emerged across the American landscape in any of these periods. Scholars who study political development around the world have long identified the cleavage between cities and the periphery as consequential for politics in other nations. In the United States, it materialized only in particular localities or regions, but not nationwide. Why?

In this chapter we explain why a rural-urban cleavage was avoided in the United States, both historically and in particular when it might have most been expected, starting in the 1930s.[3] We show how both American political parties and public policies managed to incorporate rural people in ways that diffused conflict and addressed at least some of their needs. American political parties grew to be big and decentralized, enabling them to accommodate diverse constituencies, including residents of both rural and urban areas. From early on and most strikingly in the New Deal, a vast array of public policies prioritized rural places in clear and visible ways, and tied them to the growth of the national economy. The legacies of both party and policy developments remained powerful in incorporating rural Americans into the polity for decades, until finally by the late 1990s, circumstances had changed.

Here we also highlight how change in political behavior can occur as a result of the interplay between political parties and public policy. For long periods of American history, groups of people with shared social networks or identities—for example, those who lived in particular places or belonged to a certain religious or ethnic group—steadfastly supported the same political party and passed the tradition on to their children. The reasons for this are well established by political scientists, as we noted in chapter 1. Yet on occasion, significant change occurs, and members of some groups turn away from the party their forebears have long supported, potentially switching their support to the opposing party. Drawing on a rich historical literature, we argue that several New Deal policies made their benefits obvious to many rural dwellers, and also made it clear that government was the source of these beneficial policies.[4] In so doing, they won the support of many rural people, and that legacy was passed down to subsequent generations through the typical dynamics of party affiliation.

The Structure and Development of American Political Parties

In the past, although rural-urban differences occasionally existed in the United States or flared up in particular states and regions, they failed to develop into a uniform, pervasive national political cleavage. A primary reason is that American political parties became well established, even though they were not envisioned by the framers of the Constitution, and they did so in ways that gave rise to two "big tent"–style parties. Their decentralized character subsumed many potentially explosive cleavages, including religious, class-based, and, not least, rural-urban divisions.[5]

The nation's tendency to foster a two-party system owes to its system of single-member districts in which one candidate wins, rather than votes being allotted proportionately among parties. The two parties, in turn, relied on building internal coalitions between all sorts of interests to represent a large and diverse nation.[6] Many institutional and practical arrangements promoted such development. The separation of powers effectively encouraged members of each branch of government to prioritize the interests of their own institution over that of their party: For instance, members of Congress often sought to assert the autonomy of the legislature even when a fellow partisan held the presidency. Perhaps most importantly, the parties were shaped by federalism in ways that promoted decentralization and internal variation between states. Each party was in effect a coalition of fifty separate parties, which coordinated among themselves for the sake of securing victory in national elections while retaining a high degree of internal diversity as they accommodated local and regional interests.[7]

As a result, instead of each party having a uniform policy agenda and identical stances on issues nationwide, these positions varied between the states and regions.[8] Furthermore, resources for parties were dispensed at the state level, where parties controlled nominations, creating strong incentives to maintain these arrangements. The state parties persisted even as national state-building advanced.[9] As political scientists Paul Pierson and Eric Schickler explain, parties in the United States acquired "the form of catch-all organizations that accommodated a range of ideologies and social groups."[10] The resulting party system reduced the stakes of party conflict.

The upshot of these decentralized parties, while they prevailed, is that both major parties gained some support from rural areas and some from urban ones. From the New Deal through the early 1990s, rural people in certain places were devoted Democrats, elsewhere they were devoted Republicans, and in still others they tended to vote split ticket or to vacillate from one election to another in which party they supported. Neither party, in other words, had a lock on rural areas.

In addition to these features of the party structure, the national rural-urban divide was forestalled by sectionalism, meaning the regional distinctions that divided U.S. politics, particularly separating the South from elsewhere.[11] Throughout the contestation over slavery, preceding and through the Civil War, followed by postbellum Southern resistance to extending rights to Black Americans, these conflicts trumped most other divisions. Of course, the South was more rural than the Northeast; its political economy was particularly reliant on agriculture, and many Southern grievances were expressed against the bankers and industrialists of the Northeast. Yet the North-South divide was never truly articulated or crystalized as a rural-urban divide; it was organized around the question of chattel slavery and the political incorporation of Black people as full and equal citizens. Nor were the rural people of the North, a significant bloc of voters, consolidated into the same party as rural people in the South.

To be sure, rural radicalism did permeate the nation's politics from time to time. The most powerful and widespread example in American history was the agrarian populism of the latter decades of the nineteenth century. It was fueled by rural people who sought better terms in their relationship with the industrialists in core cities who relied on them to produce the raw materials that were the basis of their growing wealth. Farmers faced sharply falling prices due to both monetary issues and rising competition, and many were deeply indebted, facing the risk of foreclosure. The Farmers' Alliance formed in the 1870s to promote both economic cooperation between farmers and their political representation. By 1890 it endorsed candidates who supported its platform, and soon after formed the Populist Party, which mounted a national campaign.[12] In 1892, it did well for a third party, with its presidential candidate, James Weaver, carrying four states in the plains and the West, and netting three governorships, eleven House seats, and three Senate seats.[13] In the 1894 elections, it made greater inroads in the South, endorsing candidates at all levels.

The Populist Party's ascent culminated in the Democratic Party's nomination of William Jennings Bryan, who embraced the Populist platform, as its presidential candidate following his rousing Cross of Gold speech. "You come to us and tell us that the great cities are in favor of the gold standard," Bryan said. "We reply that the great cities rest upon our broad and fertile prairies. Burn down your cities and leave our farms, and your cities will spring up again as if by magic; but destroy our farms, and the grass will grow in the streets of every city in the country."[14] Yet Bryan faced defeat. He lost largely at the altar of sectionalism as Northerners, both rural and urban, mostly allied themselves with the party that represented industrialists, rallying behind Republican William McKinley.[15] Bryan and the Populists' success proved fleeting. Indeed, no major presidential candidate or party sought to organize politics around rural or urban poles for more than a century.

Finally, various other social divisions *within* regions also diffused what might otherwise have been a more distinct rural-urban divide.[16] Even within the largely rural South, some sparsely populated areas did not become dominated by the Democratic Party; several counties in the Appalachian Mountains, for example in western North Carolina, routinely supported Republicans, as did those in the Texas Hill Country. Because immigrants and Catholics were drawn to the Democrats on class lines, some native-born working-class people who yearned for respectability supported the Whigs as a way to distinguish themselves.[17]

In short, the characteristics of political parties in the United States have historically helped to deter the emergence of a widespread, national rural-urban cleavage. Both parties developed as large coalitions of numerous groups, featuring cross-cutting divisions within them. Rural and urban people in different parts of the country varied in terms of which party they supported. When potential rural-urban frictions did flare up, they failed to crystallize into enduring or national divisions, being subsumed instead by other identities. But on occasion, party builders managed to attract new groups to their party, disrupting the usual patterns of stasis in party support, as we shall see.

Making Rural Needs a Priority: American State-Building Through the New Deal

American state-builders historically gave rural areas a prominent place in policy developments. Early on, this was no surprise, since rural people constituted the majority of the country. Yet, strikingly, even as industrialization marginalized many rural people, lawmakers found ways, through public policy, to keep them integrated into the American polity and economy.

In the nineteenth century, rural areas benefitted from numerous policies promoting economic development. Agriculture in particular garnered attention, as it accounted for the livelihood of most Americans. The U.S. House of Representatives established an Agricultural Committee in 1820, and the Senate followed in 1825. Their wide array of responsibilities, in time, ranged from overseeing the Morrill Land Grant College Act to the agricultural experiment stations, which engaged in research that helped fight diseases and established antibiotics.[18] The U.S. Department of Agriculture came about in 1862, eventually evolving into what Kenneth Finegold and Theda Skocpol called an "island of state strength in an ocean of weakness."[19] Also in 1862, President Abraham Lincoln signed into law the sweeping Morrill Act, which granted federal land to states for the purpose of establishing agricultural universities, and thus gave rise to a vast network of institutions of higher education. That same year, he also signed the Homestead Act, which distributed public land in the West to those willing to farm it. By 1887, the Hatch Act promoted cooperation between the federal and state governments in agricultural research through the establishment of the experiment stations.[20]

Other policies served rural Americans generally, not just those involved in agriculture. Perhaps no nineteenth-century government initiative did more for rural places than the establishment of the U.S. Post Office, which reached far-flung communities as early as the Jacksonian Era through a system of stagecoaches that delivered mail to rural post offices. A far more systematic and comprehensive approach began with the establishment of Rural Free Delivery in 1898.[21] Through such policies, lawmakers provided a crucial system of communications to Americans living even in the most remote locations.

In the early twentieth century, lawmakers in Congress established many of the regulatory policies that the populists had favored. These goals were achieved by a coalition of rural Democrats, Northern urban Democrats, and Midwestern and Western Republicans. They enacted railroad regulation with federal rate controls, important for farmers who sought affordable means to ship their goods to market. In 1913, once President Woodrow Wilson was elected and Democrats enjoyed a united government, they advanced tariff reforms, trimming duties on manufactured goods and excluding them on farm machinery and supplies. To make up for lost revenues, they introduced the progressive income tax, applied to incomes over $3,000, an amount high enough to exclude most lower- and middle-income people, both rural and urban. That same year, the Federal Reserve System was established with a decentralized structure that rural people favored, making it easier for farmers to get credit. In order to break up corporate mergers and monopolistic practices, the coalition created the Clayton Antitrust Act in 1914, which expanded the Sherman Antitrust Act of 1890 and allowed small businesses to thrive.[22] A hallmark of each of these policies— which would set them apart from the redistributive social welfare policies that serve as the main sources of government help for rural and urban Americans today—is that they addressed inequality through *regulatory means,* by attempting to foster fair competition and decent employment. In doing so, they helped stave off the massive rural-urban inequalities we see today.

In this period, Congress also created a national extension service through the Smith-Lever Act of 1914, funding county agents who would demonstrate farming techniques. Three years later, the Smith-Hughes Act set up vocational schools for the purpose of teaching agricultural techniques as well as skills for industry and home economics. Through all these policy developments, farm households—which still included one-quarter of the public—as well as rural people more broadly saw government acting on their behalf.[23] But as the twentieth century proceeded, economic trends would make rural life increasingly challenging, and policymakers would need to find new ways to respond effectively.

Rural Despair and Political Shifts in the 1920s

As industrialization intensified, rural dwellers grew more peripheral to the nation's economic life. Between 1900 and 1930, the nation evolved from being predominantly rural to mostly urban. According to data from the U.S. Census, the rural population fell from 60 percent to 44 percent, and the percentage of the workforce employed in agriculture decreased from one in three to one in five.[24]

These downward trends were exacerbated by the 1920s farm crisis. While urban areas experienced the "Roaring Twenties," the price of agricultural products fell sharply and rural Americans suffered. The problem stemmed from overproduction: Farmers had increased the crops they raised to meet needs during the Great War, but once the war ended, demand fell and so did prices. Republican President Calvin Coolidge expressed little interest in a government response, remarking, "Well, farmers have never made money. I don't believe we can do much about it."[25]

Two members of Coolidge's party thought otherwise. Senator Charles L. McNary of Oregon and Representative Gilbert N. Haugen

of Iowa introduced a bill in 1924 through which government would sub-
sidize agriculture, raising the prices that farmers received and protecting
them through tariffs. The bill gained endorsements from hundreds of
farm organizations, including, most prominently, the American Farm
Bureau Federation and the National Grange. In 1927, it passed with the
support of a bipartisan farm bloc. Coolidge vetoed it that year, however,
and he did so again in 1928.[26]

In the midst of this tumultuous period, Al Smith ran as the Democratic nominee in the presidential election of 1928, and some rural
Americans who typically leaned Republican chose to support him.
Smith may have seemed an unlikely candidate to attract rural Republicans. As political analyst James L. Sundquist notes, he "had scarcely
even visited the West or South and admittedly knew nothing about agriculture," and "besides being a Catholic and a wet [meaning he supported repeal of the Eighteenth Amendment, which prohibited the
manufacture and sale of alcohol], he was a product of Tammany Hall
and his manner of dress and speech could hardly have been more alien
to rural and small-town America." In sum, "He was not the man to lead
thousands of disgruntled Republican farmers into the Democratic
party," or so it appeared. Yet Smith made efforts to woo farmers and saw
a fair amount of success: He carried forty-four counties in Illinois, Iowa,
Minnesota, and North Dakota, most of them rural, and only about half
with large Catholic populations.[27] Democrats took note of how Smith
managed to subdue place-based antipathies with economic programs,
possibly creating an entering wedge for the party in rural areas.

Yet Republican Herbert Hoover won the election, and as the Great
Depression set in, he proved to be insensitive to the economic distress
in rural areas and was opposed to a stronger government role in response.[28] Farm incomes worsened, and by the time Franklin D. Roosevelt was inaugurated as president in 1933, farmers were earning just half
what they had in 1919. A full one-third had lost their land. Despite the
inroads made by Smith in the Midwest, rural allegiances on the Democratic side remained precarious. Indeed, the massive upheavals in rural
life wrought by the Great Depression, along with indifference from
most major political leaders, threatened to fuel a rural-urban divide.

Roosevelt Seeks to Build a Rural-Urban Alliance

Into this precipitous political moment stepped then–Governor of New York Franklin D. Roosevelt, who would orient his presidential campaign and his presidency around serving the needs of lower- and middle-income Americans. Certainly much of that effort would benefit urban areas, which in turn became crucial supports of the Democratic Party.[29] Less well appreciated, however, is that he would also put in the very center of his focus rural dwellers, who still represented roughly two out of five Americans.[30] It turned out to be not only a successful political strategy for getting elected, but also one that would forestall the emergence of a rural-urban divide for more than another half century.

In June 1931, when Roosevelt addressed a national gathering of governors about the economic crises facing the nation, he explicitly chose to focus his remarks on what he called "the dislocation of a proper balance between urban and rural life." As historian Sarah T. Phillips has documented, he described how many farmers toiled just to subsist at a level far below the "American standard of living," often trying to work exhausted land. One year later, as he campaigned for president, Roosevelt further developed his vision for, as Phillips put it, a "rural renaissance built upon the proper use of land and the availability of hydroelectric power." He believed that the farm crisis of the 1920s had played a major role in causing the Great Depression and that rural poverty sustained it. Roosevelt insisted, "Our economic life today is a seamless web. If we get back to the root of the difficulty, we will find that it is the present lack of equality for agriculture." He saw rural economies as intertwined with those of urban areas—and he considered policy solutions accordingly. While he thought that the reduction of surplus production would provide short-term relief, he stressed the need for permanent measures such as national agricultural planning and rural electrification to lessen inequality between rural and urban areas.[31]

Roosevelt's "Brain Trust," in considering what should be the top priority among his campaign themes, selected not the problems of industrial production in big cities, but instead agriculture. Raymond Moley, who headed up the group, said that Roosevelt "advocated reforestation, land utilization, the relief of farmers from an inequitable tax burden, and the curative possibilities of diversifying our industrial life by sending a proportion of it into the rural districts." Columbia University economist Rexford Tugwell, who served as architect of the farm strategy, emphasized the interdependence of rural and urban Americans. He argued that farmers were subject to what he called a "deranged" disparity between the price of farm and industrial goods such that they lacked the ability to be consumers themselves, and this led in turn to unemployment among industrial workers in cities. Roosevelt also recruited Henry A. Wallace from Iowa, an agricultural journalist and plant geneticist whose father—a Progressive Era Republican—had served as secretary of agriculture under Harding and Coolidge, and who himself would serve as Roosevelt's secretary of agriculture. At the urging of these advisors, in an address to farmers in Topeka, Kansas, Roosevelt declared, "This Nation cannot endure if it is half 'boom' and half 'broke,'" and he called for agricultural benefits on par with the tariff protection bestowed on industry.[32]

When 1932's Election Day came, farmers in the Midwestern Plains states who typically voted Republican threw their support to Roosevelt, helping to fuel his victory.[33] The president's coattails enabled Democrats down the ballot to prevail in many previously Republican-held seats. The election yielded the largest Democratic majorities ever to have served in Congress up to that point, with 60 in the Senate and 311 in the House.[34]

Now it was time for action to address the needs of rural America, and none too soon. Increasingly angry farmers appeared on the verge of turning violent, as noted at the start of this chapter. The Roosevelt administration arrived in Washington, DC, ready to rise to the occasion, with policies that would forestall a rural-urban cleavage.

A New Deal for Rural America

In the flurry of the administration's first hundred days, lawmakers enacted several new policies aimed at raising rural incomes. These were based on the conviction that, as Phillips puts it, "the nation's prosperity rested on an agricultural base."[35] The Agricultural Adjustment Act (AAA) aimed to tackle the problem of overproduction to raise farm prices and incomes;

it did so by permitting the federal government to set production quotas on major crops and by paying farmers to plant less. The Federal Emergency Relief Administration channeled a large portion of its efforts to rural areas, and by the end of 1933, officials announced that over five million people in farm families had benefited from the program's relief checks.[36] Trying to stall the farm foreclosure crisis, Roosevelt used an executive order to consolidate all federal agencies dealing with agricultural credit into the Farm Credit Administration.[37] The Soil Erosion Service, by establishing demonstration projects, helped farmers learn about and implement conservation measures such as contour plowing and strip cropping. The move was considered highly successful in elevating farm income and land values.[38] The National Industrial Recovery Act also contained several rural resource provisions. These programs ensured that rural areas remained tied to the nation's economic growth.

Also, like New Deal programs generally, they made a profound impression that government mattered in the lives of everyday people. As observed by Paul Landis, writing in the *American Sociological Review* in 1936, "National politics is no longer an abstract distant affair in Washington. . . . The hand of the federal unit reaches every family. It meets them where they live. . . . It has brought the activities of government into the concrete world of Mr. Everyman. The average farmer may not understand the intricate details of the 'New Deal,' but when he gets his check for fifty dollars as a result of letting some of his acreage lie fallow, he feels that government is a real part of his life."[39] The Farm Credit Administration prevented an estimated three hundred farms from foreclosure daily. One farmer wrote, "I would be without a roof over my head if it hadn't been for the government loan. . . . God bless Mr. Roosevelt and the Democratic party who saved thousands of poor people all over this country from starvation."[40]

Other innovative policies achieved Roosevelt's goal of bringing electricity to rural areas. Through the Tennessee Valley Authority (TVA), started in 1933, cheap electrical power was quickly provided to homes, farms, and factories across seven states.[41] Owing to the Rural Electrification Administration (REA), the proportion of farms with electricity increased from one in ten at its inception to nine in ten in 1950. As historian William E. Leuchtenburg wrote of the REA, "Perhaps no single act of the Roosevelt years changed more directly the way people lived." At its inception, "the lack of electric power divided the United States into two nations: the city dwellers and the county folk." Farmers "toiled in a nineteenth century world," and their wives "performed their backbreaking chores like peasant women in a preindustrial age."[42] The policy "revolutionized rural life," and it did so in a strikingly visible manner.

"Finally, the great moment would come," Leuchtenburg wrote. "Farmers, their wives and children, would gather at night on a hillside in the Great Smokies, in a field in the Upper Michigan peninsula, on a slope of the Continental Divide, and, when the switch was pulled on a giant generator, see their homes, their barns, their schools, their churches, burst forth in dazzling light. Many of them would be seeing electric light for the first time in their lives."[43] The policy likely made evident to many rural people the value of government generally and conveyed to them that public officials in the Roosevelt administration cared about people like them.

Some regulatory policies were used to ensure fair competition and to bolster the economy in smaller cities and rural places across the country. During his first hundred days in office, Roosevelt signed into law the Banking Act of 1933, otherwise known as Glass-Steagall. For the first time in American history, it regulated Wall Street, requiring a division between commercial banking and investment banking, and putting limitations on "speculative" activities. It also protected Americans and prevented bank failures by creating the Federal Deposit Insurance Corporation (FDIC), which guaranteed small bank deposits.[44] In two subsequent laws, Congress strengthened antitrust policies enacted earlier in the century. Namely, in 1936, the Robinson-Patman Act prevented the formation of large chain stores by prohibiting the practice of selling items below cost. One year later, the Miller-Tydings Act required minimum pricing to prevent large chain stores from undercutting small businesses that were commonplace in rural America. Roosevelt also pursued rigorous antitrust enforcement to promote competition.[45] Over the next half century, these politics fostered stability in the economy and helped rural communities to thrive.

Although the AAA benefited only property-owning farmers and especially those with more land, the Roosevelt administration also tried to help small farmers, tenant farmers, and sharecroppers. These efforts were less successful. The Resettlement Administration, created in 1935, aimed to give relief to poor farmers who worked unproductive land by purchasing their land, converting it to other purposes, and moving the inhabitants to better farms. In 1937, the program was replaced by the Farm Security Administration (FSA), which shifted the emphasis to rehabilitating existing land. The FSA issued a loan or grant to one in nine farmers in the nation, particularly higher-risk families in the South, and it aimed to help tenants become owners.[46] Still, the rural policies of the Roosevelt administration reflected the exclusionary tendencies of the New Deal, of which several key programs marginalized Black citizens.[47] As Phillips observes, "When looking at the numbers, especially the racial differentials, it is hard to escape the conclusion that the rural New Deal," at least in "the South . . . served white rather than black, rich rather than poor."[48] Owing in part to such policy differences, Black Americans would continue to suffer for generations.

No presidential administration before or since, however, has focused so deliberately on the problems faced by rural people, and the help it provided endured for decades.[49] While a couple of the early laws were thrown out by the Supreme Court, one of them—the AAA—was replaced with a new version in 1938, and it survived, with price supports becoming a fixture of midcentury policies. Other programs were combined or renamed, but their basic purposes were carried on. Remarkably, a half century later, the fundamentals of the rural New Deal remained intact.[50]

Parties, Policies, and Political Change

The onset of the Great Depression represented a perilous political moment when a rural-urban divide certainly could have emerged in the United States, had rural people continued to perceive themselves to be marginalized by changes in American society and ignored by political leaders. Instead, something remarkable occurred: Capable party leaders during the New Deal effectively responded to rural needs and quelled the resistance that had been brewing since the 1920s. In the process, they not only prevented the emergence of a rural-urban divide; they also disrupted some long-standing political allegiances and fostered what turned out to be long-enduring support for the Democratic Party among many rural people.

Rural Americans had long sought a party that would do their bidding, and the New Deal Democratic Party rose to the occasion. At a time when rural residents were under duress and shrinking as a portion of the electorate, Roosevelt and his administration put them front and center in plans to stabilize and improve the U.S. economy and democracy itself. Through a wide array of policies, the New Deal shored up rural communities. In the process, it conveyed to their inhabitants that public officials cared about people like them. It also ensured that rural and urban dwellers remained interdependent in the economy and polity. Many rural people never forgot how the New Deal had rescued their family in a time of need or brought electricity to their farms, and they became devoted Democrats.

The Democratic Party subsequently enjoyed the support of rural people in many different parts of the country. This included lower-income producers, particularly those engaged in cotton, tobacco, rice, and peanut production in the South, as well as wheat growers in the Dakotas, Kansas, Nebraska, and the Pacific Northwest, who had to deal with the risks of a semiarid climate and highly variable yields.[51] Such political patterns in rural areas did not emerge in the course of a single election, either in 1928 or in 1932. They took longer to coalesce, as partisans in specific states continued to re-sort themselves politically in what Sundquist calls the "aftershocks of the New Deal earthquake." Roosevelt sought to build a coalition broader than Democratic Party stalwarts, and he reached out to Progressive Republicans and Farmer-Laborites in various states in the process.[52] By the early 1950s, Northern states that had supported FDR but still elected Republicans further down the ballot shifted increasingly to supporting Democrats. Voters in the upper Midwestern states of North Dakota, Wisconsin, and Minnesota, where Farmer-Labor parties had previously supported Republicans, shifted their alliances to Democrats in a reaction against Eisenhower's farm policies.[53]

To be sure, not all rural dwellers became Democrats. Many upper- and middle-income farmers remained stalwart Republicans throughout the period. Some others, after deviating from their usual Republican loyalties to vote for Roosevelt once or twice, returned to the fold. Likewise, many rural counties that had shifted away from their typical Republican leanings to support Roosevelt in 1932 subsequently returned to the party. Moreover, some white Democratic rural voters in border states could not take "the spending, farm, and civil rights policies of the New Deal," and thus began supporting the Republican Party.[54]

In the South, the political aftershocks of the New Deal occurred in urban areas, where the Republican Party made gains. This process intensified in 1948, when presidential candidate Harry S. Truman came out in support of civil rights. In response, some white Southerners formed a "States' Rights Democratic Party," otherwise known as the Dixiecrats, and supported Strom Thurmond for president. As Hood and McKee note, the Dixiecrats' "fervent defense of white supremacy perhaps unwittingly eclipsed" the importance they also placed on "a conservative laissez-faire capitalist/free-market economic philosophy," with a platform that stressed the importance of "private employment without government interference."[55] In later years, when Republican presidential candidate Dwight D. Eisenhower campaigned in the region, he specifically courted urban dwellers by stressing economic conservatism instead of segregation.[56] Strikingly, however, many rural white Southerners continued to support Democrats.

As a result, rural America of the mid-twentieth century was a political patchwork. Democrats won elections not only in rural counties throughout the South but also in numerous ones in the Midwest as well. Republican candidates typically prevailed in other rural areas besides these, but even in many places where they did, Democrats gained a good share of the vote, and residents voted split ticket on occasion.

The fact that both parties remained competitive in some rural places helped residents gain lawmakers' attention. In Congress, over the next several decades, policymaking pertaining to rural areas typically involved bipartisan coalitions and logrolling. Certainly Republican elected officials tried to scale back New Deal farm programs. Most serving in Congress had voted against them in the 1930s.[57] Subsequently, the Eisenhower administration sought unsuccessfully to reduce agricultural subsidies. Then–Secretary of Agriculture Ezra Taft Benson later wrote, "We could not go on indefinitely under the old programs without piling up mountainous surpluses, losing markets, wasting resources, running up heavy dollar losses and, most important of all, endangering the economic independence of our farm people." What the Republican administration most worried about, according to Bensel, was not just the size of federal spending on such programs or the limits they placed on the free market, but also the political ties they established between "the agrarian periphery and labor-oriented lower classes of the industrialized core." The GOP's aim was "to split asunder one of the political supports for the bipolar Democratic coalition."[58] The party failed to do so, however, and subsequently, Democratic presidents John F. Kennedy and Lyndon Johnson continued to protect such programs.

Through the New Deal, from the perspective of many rural Americans, government delivered. In the process, they gained an advocate to which they entrusted their political support. Simultaneously, the politics of the era helped stave off the formation of a rural-urban divide and held it at bay for over a half century.

The Legacy of Rural and Urban Cooperation

Several long-serving Democratic party leaders we interviewed noted the legacy of the New Deal in transforming their regions. Margaret Simpson, in Marjorie Taylor Greene's district of northwest Georgia, said, "We'd still be living in the Dark Ages around here if it had not been for FDR and the TVA and [rural] electrification and the GI Bill, with education [for veterans] after serving."

The New Deal's legacy, combined with the continuing catch-all style of political parties, yielded political effects that lasted for over half a century.[59] Certainly some rural Americans who had been longtime Republicans prior to the 1930s voted just once or twice for Roosevelt but otherwise stuck with their party. Many others, though, became staunchly devoted to the Democratic Party and remained so for decades. And from the 1940s to the 1970s, New Deal policies that helped rural areas remained largely intact.

The rural investments of the New Deal certainly had limitations, and generally, people of color and poor people of all races benefited less than other rural dwellers. The Democratic Party's coalition between conservative white Southern Democrats and urban ethnic liberals meant that policymakers avoided policies that threatened to upset white supremacy and Jim Crow in Southern states. In time, reformers would seek to overcome the limits of the New Deal in the pursuit of racial equality and justice, efforts that would challenge these long-standing alliances.

In the meanwhile, however, many rural Americans came to perceive that the Democratic Party stood up for ordinary people, themselves included, and they either gave the party their support or at least voted split ticket on occasion. That impact endured for over a half century. By the late twentieth century, politics changed, and with it the relationship between rural and urban Americans.

PART II

Causes

3

Political-Economic
Transformation

RURAL-URBAN POLARIZATION BEGINS

GOODYEAR, CHRYSLER, Ford, GM, Merck. When we asked rural
political party leaders how the local economy had changed since the
1990s, those in many counties—regardless of party—ticked off a litany
of major companies such as these, along with lesser-known but once-
major American textile, rug-manufacturing, or mineral-extraction companies. As recently as the 1990s or early 2000s, they explained, these
employers had provided large numbers of jobs with good pay and benefits in their communities. Some mentioned their own relatives who
had earned livings in those plants. But then the employers downsized
their workforces or packed up and left for good. Now, these company
names seem like ghosts of the employers whose departures still haunt
the communities left behind.

Richard Smith, a Black Democratic county chair in eastern North
Carolina, said, "Well, you know the whole southeastern part of the
country suffered . . . and industries have pulled out." Some urban parts
of the state had flourished by attracting information technology and
banking, he noted, but in his own rural region, "for those who have not
taken advantage of education, they have had a difficult task from the
closing of so many plants. This particular county put all its marbles in
plants, in industries, and industry that just dried up. Back in the sixties,

seventies, and eighties, the plants were king, [offering] a very high median level of salary for folks who did not have more than a high school education, so they did quite well." But, he continued, "Then the bust came after the Clinton Administration, NAFTA, and all of those changes in textiles, and then China, with Walmart, took all of those industries away from us. We have a few still here but nothing like the lavish industries we had in the eighties and nineties."

In the latter part of the twentieth century, dramatic changes swept the American economy. Technological advances and global competition each played a part, but crucial policy decisions created or at least accelerated these trends. Lawmakers deregulated numerous sectors of the economy, from finance to transportation. They relaxed antitrust enforcement and liberalized trade. In many instances, Republicans had long pursued these goals; what changed in this era was that some Democrats also lent their support, enabling the policies to succeed.

As a result, jobs vanished in older industries—manufacturing, mining, and other forms of natural resource extraction—that had long been pillars of the economy. Family farms went out of business, and agriculture became dominated by huge conglomerates. Meanwhile, employment and economic activity flourished in the knowledge economy, including technology, business services, and other high-end sectors such as finance. Democrats advanced policy interventions that helped promote these new components of the economy.

These seismic shifts, which economists have likened in impact to the Industrial Revolution, were felt far and wide, but many rural areas bore the brunt of them. Rural places lost jobs in farming, goods production, and resource extraction, and gained little. Many urban areas, meanwhile, more readily adjusted to deindustrialization by becoming hubs of the new knowledge economy, even as they confronted high levels of poverty and inequality. Further, rural and urban economies became far less interdependent and reliant on one another: The decline of raw goods production, the rise of foreign imports, and the concentration of economic activity in urban areas severed the longstanding ties that had held the two loosely together. In combination, these dramatic shifts increasingly cordoned off rural areas from the center of the nation's economy and gave rise to a new form of geographic inequality.

The changes, Richard Smith explained, sparked another transformation: "And so with that, you had change in the political climate. Once upon a time the Democratic Party was king. As industries left, there were lots of disgruntled folks and I think a lot of lack of insight. . . . I can tell you that ten years ago, North Carolina was a blue state, and now we are red, and our county was blue until 2016 and now we are red. So it's been a tough scenario in terms of what's going on."

In this chapter, we show how the transformation of the political economy in the closing years of the twentieth century and the early years of the twenty-first spurred the rural-urban divide in the United States. This is the first step in the process we call "sequential polarization": the rise of place-based inequality. Urban places came to be the powerhouses of the nation's economy, and in the process they further solidified their loyalty to the Democratic Party. Rural places, by contrast, found themselves on the outer margins of the economy, and as a result they moved sharply in support of the Republican Party. Now we turn to how these tectonic shifts created our contemporary place-based divide.

Growing Economic Inequality Between Rural and Urban Places

A few scholars have immersed themselves in particular rural places and helped us to understand the challenges faced by residents given their limited employment opportunities. Political scientist Katherine Cramer, for example, found that many rural Wisconsinites resent urban people, whom they perceive to have jobs that offer better pay and benefits and are more comfortable, requiring less work and hardship. Sociologist Jennifer Sherman describes how recent economic dislocation in the rural Northwest has created tensions within rural families, particularly when a male breadwinner loses a job, as well within communities, especially as inequality has grown.[1] These insights raise the question of how rural economies nationwide have fared compared to urban ones in recent decades.

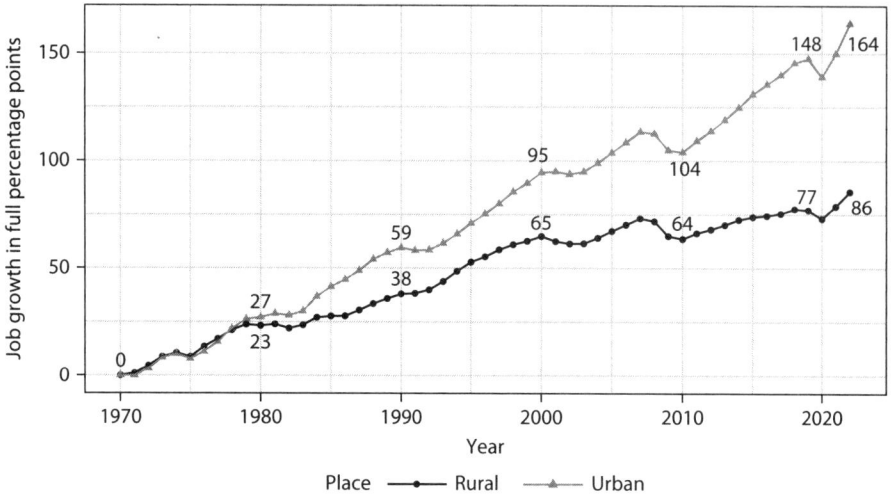

FIGURE 3.1. Private-sector employment growth, 1970–2022, rural and urban counties
Source: U.S. Bureau of Economic Analysis (BEA); measure of rural from OMB

We explore this first by comparing the growth of private-sector jobs in rural and urban places over time (figure 3.1; see appendixes).[2] Since the late 1990s, when the rural-urban political divide began to open up, rural areas have seen relatively stagnant employment growth. Meanwhile, urban areas have continued their economic ascent. Indeed, while employment in all rural counties has grown by roughly 35 percentage points since the mid-1990s, it has more than doubled in urban counties over the same period. During that time, furthermore, many rural counties have actually experienced net job *loss*.

Many rural areas have also encountered population stagnation and even loss, as young people leave and don't return and newcomers are rare. Due to such trends, sociologist Robert Wuthnow describes the many small towns that he visited for his research as pervaded by an "unspoken sadness" and full of "anger and frustration."[3] From 1970 to 2020, we find that urban areas nationwide grew at a fast and continuous clip, while rural ones overall tended to stagnate (figure 3.2; see appendixes). The disparity has been greatest during recent decades. From 1990 to 2020, urban counties grew by 39 percent, compared to rural areas at just

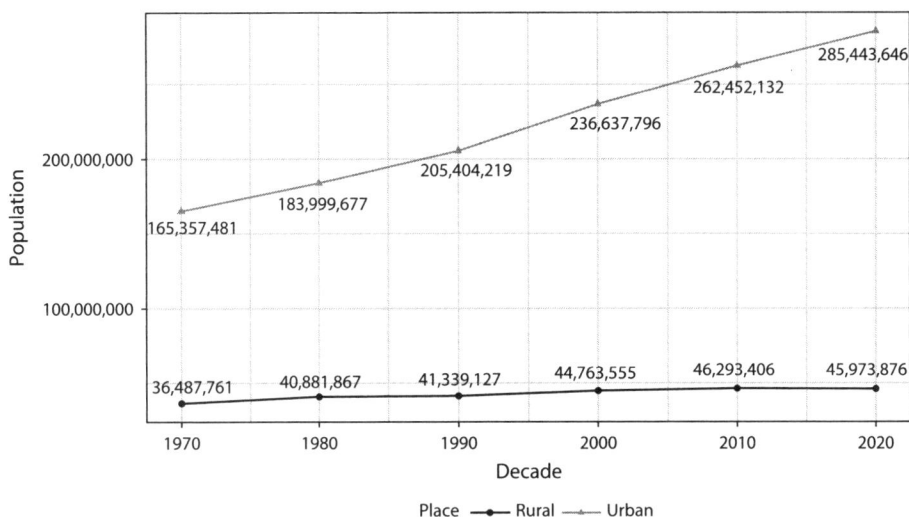

FIGURE 3.2. Population by rural and urban counties, 1970–2020
Source: U.S. Census Bureau; measure of rural from OMB

11 percent. Indeed, from 2010 to 2020, counties designated as rural by the Office of Management and Budget actually *lost* population, on net.[4]

Rural areas also tend to be poorer than urban ones. On the eve of the COVID-19 pandemic, 15 percent of the rural population lived below the official poverty line, while 12 percent of all urban people did.[5] In 2019, rural areas had a per capita income of $42,600, compared to $57,580 in urban areas.[6]

Beyond each of these indicators of economic deterioration, rural counties today suffer from poor and worsening social and economic conditions in other respects as well. Population stagnation and loss lead to the shuttering of local businesses, a decline in services and gathering places, and in some instances even the closing of schools and/or hospitals. Bob Kerrey, who served Nebraska as governor from 1983 to 1987 and as U.S. Senator from 1989 to 2001, explained to us that declining population harms the local tax base, which in turn hurts local services.[7] "If you support your schools with property tax funding, as most schools in America do, you've got to struggle to make the budget if the population moves. The income tends to drop. Moreover, a young person coming into a community:

Among the first questions they ask is, do you have a good hospital, in case I have a baby? Are the schools any good? . . . I think that rural communities have a very difficult time, given the way we support health care and education, maintaining the kind of level that young people want."

Indeed, many rural places have suffered from the closure of medical facilities in recent years, and in fact, according to the U.S. Department of Agriculture, the most rural counties tend to have the fewest health care providers per resident for a number of services.[8] Several county chairs we interviewed in Georgia and North Carolina mentioned hospital closures in their areas, leaving the local aging population in a precarious situation if they need emergency care. One in rural Missouri reported that six hospitals had closed in the region in recent years, and now it is necessary to drive an hour and a half just to get to an urgent care facility. Most troubling, the life expectancy of rural Americans, which had been increasing since 1980, fell between 2010 and 2019.[9]

Rural schools, according to education scholar Mara Casey Tieken, also play important roles. According to her, they "build and maintain these communities, communities rooted in a place, . . . defined by social interaction, . . . with a degree of power and voice." When they are closed, conversely, "the message is again starkly plain: no school, no community."[10]

How did such severe place-based inequality emerge across so many dimensions?

The Fall of Rural Economies, the Rise of the Knowledge Economy, and the Making of a Place-Based Cleavage: 1980s to the Present

Some shrug off the widening rural-urban gap in economic performance as if it stems from technological change and economic shifts that are immutable forces of nature.[11] In his study of the growth of the knowledge economy in big metro areas, for instance, Enrico Moretti (2012) chalked up regional inequality to historical accidents and elements of the modern economy that tend to feed on themselves. In a classic example, Bill Gates and Paul Allen decided somewhat arbitrarily to move the headquarters of their new business, Microsoft, from Albuquerque, New Mexico, to Seattle, Washington, in January of 1979. Microsoft's growth and profitability then attracted talented engineers, venture capital, and other innovative software companies to the Seattle region and subsequently caused the area's economic path to significantly diverge from Albuquerque's.[12] We do not dispute the importance of such factors. Instead, we argue they do not tell the entire story: The economy does not operate in a vacuum, and its development is not inevitable.[13] Rather, it is fundamentally shaped by political institutions, public policy, and political actors.[14] Over the final decades of the twentieth century, policymakers made crucial decisions that exacerbated place-based economic inequality, spurred rural backlash, and sowed the seeds of our contemporary political divide.

Deregulation and the Demise of Antitrust Enforcement

For nearly a century, many American lawmakers tried to fashion a political economy that prioritized competition, allowing small businesses to thrive and, along with them, smaller places, including towns and rural areas. From the creation of the Interstate Commerce Commission in 1887 to the Sherman Antitrust Act in 1890, the Clayton Antitrust Act of 1913, the regulatory policies of the New Deal, and strong antitrust enforcement in the 1950s and 1960s, policymakers attempted to ensure that the nation's economy would not become dominated by a few of the largest cities but rather would allow people in all sorts of places to enjoy economic opportunity.[15] Yet all of that began to change, piece by piece, in the latter twentieth century.

The transformation began with deregulation in transportation, including rail, air, and trucking. Previously, lawmakers had established regulations protecting travel to the most out-of-the-way places, and, importantly, ensuring that the costs to those who lived there of shipping their goods to market would not be exorbitantly expensive. The underlying principle was that some regions and places should not receive a competitive advantage over others. Yet following the economic downturn of the 1970s, lawmakers began to pursue deregulation in numerous areas, convinced it would help to lower costs. This view was promoted by the then-ascendant Chicago school of economics, which encouraged the demise of subsidies and special treatment for more remote locations. The deregulation of airlines, for example, lowered the cost of travel between some of the largest cities but increased the cost of flying to less-populated places and discouraged airlines from retaining such routes.[16] Some rural lawmakers supported these policy changes and later wished they had opposed them. Democratic Senator Robert Byrd of West Virginia, for example, in 1986 said of himself, "This is one Senator who regrets that he voted for airline deregulation. It has penalized States like West Virginia, where many of the airlines pulled out quickly following deregulation and the prices zoomed into the stratosphere—doubled, tripled and, in some instances, quadrupled. So we have poorer air service and much more costly air service than we in West Virginia had prior to deregulation. . . . I would welcome the opportunity to vote for reregulation because we people in the rural States are paying the bill."[17]

But rather than deregulation fading, it gathered momentum, spreading across sectors of the economy. Lawmakers loosened regulations on the financial sector through several policy changes. Majorities of Republicans had long favored such changes; what was new in the late twentieth century, as mentioned, was that they were joined in these efforts by some Democrats, rural and urban alike.[18] By the 1990s lawmakers eliminated prohibitions on interstate banking, and local banks either went under or were bought up by larger banks located farther away, often across the country. The Federal Reserve repeatedly reinterpreted the Glass-Steagall Act to limit its scope, and lawmakers finally terminated it in 1999. These and other policy changes promoted record profits in the financial sector and with it the escalation of wealth in large cities.[19] For small businesses in rural places, it became more difficult to borrow funds to get a business up and running or expand it.[20]

Courts and lawmakers also shifted away from strict enforcement of antitrust laws, which further exacerbated economic consolidation. Academics associated with the Chicago school, such as failed Supreme Court nominee Robert Bork, criticized the nation's antimonopoly laws, arguing that conglomerates were not to be feared, and should even be encouraged because they might produce lower prices or better services for consumers.[21] By 1982, the Justice Department applied this doctrine and relaxed its approach to antitrust enforcement, and the number of staff at the Federal Trade Commission declined. Mergers subsequently proliferated under presidents of both parties.

Many of the small towns and villages we visited featured boarded-up buildings and few thriving businesses. As recently as the 1980s, these places still contained restaurants, hardware stores, feed and seed stores, and numerous other small enterprises. As jobs and the population stagnated, it became increasingly difficult for businesses to stay afloat.

Although Patrice Hawkins complained about the fast-food restaurants in her area, other rural counties looked with envy on such places that were near major highways and could attract national chains. In Georgia, communities without a Dollar General felt deprived. Fred Donovan, an educator and party chair in northeastern North Carolina, commented that nowhere in his county could a person purchase a television. "We make our money here but we spend it elsewhere," he noted. It was as if a devastating storm had passed through and rural places had never recovered.

The Decline and Consolidation of Agriculture

Even though farming has been in decline since industrialization, as recently as the 1970s the agricultural industry served as an important source of economic security for rural areas. But it was a precarious arrangement that was held together in large part by public policies. During the Nixon administration, tax policies and low interest rates made investments in large-scale farming, including through the acquisition of land and machinery, particularly attractive. The ethos of the decade was captured by Nixon's secretary of agriculture, Earl Butz, who famously told farmers to "go big or get out."[22] Shortly thereafter, however, farmers were hit with a downturn the likes of which had not been experienced since the Great Depression. On the one hand, the Federal Reserve raised interest rates to curb inflation; this made the massive debt farmers had taken on to acquire more land and machinery even heavier and difficult to repay. On the other, Nixon strengthened the dollar internationally, rendering commodities far less competitive in the global marketplace.[23]

Subsequently, during the Reagan Administration, between 1980 and 1988, some two hundred thousand to three hundred thousand American farms—8 to 12 percent of all U.S. farms at the time—went bankrupt, were foreclosed on, or financially restructured.[24] Their demise became widely known as the Farm Crisis. It drew attention from national news outlets—including *The New York Times* and *The Washington Post*—and federal lawmakers.

In short, technological changes and policy decisions combined to foster consolidation and with it greater inequality in rural farming communities. Large farms and companies continued to grow, but many midsized farms and businesses that supported them were squeezed out, and small ones barely survived except as "hobby farms," or farms that are not used as primary sources of income.[25] Most food that is produced in the United States, from dairy products to major crops, became the province of "big agriculture," as did most stages of production, including seed sourcing and retail.[26] Horizontal integration, meaning concentration of businesses in the same stage of the production process, was joined by growing vertical integration, meaning concentration across areas of production.[27]

As with other industries, the consolidation of agriculture was intensified by deregulation and lax enforcement of antitrust laws.[28] By 2015, 51 percent of the value of U.S. farm production came from farms with at least $1 million in sales, compared to just 31 percent in 1991, adjusted for price changes.[29] As agriculture became more concentrated, overall employment and income derived from farming continued to decrease in rural areas.[30] Indeed, by the end of the twentieth century, the sector employed fewer than 2 percent of the nation's workforce and had become archetypical of what scholars have called the "new Gilded Age," featuring concentrated economic power and wealth and diminishing opportunities for small producers and workers.[31]

The demise of family farms, in turn, harmed businesses in small towns in rural areas. Congressman Earl Pomeroy, who represented North Dakota from 1993 to 2011, explained to us that his father had owned a farm store in the small town where he grew up, which was not far from Fargo, the trade center, which kept growing. These "communities suffer because the farms consolidate. So my dad's farmers, my dad's clientele, would have been chopped in half and maybe in half again. As the small farms ultimately sold out to the larger farms and [with] ag consolidation pounding Main Street, . . . people [started] going elsewhere for greater shopping alternatives." Similarly, John Maddocks, a local political leader in southwestern Georgia, explained, "The big companies now own the farms: it's not like you have your family farm and you come in and buy your seeds at Johnny's feed and seed store in [town]. So a lot of places have dried up . . . so buildings deteriorate, and it's just hard to get by." The closing of businesses, in turn, engendered despair in such towns.

The farm crisis of the 1980s and 1990s likewise spurred rural backlash. Farmers mobilized en masse, to resist foreclosures at the grassroots level and cuts to aid at the federal level. They banned together in state, local, and national organizations, traveling to sheriffs' departments, state legislatures, and even Washington, DC, to call for relief.[32] As historian James Leiker sums up farmers' activism, "Each [movement] provided expressions of rage, manifestations of anger against government, consumers, and urban elites who understood little about farm life yet appeared to hold farmers' destiny in their hands."[33] While many of the cuts were eventually reversed, the farm bills of the 1980s and 1990s—all featuring some level of bipartisan support—included provisions that eviscerated support for farms and moved agriculture policy from the New Deal paradigm to a more market-oriented approach. Dairy farmers were especially vulnerable. The frustration and anger caused by the farm crisis and related economic policies of the 1990s endured for decades, particularly in the Midwest.[34] The heightened stress and depression among farmers became tragically obvious in a rash of farmer suicides.[35]

The Boom and Bust of Natural Resource Extraction

Particularly in the West and the Appalachian regions, rural areas have been disproportionately reliant on the extraction of natural resources, including timber and natural energy. These industries have also been buffeted by technological change and global competition, both of which placed downward pressure on employment.[36]

Even when such industries flourish, they are highly subject to boom and bust cycles. This can wreak havoc on communities that become overly reliant on them, a phenomenon described by scholars as the "resource curse."[37] County chairs in northern Michigan described to us how their area had prospered and declined time and again through such cycles, from logging early on, through the oil industry in the late twentieth century. Once Amoco and Shell Oil pulled out by the early 1990s, smaller "mom and pop stores" subsequently closed as well, and the unemployment rate ballooned. In southeastern Ohio, county chair Bill Whittaker told us, "It's been a roller coaster here. . . . The highs and lows have a lot to do with natural resources here. In the 1970s through the 1980s, coal mines were huge. . . . When they mined those places out, ran out of seam, they closed; there was a big shift in the economy. They [had been] some of the higher-paying jobs in the county; those were all union jobs, which makes a big difference in everything." Next came a "shallow-well oil boom," but that "ran its course." Two aluminum plants and shale have propped up the economy since then. "We went through a lot of lean times in the county," he concludes, noting cycles of high unemployment. In short, although jobs in extractive industries have declined nationwide for more than a century, their numbers in certain rural localities have waxed and waned, often wreaking havoc on those communities.

Meanwhile, in recent decades, federal policies that aimed to regulate greenhouse emissions yielded highly visible examples of government intervention that, at least ostensibly, seemed to threaten local economic activity.[38] While economic evidence is mixed on the true employment effects of such regulations, some—such as the Clean Air Act—do appear to have negative impacts.[39] Moreover, Republican lawmakers have made rhetorical appeals against these laws on the basis that they "kill jobs." From the perspective of local residents, especially when they are not consulted in the process, such regulations also seem invasive, sparking political resentment.[40]

The Deindustrialization of Rural America

Though manufacturing is typically associated with urban areas, in fact it has long been a crucial component of the rural economy. It became even more so in the late twentieth century, when jobs in agriculture and other sectors declined.[41] As manufacturers fled urban areas, they often landed in rural ones; this included particularly industries in which production was done more efficiently in single-story facilities with larger footprints.[42] Rural areas attracted industries also because of their low-wage labor markets, cheap land, and often hands-off regulatory environment. For a time, therefore, manufacturing employment grew at a higher rate in rural areas than urban ones.[43] Congressman Richard Gephardt, who represented Missouri from 1977 to 2005, explained that many "industries put their factories in small towns and rural areas, and that cushioned the blow when so many workers left agriculture: They could move over to manufacturing." Where he'd grown up, for example, "shoe factories and auto-parts plants went into areas that were losing agriculture."

Rural manufacturing was not necessarily ideal for workers: Many plants fled to rural areas to avoid union drives and other forms of regulation aimed to protect workers. Nevertheless, the sector did offer many rural dwellers employment, typically in jobs with decent pay and benefits, particularly relative to other industries that employ people with lower levels of education.

Starting in the 1990s, however, rural manufacturers became vulnerable to growing global competition and began to hemorrhage jobs. This occurred due in part to trade liberalization and the rise of East Asian countries—first Japan and then China—as producers of electronics, furniture, and other consumer goods.[44] The North Atlantic Free Trade Agreement (NAFTA), ushered into law with bipartisan support in the mid-1990s, brought the United States into greater competition with Mexico, resulting in job losses and broader economic harm.[45] Indeed,

such deals allowed foreign competitors to bypass the very conditions—
low labor and regulatory costs—that made rural areas attractive to
manufacturers to begin with.

Mexico had initiated NAFTA during the 1980s, and President
George H. W. Bush took the lead on promoting the negotiations, aiming
primarily to protect the interests of U.S. corporations. Democratic presidential candidate Bill Clinton adopted an ambiguous stance of "qualified
support, but only with side agreements on labor and the environment."[46]
This left room for billionaire Ross Perot to launch his third-party campaign focused in part on the damage NAFTA would do to the U.S. economy. He won 19 percent of the vote, the most any third-party candidate
had won since 1912, and attracted public attention to the issue.

Once Clinton was inaugurated, his ambivalence about NAFTA faded
and he turned his attention to securing its ratification.[47] Gephardt—by
then the House majority leader—met with him and said, "We need
trade, but we also need an ironclad commitment from Mexico" to abide
by strong labor protections and environmental standards. Clinton sent
Gephardt to Mexico to strike a deal, but to no avail. Upon his return,
Gephardt and House Majority Whip David E. Bonior worked hard to
organize congressional opposition to NAFTA, creating a high-profile
intraparty conflict that spotlighted the president's role in defying those
who were advocating on behalf of American workers.

This conflict was amplified by a major grassroots effort that emerged
to fight ratification. All major labor organizations opposed NAFTA vociferously, playing a "long overdue game of outside-the-Beltway hard-
ball" that "successfully captured broad working-class anxiety and anger
over the state of the economy."[48] Labor unions, alongside environmental, consumer, human rights, and church organizations from across the
country, invested millions in running television and radio ads against
the agreement and highlighted lists of jobs and companies that would
be lost to Mexico.[49] The Clinton administration promoted a debate on
the subject between Vice President Al Gore and Perot; televised on
CNN in November 1993, it attracted the highest number of viewers
CNN had ever had, and they heard Perot argue that the agreement
would force blue collar jobs to depart the United States for Mexico.[50]

Ultimately, the opposition failed, and Congress ratified NAFTA. Many Democratic members felt cross-pressured by strong support for Perot in their districts and opposition to the trade agreement from organized labor on the one hand, and Clinton's support for it on the other.[51] In the House, Democrats brought the agreement to the floor for a vote, where it passed 234–200, with 102 Democrats in favor and 156 opposed. In the Senate, NAFTA passed 61–38, with 27 Democrats voting for it, 28 against it, and one abstaining. According to our analysis of roll call votes, several dozen Democrats from relatively rural districts voted in favor of it.[52] NAFTA had been a highly visible and deeply bruising battle, one that likely seared into the minds of many Americans that the Democratic Party was no longer the staunch defender of workers' interests that they had long assumed it to be.

Alongside the competition resulting from NAFTA, China emerged during the 1990s and early 2000s as one of the world's largest exporters and fiercest producers in manufacturing.[53] This development, known as the "China Shock," led to economic displacement and stagnant wages, as several economists have shown.[54] It has also been linked to higher community-level mortalities from alcohol and drug abuse, mental health issues, and suicide.[55] These deaths, in turn, have been disproportionately located in rural counties.[56]

To probe the relationship between place-based employment trends and trade, we examine claims for the Trade Adjustment Assistance (TAA) Program, the major U.S. program that aims to help workers who have been displaced.[57] Enacted in 1962 and bolstered in the early 2000s, the program offers training, employment management services, and various forms of income support to workers who are able to demonstrate that they have been laid off or their employment terminated as a result of U.S. trade policies. Layoffs related to TAA claims, an admittedly limited measure for reasons we discuss in the appendixes, suggest that rural counties, relative to urban ones, have been disproportionately harmed by recent trade policies (figure 3.3; see appendixes).[58] Increases in claims were especially high in the mid- and late 1990s, following the implementation of NAFTA, when they often dwarfed rates in urban areas. In fact, adding up all TAA-related claims from 1994 to 2020, we find that rural areas lost nearly twice as many jobs per person—85 percent

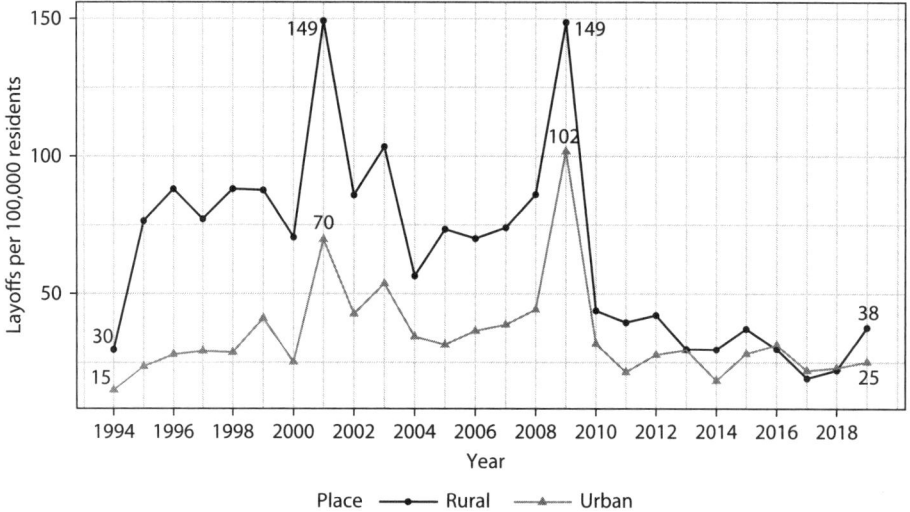

FIGURE 3.3. Trade-induced layoffs, rural and urban counties, 1994–2019
Source: U.S. Department of Labor; measure of rural from OMB

more, in fact—than urban counties. As Senator Bob Kerrey remarked, "There's no question rural communities have borne the brunt of . . . the movement of jobs to Mexico and China. . . . They have been punished by free trade."

The loss of jobs in manufacturing, like losses in agriculture, triggered rural backlash. The ratification of NAFTA in particular galvanized disappointment with the Democrats among many longtime party supporters, given the visibility of the campaign against it and its ultimate support by many congressional Democrats and of course President Clinton himself. This likely pushed many rural dwellers to see the Democratic Party as no longer representing their interests. Rage ensued in small rural towns that were rocked by the decline of manufacturing and other goods-producing industries.[59] Communities felt betrayed not only by large corporations that outsourced jobs, but also by policymakers in Washington and even in their own districts, whom they viewed as undermining their economic security.

To be sure, manufacturing continues to provide an important economic base for rural areas. According to estimates for the year 2019 from the USDA, 21 percent of nonfarm income in rural areas comes from manufacturing, compared to just 11 percent in urban counties.[60] According to the Federal Reserve, manufacturing offers a better wage premium—that is, higher pay relative to comparable private sector, nonmanufacturing wages—in rural areas, where it is 30 percent, compared to urban counties, at 7 percent.[61] Yet rural communities' reliance on manufacturing and the waning importance of goods production to the U.S. economy underscore the very vulnerability of rural areas. As deindustrialization continued during the first decades of the twenty-first century, rural workers in manufacturing were disproportionately affected.[62] Further, on January 1, 2005, protections for domestic apparel and textile industries—which were located particularly in the rural South—expired as a result of trade negotiations reached in the 1990s under President Clinton. From 2000 to 2017, more than three-fourths of nonmetropolitan counties lost manufacturing jobs.[63] It is perhaps no surprise, then, that politicians' calls to "bring jobs back to America" appear to especially resonate in rural areas.

The Place-Based Rise of the Urban Knowledge Economy

As policy changes hastened the decline of rural areas, they also bolstered the growth of urban ones. The knowledge economy did not just develop naturally. Instead, as several scholars have argued, it was deliberately constructed by policymakers at the national- and state levels.[64] They created it by making technological investments in coordination with high-end technology firms.[65] Beginning in the 1980s and through the 1990s, policymakers commenced aggressive national and state-level policies to "incubate" urban knowledge-economy hubs. Some Democratic officials envisioned future national economic fortunes as dependent on the involvement of venture capital and the creation of university-industry consortiums in major cities, and they joined forces with Republicans to promote such efforts. The knowledge economy propelled growth in many metro counties—and in doing so it spurred high levels of geographic inequality.

Several features of the contemporary knowledge economy exacerbate rural-urban disparities. First, the knowledge economy relies on a highly educated workforce, which rural areas have struggled to cultivate and retain. Whereas the workforces in rural and urban counties had very similar levels of postsecondary education in 1970, since then the gap has grown tremendously—by roughly threefold. This has occurred as young people from rural areas who acquire more education—a potential resource for local economies—tend to migrate permanently to urban areas precisely for better job opportunities.[66] This so-called brain drain only hastens the decline of rural economies, contributes to population stagnation, and promotes resentment among residents who remain. One party chair after another, in disparate states and in both parties, told us that young people move away to go to college and don't return. "There is no future for them here," a Democratic Party county chair in Texas put it after describing the deep poverty and lack of good-paying jobs in the area. One lawmaker shared that in recent years, trips back to what had been his cherished rural hometown now fill him with sadness and bring to mind the lyrics from Paul Simon and Art Garfunkel: "Nothing but the dead and dying back in my little town." For those who remain behind, circumstances can feel bleak.

Beyond the frustrations created by the brain drain, the material inequalities created by the knowledge economy are especially trenchant and can be self-reinforcing. Firms in this sector typically cluster in particular places. That is because they benefit from and even thrive off so-called agglomeration or spill-over effects that result from being in close proximity. This allows them to partner with and learn from one another, engage in idea formation, and draw on potential employee pools. Cities, because of both their physical infrastructure and their amenities that draw in highly educated workers, are especially well suited for such industries. After an urban area has developed a solid base of the knowledge economy, it tends to build on its successes, exacerbating place-based inequalities between cities and outlying areas.[67]

Rural areas are far less well equipped to draw in such economic activity. Despite recent efforts to expand broadband to sparsely populated communities, rural areas still lag behind urban ones in terms of having the physical infrastructure necessary to support knowledge-based economies. As a result, many rural areas have been forced to rely disproportionately on the low-wage jobs that are common in the contemporary economy.[68]

Urban areas that are home to bustling knowledge economies are certainly not without their problems. These include high levels of economic and racial inequality, as well as other forms of dislocation, such as gentrification. And not all rural areas have been totally left behind. Some have successfully exploited their closeness to natural amenities to foster economies based in tourism and recreation.[69] Yet such rural economies can create their own divides and frictions, pitting more affluent newcomers and vacationers against long-term residents, who may find themselves squeezed out of the housing market and other aspects of the economy.[70] Moreover, economies rooted in natural amenities are simply not robust enough to foster sustainable, widespread growth.

In brief, while rural areas have been secondary to urban economies for most of American history, the rise of the knowledge economy as the central engine of economic activity has pushed place-based inequality to new heights. These dramatic shifts—combined with the perception that the Democratic Party is advancing primarily the interests of those in urban areas—have alienated rural people. This raises the question of the political consequences, to which we now turn.

The Political Effects of Rural Decline and Restructuring

Several economists and political scientists have shown that job displacement produced by trade and other forms of economic decline has shaped the politics of those living in affected localities. They link job loss induced by NAFTA, the China Shock, and deindustrialization more broadly with an increased likelihood that those who are adversely affected—particularly those who are non-Hispanic white—will support the Republican Party.[71] What we want to know more specifically is how—and when—such economic trends have affected politics in rural areas compared to urban areas.[72]

To investigate these questions empirically, we collected data on all 3,143 counties in the United States for each election year running back to 1976.[73] We analyze how specific trends—starting with employment growth—influenced the share of the vote in each county for the Republican presidential candidate. We examine three specific time periods: 1976 through 1988, when the divide had yet to emerge, as a baseline or reference point; 1992 to 2004, when the divide opened up; and 2008 through 2020, when it intensified and became deeply entrenched. We do so using multivariate regression analysis, a technique that social scientists deploy to see if two phenomena are systematically related to each other. We control for other important county-level factors, including race, ethnicity, and age, to ensure they do not account for the relationships we uncover (see appendixes).

In examining the data, we are interested in two ways that certain factors might relate to the rural-urban divide. In some instances, rural and urban people may face similar circumstances, but if those circumstances are more prevalent among the population in rural places, they may be particularly consequential there. We refer to these as *compositional factors*. In other instances, rural and urban people may confront different experiences because of the particular ways that trends interact with circumstances in each place. We refer to these as *contextual factors*. In either case, such factors may influence residents' behavior at the ballot box and account for differences in how they vote.

Turning to the systematic relationship between employment growth and county vote share for the Republican presidential candidate, we find a significant relationship, but one that changes with each time period. Figure 3.4 plots the relationship between job growth (x-axis) and presidential voting (y-axis), comparing rural and urban counties (the two different lines), across each time period (for full results, see table A3.2 in the appendixes). In the first period, employment growth is positively associated with Republican vote share, meaning that counties with stronger economies were more likely to support the Republican presidential candidate. This was much more

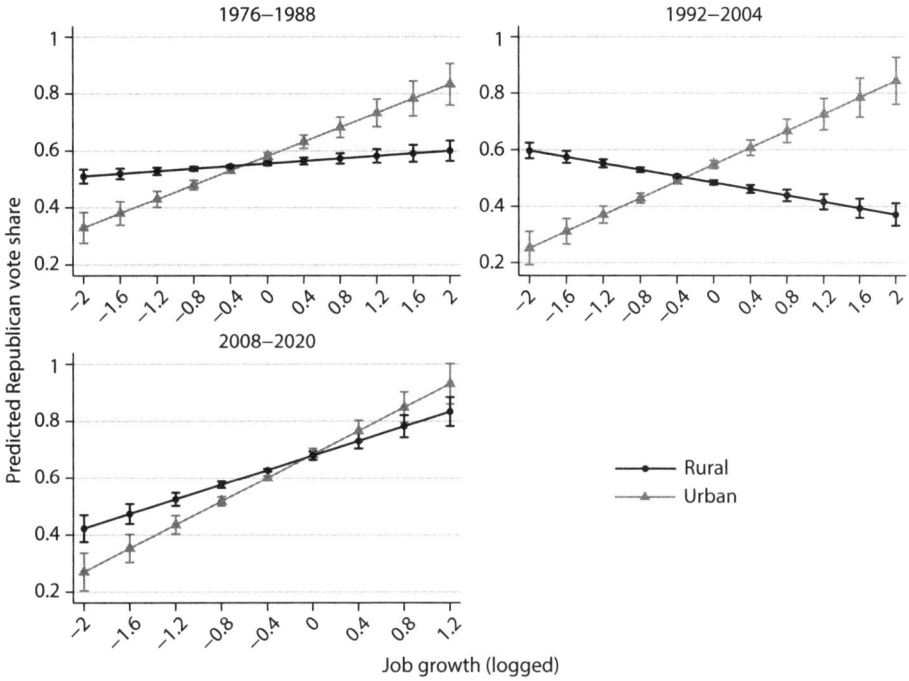

FIGURE 3.4. Employment growth and Republican vote share, rural and urban counties
Note: Estimates were generated using multivariate regressions, including county-level controls for education level, racial and ethnic demographics, and age, among other factors. Full results, model specifications, and sources are in appendixes.

the case in urban areas than rural ones. In the second period, when the rural-urban political divide emerged, we note a striking change: Rural areas with *lower levels* of job growth became more likely to vote Republican, while the opposite remained the case in urban areas. In the third period, both rural and urban areas once again exhibit a positive relationship between job growth and Republican vote share. This indicates that in the second period—when the divide emerged—rural dwellers in places that were facing lower economic performance turned to the Republican Party.

When it comes to population growth, other scholars have shown that it can shape politics, including by spurring resentment and backlash.[74] Those studying other countries, for example, have linked

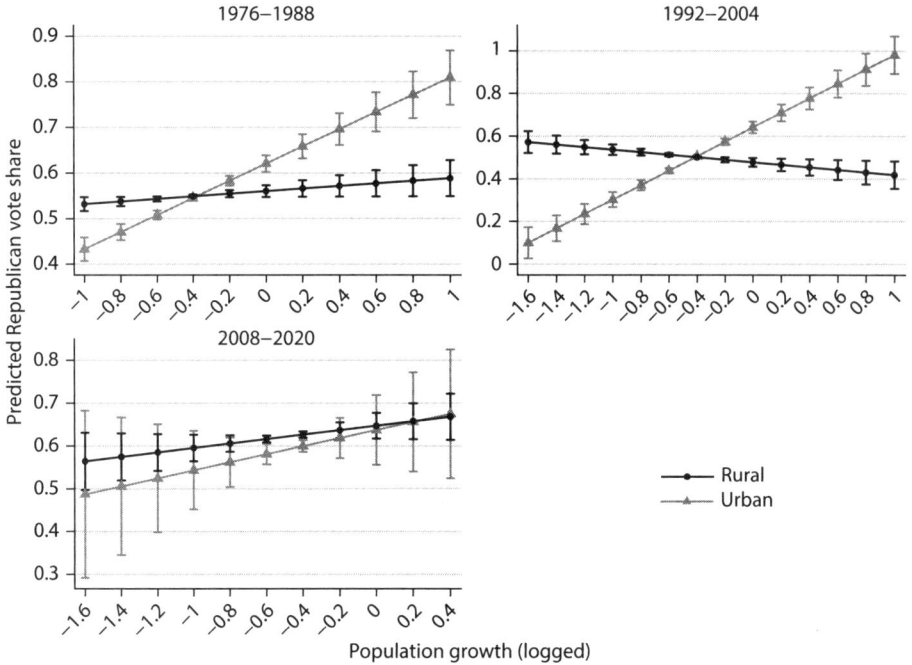

FIGURE 3.5. Population growth and Republican vote share, rural and urban counties

Note: Estimates were generated using multivariate regression, including county-level controls for education level, racial and ethnic demographics, and age, among other factors. Full results, model specifications, and sources are in appendixes.

population decline to right-wing populism.[75] How have population dynamics affected voting patterns in rural versus urban places in the United States?

Investigating this, we find a very similar pattern as we did for job growth (figure 3.5; for full results, see table A3.3 in the appendixes). In the first period, when no national rural-urban divide existed, population growth in urban areas is positively associated with Republican vote share, and in rural areas, the flat line suggests there is not much of a relationship. From 1992 to 2004, however, we find that population decline is associated with greater Republican vote share in rural areas—as is evident by the downward-sloping line. This is very noteworthy given that more than one-fifth of all rural counties between the years 1992 and

2004 lost population. Urban areas, by contrast, continued behaving the same as in the earlier period. In the third period, 2008 to 2020, we find that population growth is once again associated with greater Republican vote share, in both rural and urban areas, at similar rates.

In short, our results indicate that as the political economy of the United States was transformed in the late twentieth century, it spurred the opening of the rural-urban divide. As shown above, the key moments of transformation were the 1990s and early 2000s. During this time, as many rural areas hemorrhaged jobs and faced population stagnation, rural voters—many of whom had long viewed the Democratic Party as the one that best represented them—increasingly began to support Republican presidential candidates instead.

The Demise of Rural Support
for Democratic Candidates

Like other county chairs, Bob Hopkins, a Republican in southern Ohio, recited a list of six or seven major companies that had employed local people into the 1990s. He mentioned the products they made and the parts of the country to which they were shipped. "So when you were in high school, and the teacher says, 'What are you gonna do when you get out?' the answer would be, 'Uncle Bob's gonna get me [a job at] GE,' or 'Uncle Jake's gonna [get me a job] at Goodyear.' Then the economy changed and everything. Now this county is probably 75 percent driven by tourism. We have no industry here. So people live here, but they drive to Columbus to work. That's the biggest change: We went from, 'We make stuff, people stay here, their kids all play ball here,' to 'I live in [this] county, but I work in Columbus or Cleveland or . . . other places.' So probably the biggest employer in the county right now is Walmart, or the county itself, and state jobs."

The transformed political economy that created greater place-based inequality did not emerge naturally or inevitably, nor was it purely the result of technological change. Rather, it was in large part the result of politics, produced as lawmakers embraced policies that helped build up urban economies but in the process harmed rural ones. While many urban areas have been able to transition to new sources of economic growth, rural areas have indeed been left behind. Job losses and population stagnation in rural areas figured heavily into the political shift toward supporting Republicans in presidential elections. As conditions worsened, residents called to restrict trade, bring manufacturing jobs back home, and exploit natural resources such as oil and gas.

After six decades during which many rural dwellers were either devoted Democrats or occasionally voted for the party, why would these changes have driven them away from it? After all, Republicans generally had long favored the key policy changes that ended up harming rural areas, and it was only when a handful of Democrats joined them that changes were enacted. We reason that Democrats caught the blame largely because they held the White House during most of this period, and a Democratic president signed into law some of the most highly visible policies signifying these changes, such as NAFTA. In fact, it was congressional Democrats themselves and their allies in labor unions and other organizations that highlighted for the general public how harmful these policies would be for everyday Americans and smaller communities. Tragically for the party, that political activity not only failed to yield its desired policy impact, but worse yet, it boomeranged in ways that harmed it deeply, for years to come.

Stepping back, we can see the interplay of policy and party dynamics that induced political change. In the 1930s, New Deal policies had spurred many rural dwellers to shift to the Democratic Party. Then, for decades, a new partisan status quo persisted, as we saw in chapter 2, with rural Americans split between the two parties depending on region and other aspects of their identity. The late 1990s and early 2000s upset the partisan divide once again, as the demise or weakening of long-existing policies that had protected rural economies provoked many white rural dwellers to desert the party en masse.

To be sure, not all urban areas have been buoyed by the knowledge economy, and those metropolitan areas that have become the nation's center of growth have also featured growing inequality.[76] Moreover, some postindustrial urban areas have shifted in recent years away from the Democratic Party. In his study of Youngstown, Ohio, for example, Justin Gest finds that economic decline in what was previously a Democratic stronghold has, in combination with concerns over status threat, pressed many working-class white people to abandon the party.[77] Yet such areas tend to be the exception rather than the norm, and the people who inhabit the most urban areas have not shifted to the Republican Party for various reasons.[78] For one, in booming metropolitan areas, as fellow political scientists Jacob Hacker and Paul Pierson show, the Democratic Party has managed to piece together a relatively progressive economic agenda that addresses many of the concerns of lower-income residents without upsetting wealthier urbanites.[79] Second, those urban areas that are not doing as well tend to be inhabited by residents who are loyal to the Democratic Party owing to its stand on other issues, such as civil rights. These include Black Americans, who have remained "steadfast Democrats," as political scientists have shown.[80]

But the political-economic forces themselves prompted only the first step in the formation of the rural-urban divide. They would set into motion others as well, to which we now turn.

4

Overbearing Elites
and Rural Resentment

POLARIZATION INTENSIFIES

MATTHEW NOVAK, a Republican Party county chair in the Lower Peninsula of Michigan, explained that not long ago, moderate Democrats typically won elections in the region. He described those political leaders generally as "progun, prolife, and prounion," and "very respected." A prominent example was Democrat Bart Stupak, who served in Congress from 1993 to 2011. He represented the immense, sparsely populated rural congressional district that spans the Upper and Lower Peninsulas and takes more than seven hours to drive across. Democrats like Stupak benefited from the long-enduring support of an "older generation [of voters that] was very prounion, because of GM in Flint and Saginaw"—which offered, within commuting distance, jobs with good pay and benefits. Even when many other rural counties veered toward the Republican Party in presidential elections in the late 1990s, Democrats still prevailed in the area right up to and including Barack Obama's 2008 victory.

But after that, things changed. In 2012, Republican candidate Mitt Romney won Novak's county with 51 percent of the vote, and the GOP continued to make inroads subsequently. Explaining the shift, Novak said, "You saw the Democrat Party kind of leave those people. . . . The quote from [Obama] that encapsulated why people then switched their vote [was when] he kind of sneered and said, 'These people are clinging to their guns and their religion.' That's a quote for the East and West Coasts, the base of the Democrat Party. . . . That's not going to go over well here. I think a lot of those folks felt abandoned under Obama, and so they were upset. And then Trump comes in and gives a big [middle] finger to that kind of leftist elitism," he continued. "And they loved it. . . . They're like, 'Yes, I'm upset. And you're channeling my anger in some way.'" Now, he explains, the region is "very solidly Republican."

The mention of "leftist elitism" was striking to us, and as we will see, it was a theme that came up repeatedly in describing how rural dwellers had come to view Democrats, the party that many once supported. Explaining why politics had changed locally, Novak observed that Democrats "seem completely detached from the reality of how people live here. I think the environmental side of it is big. . . . You know, they talk about electrification in green energy, and burning gas stoves, and all these sorts of things. And people here are like, 'I can't afford higher electricity bills! I can't afford a $60,000 to $70,000 electric car, and if I could, I can't drive it because I need to commute, and its range isn't enough.' . . . The dynamics of the policies that they're pushing don't connect and don't resonate with people's everyday lives here."

Already in the 1990s and early 2000s, the continuing transformation to a postindustrial economy had exacerbated the inequality between rural and urban areas, elevating the standard of living in many urban places while leaving rural ones far behind. As the twenty-first century continued, a second wave of changes followed. Once many rural voters had lost their faith in Democratic politicians to represent their economic interests, anger spurred by other matters repelled them further. What drove them away from the party at this stage stemmed less from its stance on any particular issue—in fact, as we saw in chapter 1, for the most part, their policy views are not very different from those of urban dwellers— than from their resistance to what they perceived as being imposed on by affluent urban outsiders who seemed oblivious to the struggles of their communities. Particularly from 2008 onward, rural people became increasingly supportive of a Republican Party that had grown more determined to push back against certain Democratic initiatives.

In this chapter, we show the second wave of dynamics that exacerbated the rural-urban divide in the early twenty-first century: rural dwellers' resistance to what they viewed as the overbearing actions of urban elites. Across numerous policy areas, rural residents came to resent people they identified as holding government power—namely Democrats from their state capitol or Washington, DC—foisting regulations or other burdens on them without consulting them. In the context of widening place-based economic inequality, this perception of power fostered resentment among rural whites toward the party they deemed responsible and heightened their support for the GOP.

A Growing Gap in Educational Attainment by Place

The transition among rural people from being willing to occasionally support Democratic candidates or even identifying strongly with the party to seeing it instead as a group of overbearing elites did not happen overnight. It began with a dynamic that grew out of the economic changes discussed in the last chapter. It then intensified through a shifting connection between education and place, which transformed how both matter for politics.

Education shapes individuals' relationship to both economic opportunities and politics. It is well established that college graduates enjoy a "premium" that boosts their incomes, employment opportunities, and other measures of well-being beyond those accessible to people with less education.[1] Education is also known to influence politics in various ways; for example, Americans with higher levels of education are likely to be more involved in civic life, in activities from voting to volunteering.[2] The amount of education individuals have also plays an important role in shaping their orientation to politics.[3]

Over the past several decades, a dramatic gap in educational attainment developed between rural and urban areas. In 1970, they differed little: Only 5 percent more adults in urban counties had attained a four-year college degree compared to those in rural ones (figure 4.1). Yet since then, urban areas have pulled away from rural areas, and the gap has nearly tripled. By 2020, 35 percent of all adults in urban areas

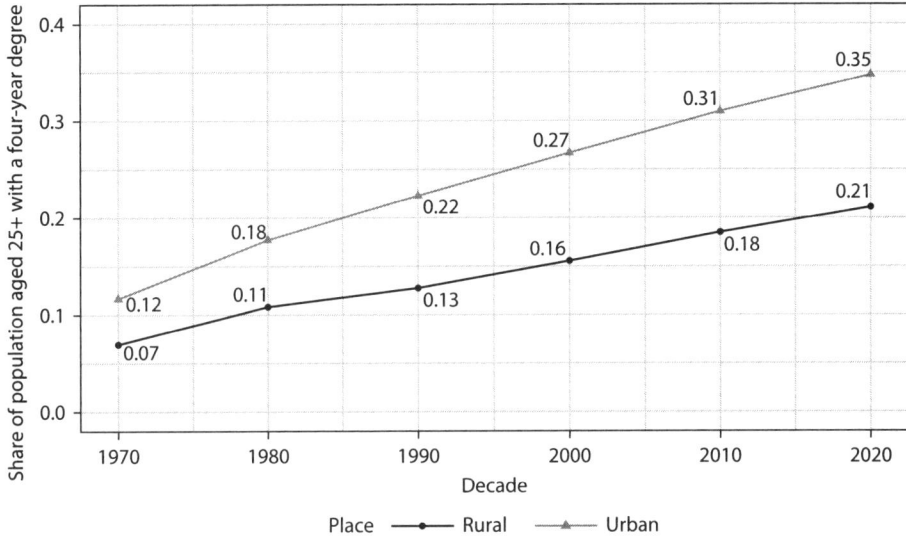

FIGURE 4.1. The rural-urban education gap, 1970–2020
Source: U.S. Census Bureau; measure of rural from OMB

had at least four years of college education, while only 21 percent of those in rural areas did. Certainly, this widening gulf indicates grow-ing disparities in the socioeconomic character of urban and rural places.

How does the education gap relate to politics? Using similar tech-niques to those we used in the last chapter—that is, multivariate regres-sion analysis examining the systematic relationship between education and presidential county vote share—we find a pronounced pattern.[4] In the late 1970s and the 1980s, areas populated by many people with higher levels of education tended to vote for Republican candidates for presi-dent, while places featuring those with more high school degrees or less education were more likely to vote for Democrats (figure 4.2; for full results, see table A4.1 in appendixes). But in the 1990s and early 2000s, urban places changed: Those with more highly educated residents began to support Democratic candidates at higher rates. Then by 2008 and beyond, rural places started following the same pattern. Given that rural places have a higher concentration of residents with less education,

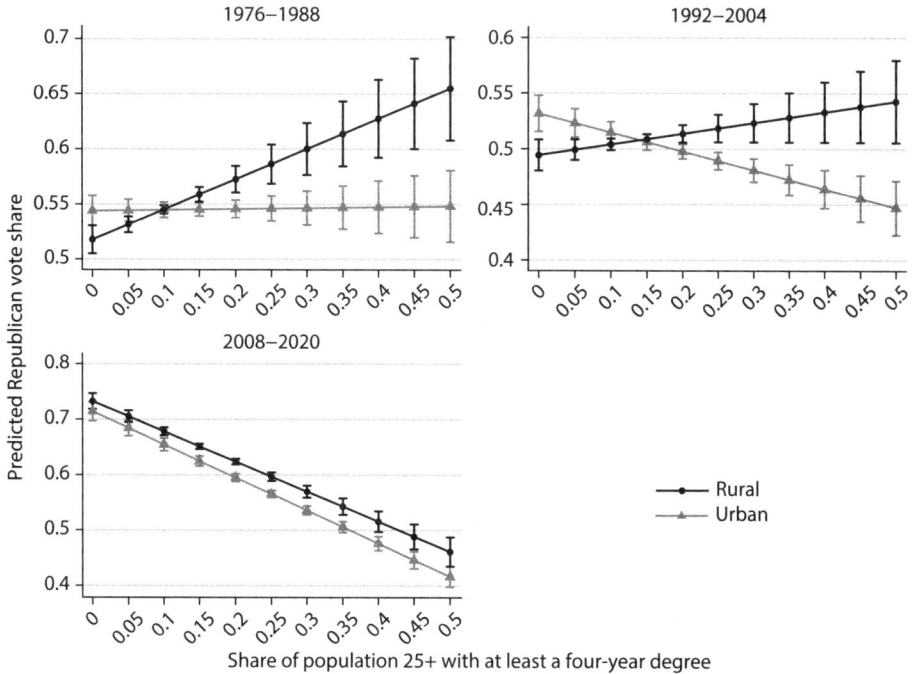

FIGURE 4.2. Education and Republican vote share, rural and urban counties
Note: Estimates were generated using multivariate regressions, including county-level controls for job growth, racial and ethnic demographics, and age, among other factors. Full results, model specifications, and sources are in appendixes.

they shifted to supporting Republicans. These new patterns exacerbated place-based polarization.

How Democrats Became Perceived
as Overbearing Elites in Rural Places

Why would the growing educational gap between rural and urban places have spurred a partisan transformation? Such shifts are very rare in politics. The first question is what might have prompted urban areas dense with highly educated people to drop their allegiance to Republican candidates and begin voting for Democrats.

While the Democratic Party had long held the reputation as the party representing lower- and middle-income Americans, in the late twentieth and early twenty-first centuries it increasingly attracted the highly educated professionals who were populating metropolitan peripheries, many of whom had higher incomes. Historian Lily Geismer points to the growing support for the party in "postindustrial, high-tech enclaves" around the country, among the "engineers, tech executives, scientists, lawyers, and academics" that filled the suburbs of Boston, New York, Philadelphia, northern Virginia, Atlanta, Chicago, Seattle, Los Angeles, numerous college towns, and the Research Triangle of North Carolina and California's Silicon Valley.[5] In fact, as the United States developed a knowledge economy, the sheer size of the highly educated white population more than tripled, making up more than a third of the electorate by 2015 and turning it into a more politically consequential group. This group has become increasingly multiracial over time, and more clustered in cities and the areas described above.[6]

Throughout this period, the two parties were themselves changing as they sought to win elections in what had become an intensely competitive political climate, and as political entrepreneurs and interest groups pushed them to become responsive to particular demands.[7] We suspect that highly educated urbanites were increasingly turned off by a changing Republican Party, and that shifts taking place in the Democratic Party enabled them to feel more at home in supporting it.[8]

For one, highly educated urban Americans may have been attracted by the new economic policies of some Democrats in Congress and, most prominently, of President Clinton himself. As politicians shifted away from their party's historical defense of antitrust policies and embraced free trade, the party likely became more appealing to highly educated and relatively more affluent voters. Offering suggestive evidence of this, political scientist Nicholas Short finds that states with higher rates of employment in the knowledge economy, such as New York, California, and Washington, resemble Republican-dominated states to the extent that they favor lax enforcement of antitrust laws, and yet they support Democrats in elections.[9] Moreover, such voters could have been attracted by the increasing emphasis Democrats placed on social liberalism, such as gay rights and gender equality.[10]

Our primary interest is in the changing relationship between education and voting in rural areas, since it is there that politics has changed most dramatically. Some scholars have assumed that what drove political polarization generally and the rural-urban divide in particular was the growing prominence of social issues.[11] They argue that issues such as abortion, gay rights, and gun control replaced so-called bread-and-butter economic issues, and that alienated rural voters.[12] Yet attributing the rightward turn of rural areas to social issues assumes that rural voters adopt dramatically different opinions on them than urban voters. As we saw in chapter 1, there is not actually a great deal of difference between rural and urban people's views on such issues, even on those we might assume to exhibit huge divides, such as gun control, spending on police, and abortion.[13] In fact, the differences have remained relatively modest even as the rural-urban divide in voting has escalated to its highest levels in recent years. Indeed, if such differences in mass opinions explained the rural-urban divide, we would expect the differences to be *especially large when the rural-urban divide solidified.* In short, differences in positions on social issues by themselves cannot fully explain how the rural-urban gap came to be a central dividing line in the American party system and society more generally.[14]

We are curious about whether what's driving the divide relates less to views about any of these social issues in particular than to an underlying thread that links several of them and other policies together in the experience or perception of rural Americans. Our interviews revealed a recurring theme: that rural people saw urban people, highly associated with the Democratic Party, as an overbearing elite. GOP Chair Bob Hopkins's county in Ohio had long been politically competitive in presidential elections, and Bill Clinton won the county in both 1992 and 1996. After major employers left in the late 1990s and early 2000s, he explains, "People just got tired of government." Republicans have won the county since 2000. "And here comes Donald Trump," Hopkins continues. "Yeah, he's rich beyond belief, and he's done all these things. But . . . he got people fired up, he got people excited. He was like, 'Dadgum it, this is America. Why are we letting it go down the toilet? Why are we kowtowing down to these elite people? They're not like you!' I think that really that hit home in rural [America]."

In thinking about this pattern, we are aided once again by Lipset and Rokkan, the authors we discussed in chapter 1 who have studied social divides and how they connect to politics. They explain, "Nation-building invariably generates territorial resistances," namely conflict between the "capital" and the "provinces," and tensions between "economically advanced areas" and the "periphery." In established nations, such opposition may emerge against "rising networks of new elites, such as the leaders of the new large bureaucracies of industry and government, those who control the various sectors of the communications industry, the heads of mass organizations, the leaders of once weak or low-status minority ethnic or religious groups," or other high-status groups.[15] When residents of rural areas perceive new laws and public policies or demands for them to be promoted by urbanites in one political party, that can prompt them to affiliate with the opposing party, in resistance.

The development of these dynamics occurred slowly in the United States. Given the particularly decentralized design of U.S. federalism, Americans lacked national rights of citizenship—meaning civil liberties, civil rights, or social rights—well into the twentieth century. Rather, states did most of the policymaking that affected people's day-to-day lives, developing a patchwork of approaches.[16] Policies featuring national standards began emerging initially in the late nineteenth and early twentieth centuries, but only in a few domains. New Deal policies promoted national standards in a wider array of areas, many of which, as we saw in chapter 2, reached rural people. Even then, however, many policies left considerable authority to the individual states to define standards, and people of color still lacked basic protections to civil and voting rights guaranteed by the federal government.[17] The civil rights movement led to the enactment of major legislation—the Civil Rights Act of 1964 and the Voting Rights Act of 1965—that established significant rights for citizens, regardless of race or ethnicity and regardless of which state they lived in. In addition, in other areas of public policy, such as environmental policy, the federal government came to play a larger role over time, and state governments, too, have sought to further policy goals emanating from the national government. Notably, the Democratic Party in particular championed many of these policy changes, and rural Americans remained about as supportive of the party as urbanites throughout.

Only after economic changes decimated many rural areas did rural dwellers begin to vote for the party that had developed more conservative stances on these issues. As the economy bottomed out in rural areas, residents began to perceive urban Americans—who were increasingly identifying with the Democratic Party—as advancing an overbearing national agenda that did not take their voices or their needs into account. It was not any one issue that tipped the scales, but rather the persistent commonality that ran across them. From 2008 onward, rural Americans perceived an urban elite that sought to impose itself on farflung places, controlling residents' lives through new rules and procedures in which they felt they had little voice.

As should be evident by now, Donald Trump did not cause the rural-urban divide. To the contrary, the gap commenced a couple of decades before he came on the political scene. The nationwide shift of rural voters toward the Republican Party occurred gradually, not in response to any particular president. At the same time, it is also the case that the resentment that had been brewing among rural dwellers—through dynamics we identify here—gained a megaphone once Trump entered the political arena. Unlike previous Republican presidential candidates, he overtly catered to such sentiments, generating heightened enthusiasm among many rural voters.

Now we will explore two examples that showcase these dynamics at work, involving environmental policies and gun control. Though Democrats have been less successful than they would have liked on these issues in recent decades, rural people feel disrespected by outsiders who do not appear especially receptive to their input or sensitive to how they live. Education comes into play here as well, as rural people perceived Democrats as wielding their formal, technocratic expertise to impose particular policies on them.

Environmental Policy and the Case
of Renewable Energy

As recently as the early 1990s, environmental policies enjoyed bipartisan support among both the public and lawmakers. Republican President George H. W. Bush signed into law amendments that strengthened the Clean Air Act and the Energy Policy Act, encouraging the use of alternatives to fossil fuels. At the Earth Summit in Rio de Janeiro, he signed the United Nations Framework Convention on Climate Change. Since 2000, however, the two parties have become polarized around such issues, and voters' partisan identity has become more strongly related to their support for or opposition to them.[18]

Yet if we scratch beneath the surface, we find that rural dwellers appear to have more nuanced opinions than those presented by party elites, and in many ways are particularly attuned to and concerned about the environment. As recently as 2020, roughly three-quarters of both rural and urban Americans told pollsters that they consider "environmental and conservation issues" to be important to them personally.[19] Rural people further exhibit a strong sense of "place identity," with most agreeing that "the area that I live in is an important part of who I am," as well as having a strong connection to nature, and this spurs them to be dedicated to environmental stewardship.[20] As researcher Emily P. Diamond found in focus-group studies with rural people across the United States, "This deep connection to nature led rural participants to recognize that their actions and behaviors have a direct impact on the health of their natural environment, and subsequently, environmental health has a direct impact on their welfare."[21]

Rural Americans have also suffered from environmental degradation that endangers residents' health in many instances and often harms the local economy. Democratic county chair Tina Wolford, who lives along the Gulf Coast in Texas, explained that fishing—previously among the primary sources of jobs in the area—had been undermined owing to pollution in the Gulf, in part because of a major mercury spill by a local industry. In North Carolina, poor rural communities in which Black Americans made up a higher share of the population than elsewhere were especially likely to be targeted for disposal of hazardous waste such as chlorinated hydrocarbons (e.g., PCBs), known to be associated with higher rates of cancer.[22] In northern Michigan, chairs in both parties mentioned concerns about unsafe drinking water, due to chemical pollution produced by local manufacturers in the past, as well as "Line 5," an aging set of pipelines in the Mackinac Straits that carries twenty-three million gallons of oil daily and the deterioration of which could cause a dangerous spill.[23] In other rural places, agricultural consolidation has been subject to lax enforcement of environmental laws, leading to a vast increase in water and air pollution.[24]

The need to care for the environment has intensified with climate change, and rural areas have an indispensable role to play in the necessary transition to renewable energy. Congress in 2005 committed the nation to reducing greenhouse gas emissions by half by 2030 and to net-zero emissions by 2050. Subsequently, national policies and those of several states have sought progress in meeting those goals.[25]

Our review of citizens' attitudes indicate support for these goals, across places. We find, for example, that majorities of both rural and urban white voters support giving the Environmental Protection Agency more power to regulate carbon dioxide emissions, raise the average fuel efficiencies of automobiles, and require the use of a minimum amount of renewable fuels (wind, solar, and hydroelectric) in the generation of electricity, even if electricity prices increase.[26]

Yet, as the United States has tried to shift away from relying heavily on fossil fuels and toward renewable energy, numerous plans for specific wind, solar, and geothermal projects have met with resistance in rural areas and thus failed to be adopted. These sites of opposition have emerged in all regions and states throughout the nation.[27] Such antipathy to the development of renewable energy in localities can act as a major barrier to its proliferation nationwide. In Indiana, for example, though wind farm development began in 2008 and has taken place in six counties, thirty other counties—encompassing a large share of the state's high-wind areas—have put moratoriums on wind farm construction or passed land use ordinances that in practice lead to the same outcome.[28]

Some might be inclined to dismiss such opposition as emerging from rural dwellers' ignorance or misinformation about climate change, parochialism, or hypocritical self-interest—otherwise known as "NIMBYism," referring to the "not-in-my-backyard" sentiment. Scholars who have studied such resistance in depth, however, argue that these explanations woefully misunderstand the underlying dynamics and therefore fail to offer insight about how to move forward constructively.[29] They find, by contrast, that resistance comes from several sources, with the commonality among them that local people feel that such projects are foisted upon them, that they have little voice in the matter, and that they are taken advantage of.[30]

Local residents' perceptions of whether renewable energy came about through a fair process is influenced by several factors, including their access to information about it; opportunities for them to participate, raise concerns, and influence decisions about siting; and whether political officials seem biased toward developers.[31] Scholars who researched opposition to wind farms in northern Indiana found that the "most pervasive feature" was that "the process by which wind developers engage with communities causes resistance, resentment, anger, and long-lasting community divisions." They learned from interviews with residents in multiple counties that developers typically operated secretly in the early stages, communicating only with a large landowner—often someone who lives elsewhere—whose land they wished to use. Meanwhile, they negotiated quietly with county officials on the basic terms of land-lease options, tax abatement, and any needed changes to zoning ordinances—all *before* news of the deal went public. By the time county residents learned that a wind farm was going to be established in their community, they felt that they were told, "It's a done deal." They experienced county governance processes as complex, often impenetrable to those opposed to the wind farms. They felt shut out from the process, while they perceived the developers to enjoy immense privileges. "We were effectively going up against a multi-billion-dollar company. We couldn't win," explained one opponent. Another said simply, "I'm not anti-wind. I'm anti-how-it-was-done-here."[32]

Similarly, residents of upstate New York perceived procedural injustice in the siting and permitting processes for installations of solar panels. The state government claimed authority for these processes, effectively allowing it to override zoning ordinances and other laws and to circumvent local input. Local people objected that hundreds of acres of solar panels could be installed in areas zoned as "residential," where other types of industrial or commercial establishments would not have been permitted.[33] The authors of a national study of failed renewable energy projects found that procedural conflicts such as these, where the public was not permitted to participate meaningfully in the process, accounted for 28 percent of their cases (though they did not distinguish between rural and urban), and nearly an equivalent loss of energy production.[34]

Besides rural residents often finding that their communities have little voice in the decision-making processes, many also perceive that on net, rural areas largely bear the burdens while the benefits are gained elsewhere, predominantly in urban areas. Residents may be skeptical that any financial payments or other resources provided by developers to the community amount to sufficient compensation.[35] Such developments can create a perception that renewable energy is extractive, delivering benefits to urbanites while placing costs on rural communities and failing to recognize their sacrifices or to compensate them adequately.[36]

Support for climate action from rural areas is crucial, given that the generation of renewable energy, such as wind and solar, requires a lot of land—in fact, ten times as much land per unit of energy produced compared to coal- or natural-gas-fired power plants.[37] Producing renewable energy will require cooperation between rural and urban areas, and rural communities' willingness to provide the extensive resources that are needed.

Yet the features of renewable energy development described above often generate a sense of burden among rural people, and it is only one of many types of environmental policy issues that have done so. Other examples include an updated rule modifying the Clean Water Act (called Waters of the United States) and aspects of the Clean Air Act. In each instance, rural people feel imposed on by urban elites, whom they blame for advancing such policies with little heed to those affected by their implementation.[38] Generating such backlash can be counterproductive to conserving the environment and addressing climate change.

Gun Control: The Case of the New York SAFE Act

As we saw in chapter 1, majorities of both urban and rural people tend to be supportive of gun control measures. Nonetheless, the process of establishing such laws can generate considerable tensions between the groups. The case we explore here occurred in New York State. Though New York is typically regarded as a Democratic stronghold in statewide races and the Electoral College, in fact the state exhibits a rural-urban divide of 12 percent in presidential elections as of 2024.

The enactment of the New York Secure Ammunition and Firearms Enforcement (SAFE) Act, touted as the "toughest gun law in the nation," epitomized the dynamics of elite overreach in the experience of many rural residents. Momentum for it began after the Sandy Hook massacre on December 14, 2012, when Governor Andrew Cuomo pledged "aggressive action." He was widely viewed as a politician with presidential ambitions, and the pursuit of a strong gun control measure would have seemed to be a major win and a positive signal to Democrats nationwide, who dearly wanted the enactment of such policies at the federal level.

Cuomo's team worked on the measure over the Christmas holiday—and did so secretly, to avoid mobilizing opposition. His administration crafted legislation that, among other things, required background checks for all who purchased guns, increased penalties for those who used guns illegally, and imposed an assault weapons ban. Despite the bill's sweeping scope, Cuomo and his team sought no input from gun owners, although it did brief the state senate's Republican leadership and heeded some of its objections. Most of those Republicans represented suburban Long Island districts, however, not the upstate rural counties in which more constituents engaged in hunting and had strong views about gun owners' rights. No public debate occurred over the bill.

On January 13, 2013, Cuomo announced that he would introduce the bill under a "message of necessity," which allows the legislature to avoid hearings and pass a bill in a shorter time period than the normal three-day minimum.[39] Yet the rationale for these expedited procedures was unclear: Crimes involving guns had been diminishing in New York for decades, and the state ranked fourth lowest in the nation in gun homicides, suicides, and accidents. The state, moreover, already had a strict assault weapons ban on the books, one of the toughest in the nation. The next evening, at ten p.m., lawmakers were given a thirty-page single-spaced law, with no staff summary, amending ten of the state's codes. The state senate voted quickly that night in favor of the bill. When the assembly reconvened the next morning, several members asked specific question about the meaning of terms in the bill, how it would treat particular circumstances, and how it should be interpreted. Few answers were provided, debate was closed after just five hours, and the bill was enacted.[40]

Cuomo may well have had compelling reasons for proceeding with such haste. He and other Democrats and their Long Island Republican allies might have rightfully been concerned about gun-related deaths, and strategically concerned that moving slowly would have allowed opposition groups, such as the National Rifle Association (NRA), to filibuster or ultimately stop the bill. Or possibly he just wanted to grab the headlines in hopes that he could become a presidential contender in 2016. In any case, the speed and secrecy with which the SAFE Act was written and passed alienated many rural dwellers. Over the next five months, a fully fifty-two of the state's sixty-two counties—including all the rural ones—passed resolutions opposing the law. Critics particularly lambasted the process of the law's enactment—for *how* it was passed. As a result, they claimed, many of its provisions lacked clarity or a clear rationale or seemed to present implementation challenges.[41]

Political scientist Robert Spitzer points out that public opinion regarding the SAFE Act among state residents was overall supportive, and even among upstate residents—including rural areas—there were nearly as many supporters as opponents. A poll of a conservative rural county—Jefferson County, in the northern part of the state—found that 50 percent of respondents said the law went too far, but 41 percent said it either did not go far enough or was about right. And in the same survey, 86 percent supported background checks for assault weapons purchasers at gun shows, and vast majorities of gun owners concurred. Yet among those who disagreed with the law, antagonism ran deep, and it provoked "vocal, visible, and angry" opposition.[42] For many rural residents, the SAFE Act signified the rise of a Democratic Party that wanted to run roughshod over them.

Of course, viewed in a national context, the enactment of strict gun control measures was the exception to the rule, both in the wake of the Sandy Hook shooting and since that time.[43] Since the 1980s, states across the nation have tended to relax or terminate their gun control policies of the past.[44] For the NRA, the SAFE Act likely served to mobilize its members by exemplifying what Democrats would do if they held political power elsewhere, a dynamic we explore in the next chapter. The organization continued to track the issue and to highlight Republican mobilization that ensued in rural areas' reaction to it, including Republican victories in many New York state races in 2014, which the state's Rifle and Pistol Association interpreted as a "repudiation of gun control."[45] The controversy over the SAFE Act, meanwhile, galvanized rural opposition to it, and bound it to the Republican Party. Signs voicing criticism of the SAFE Act continued to be displayed in rural areas of the state for years afterward, making apparent the growing place-based partisan divide.

———

Whether it was on gun control, environmental policies, or a slew of other issues, rural Americans increasingly felt that government—when run by Democrats—was telling them how to live, and they resented it. They viewed Democrats as mostly urban elites who were promoting such policy changes nationwide, through both the federal and state governments. They perceived them as better off than themselves and wielding an air of superiority, a self-righteous conviction that rural dwellers' lifestyles needed correction. In sum, rural Americans seemed to detect in Democrats what political scientist James A. Morone has shown to be a recurrent theme in American history: a moral fervor on the part of a group that understands themselves ("us") as practitioners of a superior code of conduct that they seek to impose on recalcitrant others ("them") to reform them.[46] In this case, the "us" versus "them" attitudes deepened partisan divisions.

Considering Racism and Nativism

We also aim to consider whether attitudes about race—specifically anti-Black attitudes—or responses to immigrants play a role in the urban-rural divide, and if so, how. An analysis of the Jim Crow–era South under one-party rule, V. O. Key's classic book, *Southern Politics*, showed that white people in rural areas of the region subjected Black residents to particularly oppressive political domination.[47] Some who investigate current politics demonstrate that non-Hispanic whites who identify as rural and exhibit "rural consciousness"—perceiving rural areas as deprived materially and disrespected culturally by urbanites and political elites—are more likely to hold anti-Black attitudes.[48] Yet we still don't know when such attitudes emerged, and if rural dwellers are more likely to hold them; many who score high on rural consciousness and resentment, for example, do not actually live in rural places. We are particularly curious about this question in the context of this chapter: Might rural whites perceive policies that aim to foster racial equality as the work of overbearing elites, and if so, might that be deepening the rural-urban divide?

By some indicators, the United States in the early twenty-first century seemed to be becoming a more inclusive place for people of all races and ethnicities. The Civil Rights Act of 1964 and the Voting Rights Act of 1965 had long since been enacted, both with broad bipartisan support, and the latter was reauthorized—also with bipartisan support—and signed by Republicans Ronald Reagan and subsequently George H. W. Bush. The 2008 election of President Barack Obama as the first Black president signaled impressive progress, as did his appointment of Justice Sonia Sotomayor, the first Latina to serve on the Supreme Court. The number of people of color serving in Congress was on the rise, reaching one in four members.[49]

Yet at the same time, rising partisan polarization has unleashed more visible and virulent racism and nativism into mainstream American politics than had been present for several decades. Republican political leaders had certainly long used racially coded campaign messages, such as George H. W. Bush's "Willie Horton" ad, which featured a Black criminal and appeared aimed to elicit racial bias among white voters.[50] But following Obama's election, the right-wing Tea Party formed and organized a backlash. It unleashed overtly racist and nativist popular sentiments that in the late twentieth century had been politically organized only in far-right fringe groups such as the John Birch Society; now these attitudes became infused into mainstream Republican Party politics.[51] This mobilization, in turn, paved the way for Trump's ascendance and election to the White House. Throughout, he drew supporters by promulgating racist and nativist claims, such as by spreading the "birther" claim about Obama in 2011 and depicting Mexican immigrants as "bringing drugs" and "crime," and as "rapists." He forcefully suppressed Black Lives Matter protesters after the murder of George Floyd. He actively courted white nationalist paramilitary groups such as the Proud Boys and Oath Keepers, and on January 6, 2021, they played a pivotal role in the deadly insurrection on the U.S. Capitol.

As the United States became more politically polarized, views about race diverged by party. Among white Americans, racial resentment—the measure typically used to study anti-Black attitudes—has become an increasingly strong predictor of partisan identification and vote choice.[52] Most white Democrats now feel that the United States has not gone far enough to ensure racial equality, while most white Republicans feel that it has gone either too far or far enough.[53] White Democrats are now much more likely to think that Black Americans are often treated less fairly than whites by government, such as when voting or when interacting with the police or criminal justice system.[54] Some scholars argue that support for Trump and the Republican Party has been fueled by a sense of status threat, white racial consciousness, and/or anxieties about American identity and inclusiveness.[55] In these accounts, in addition to overt racism or out-group hostility, white in-group solidarity has helped bolster support for the GOP.

This growing political polarization over views about race, overlapping in timing with the rise of the rural-urban divide, prompts us to investigate whether and how they might be related. While our analysis so far in this chapter and in the previous one rested on measures about counties—employment growth rates, share of college graduates, and so forth—here we are asking a question about individual attitudes, so we must use individual-level data. Importantly, unlike previous studies, ours considers where residents actually live, rather than subjective measures like self-identification.

Figure 4.3 uses survey data to proxy anti-Black attitudes among non-Hispanic white respondents. While we would ideally have data for racial resentment—the typical measure used by social scientists—the relevant questions are not asked for all the years in our period of study. In its place, we used the following question: "Some people feel that the government in Washington should make every effort to improve the social and economic position of Blacks. Others feel that the government should not make any special effort to help Blacks because they should help themselves. Where would you place yourself on this scale?"[56] Respondents were given a seven-point scale ranging from "Government should help Blacks" to "Blacks should help themselves." We think this question is a good proxy for racism: It picks up on the main elements of racial resentment—namely, the extent to which white people are unsympathetic to Black Americans and, moreover, deem them responsible for racial inequality.[57]

From 1976 to 2008, rural and urban white people tended to score, on average, very similarly in terms of anti-Black attitudes (figure 4.3; see appendixes). Indeed, as late as 2012, virtually no gap existed between the average rural and urban white respondents. In other words, racist attitudes were not limited to rural areas; rather, the typical white urban dweller expressed similar levels of anti-Black attitudes as those in rural areas. Beginning in 2016, both groups began to liberalize on the measure, but urban dwellers did so at a quicker pace. By 2020, the difference between them reached a modest but nontrivial 9 percentage points.[58] This means that anti-Black attitudes are more concentrated in rural areas, reflecting a compositional difference.

To what extent might this small but significant difference between rural and urban whites be driving the larger rural-urban political divide?

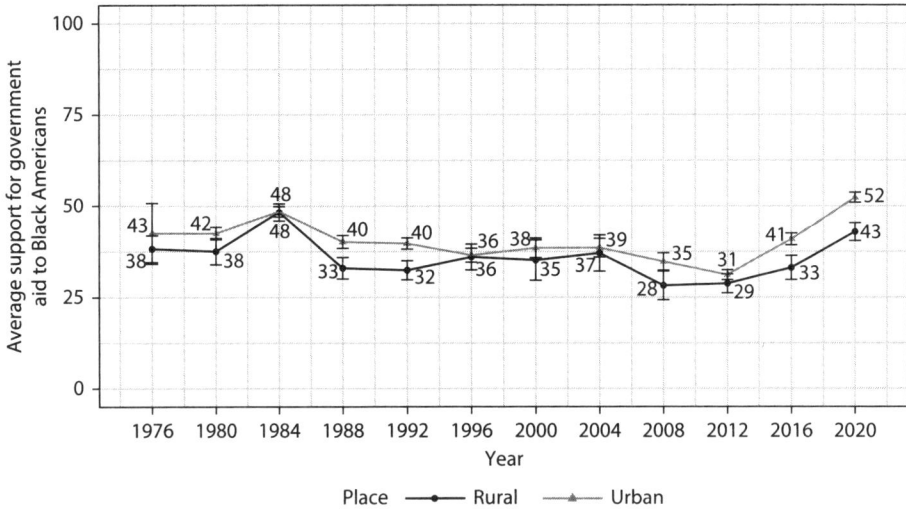

FIGURE 4.3. Anti-Black attitudes among non-Hispanic white Americans, rural and urban, 1976–2020
Source: American National Election Studies (ANES); measure of resident's rural/urban status from OMB
Note: Lines represent averaged responses to whether or not "the government in Washington should help improve the economic and social conditions of Black people," organized by respondents' places of residence. Responses range from "Government should make every effort" to "Blacks should help themselves," and are placed on a scale of 0 to 100 for interpretability. Higher scores mean greater support.

We examine the extent to which anti-Black attitudes are systematically related to one's likelihood of voting Republican, after accounting for education, income, age, and other potentially influential factors (figure 4.4; see appendixes). In all time periods under examination, higher levels of anti-Black attitudes are associated with an increased likelihood to vote for the Republican candidate, among both rural and urban non-Hispanic white people. In the period from 2008 to 2020, however, anti-Black racism is consistently a stronger predictor among rural dwellers than urban dwellers. In other words, anti-Black resentment has long been related to voting for Republicans, but up through 2004, it had no particular or distinctive role in rural areas, and it was not driving the rural-urban divide. Since 2008, however, such attitudes have been contributing to the

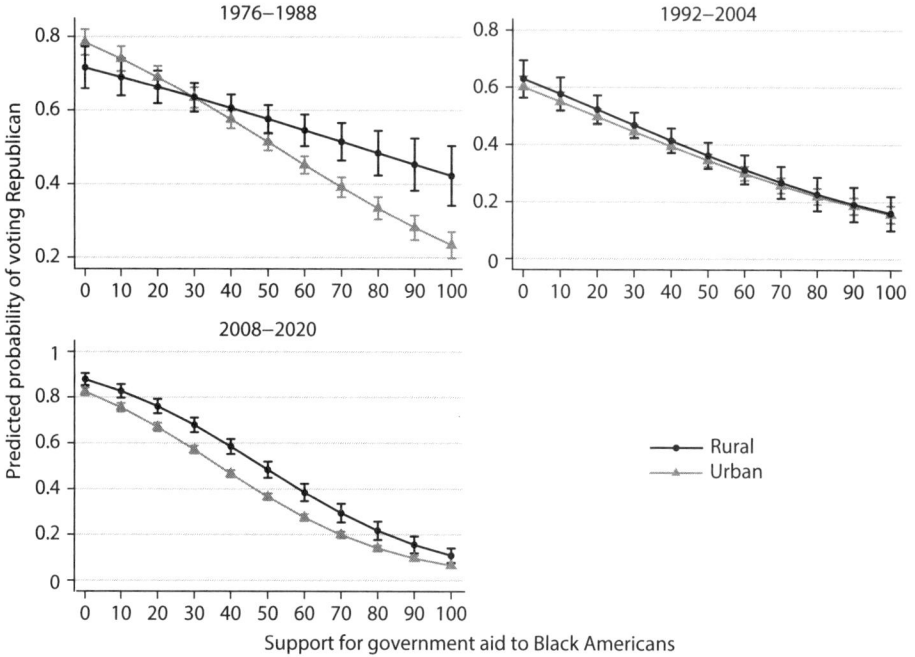

FIGURE 4.4. Anti-Black attitudes and presidential vote choice, rural and urban individuals

Source: American National Election Studies (ANES); measure of resident's rural/urban status from OMB

Note: Estimates were generated using logistic regression, including controls for age, education, and gender, among other factors. Full results, model specifications, and sources are in appendixes.

place-based divide (for full results, see table A4.2 in the appendixes). This is mostly in line with the research of other scholars who have found that anti-Black racism is an important if moderate contributor to rural-urban polarization.[59]

The timing of this rural-urban split in attitudes about race might seem puzzling. After all, the civil rights movement and its core policy accomplishments took place well over a half century ago, so why would this gap have emerged just recently? Both rural and urban whites held similar views about race in the later decades of the twentieth century, and both responded similarly to the adoption of national standards for civil rights and the implementation of such policies. We think the divergence in their views occurred, like other patterns we've observed in this chapter, as part of a two-step process of sequential polarization. After experiencing economic deterioration in their communities in the late twentieth century and early years of the twenty-first, rural white Americans felt more resentful of government efforts to expand rights to others—particularly a group they perceived mostly as urban—after the government had, in their view, been so unresponsive to their own plight. This echoes Arlie Hochschild's finding among Tea Party supporters in Louisiana, who felt that people of color were being permitted—by Democrats—to "cut in line" ahead of them.[60] As the parties polarized, white rural dwellers likely viewed these efforts as being promoted by urban Democrats.

Racial resentment probably remains more prevalent in driving the partisan divide in some rural areas than it does in others, as our interviews suggested to us. Several rural Democratic Party county chairs pointed to racism as they sought to explain how politics had changed locally in recent years. Those in North Carolina spoke of the long reach of history in local politics, and told of how white "Dixiecrats" abandoned the Democratic Party after Obama was elected. One reported being told by a local white resident that having a Black president was "not the natural way it's supposed to be." Patrice Hawkins said that once Trump was elected in 2016, "That is the most I've ever seen [white] people being rude to Black people and being very open, very vocal about it. . . . There was something underlying, and he gave them the freedom to do it." County chairs in other states, including Michigan, commented similarly that since Trump's election, some whites in the area, often including their own friends, openly expressed racist views that they had not heard from them before. Said Robert Nolan, a county chair in a coastal county of North Carolina, "Race still divides people, more in rural parts of the state than urban." A Democratic county chair in rural Missouri spoke of deeply entrenched racism in the area, and said that she could identify the local head of the Ku Klux Klan.

Some county chairs portrayed racism and nativism as primarily strategies used by Republican leaders: "They want to generate those emotions to drive people to be politically active." Or as John Maddocks of

Georgia put it, Republicans used racism to drive a divide between "the Black community and low- and moderate-income whites, when their interests might be the same."

Given the high rates of immigration in recent decades and the influx of Latinos in many rural counties, we also wondered whether growing racial and ethnic diversity might spur rural whites to vote for Republican candidates. Since the enactment of immigration policies in 1965 and 1986, the United States has grown more racially and ethnically heterogenous, including in rural areas.[61] We considered the changing racial and ethnic demographic profiles of rural and urban counties in recent decades. We found that both types of counties featured fairly similar racial and ethnic demographics in 1970, but in recent decades, urban counties grew far more diverse, and by 2020, roughly 45 percent of all urban residents identified as nonwhite.[62] Rural areas have also become more diverse, though, with one in four rural dwellers identifying as a person of color and 10 percent as Hispanic.

We wondered whether rural dwellers in more quickly diversifying counties are more likely than urban dwellers to view such newcomers as a threat to their status in society, and that in turn affects how they vote. This would cohere with scholars' findings that in some contexts, as the local population becomes more diverse, white residents view their position as imperiled by competition for scarce resources, particularly if nonwhites appear to be making political or economic gains.[63] Given the economic deterioration experienced by rural areas in the late twentieth and early twenty-first centuries, we were curious about whether white residents there might view the growing diversity in their communities as a threat, and respond by supporting the political party whose leaders in recent years have highlighted that theme.

To examine this, we evaluated whether the share of the population that identifies as Latino influenced voting among non-Hispanic white individuals. We found little support for the racial and ethnic threat hypothesis; rather, the greater racial and ethnic diversity that emerged in both rural and urban counties in more recent decades appears unrelated to the growth of the rural-urban political divide (see table A4.3 in appendixes for full results).

In sum, to the extent that racism and nativism are contributing to the rural-urban divide, it owes not to changes in the population of places, but rather to a growing gap between the views of rural and urban dwellers. Rural white people now express slightly greater resistance than urban whites to policies that aim to foster racial equality. Certainly, racism and xenophobia could be driving the divide in ways we are unable to observe given the limitations of the data available. For example, elite rhetoric on immigration could play an important role, beyond local contextual factors. Nevertheless, our findings suggest that such factors are not the only drivers of the divide, and that their contribution to the cleavage is contingent on historical processes.

Feeling Looked Down Upon

Democratic Congresswoman Cheri Bustos represented a largely rural district in northwestern Illinois that was previously home to the world headquarters of John Deere, large Caterpillar and Chrysler plants, and numerous smaller manufacturers that supported them. She says that her constituents blame NAFTA for sending many jobs to Mexico starting in the 1990s, and, subsequently, trade with China for further decimating the local economy. As employment opportunities diminished, small towns in the district lost population. Now, Bustos says, people in rural areas in her district feel "left behind by the national party, by the Democrats. They feel ignored and looked down upon . . . that Democrats think they are gun-toting hicks that like to drive F-150s. . . . They're stereotyped at every turn."

Rural dwellers increasingly perceived Democrats as an overbearing elite. They viewed them as pushing policies that would affect how life was lived in rural communities, yet without bothering to consult with rural residents in the process. White rural dwellers also began to view the Democratic Party as promoting public policies to cater to Black Americans—a group largely stereotyped as urban, and who appeared to be progressing at their expense.

In short, in the wake of economic change driven by public policies, rural dwellers came to view Democrats as an affluent group of people who sought to impose change on their lives, through policies that they themselves had little voice in and which were largely foisted upon them. They resented it and became increasingly repelled by the Democratic Party. But this transition did not happen automatically: Parties and organizations played a crucial role, as we will now see.

5

How Parties
and Organizations Matter

CEMENTING THE NEW DIVIDE

IN TALKING about how their region of southern Ohio had changed since the 1990s, Ohio county chairs in both political parties told us not only about the jobs that had left, but also about the simultaneous decline of labor unions, which in the past had bolstered the Democratic Party. In the southeastern part of the state, Bill Whittaker, the Democratic county chair said, "We had a World War II generation that we lost [by the early twenty-first century]. So many of them had not only served in the military, but they came back home, got employment in the aluminum plant, became part of United Steelworkers, . . . and their ability to fight for good wages and benefits, safety in the workplace, etc., was very much tied to the Democrats. Those guys were die-hard Democrats." Nearby, former Republican county chair Jeff Wolak acknowledged that he himself had been a Democrat earlier in his life, when he worked at the local mill where everyone was part of the union and supported the party. Once Reagan became elected, he switched his own affiliation to Republican; he subsequently ran for local office as an independent, but by 2001 ran as a Republican.

In the northern part of the state, Democratic Chair Beth Schultz listed the many auto manufactures that had closed up shop or downsized, creating "heartburn" for local residents whose "fathers and grandfathers worked there in good-paying blue-collar union jobs." As Republican Chair Connor Williams put it, "One of the big losses that we've had is that union base, and politically we [the Republican Party] attribute a lot of our success [to that]. Twenty years ago, unions had a real grapple on our politics, and a lot of that unionization has been lost through the loss of . . . private sector jobs." As unions diminished in many rural places, Democrats lost allies that had long bolstered the party's strength.

In their wake, Republican political leaders and conservative organizations stepped up to win over white rural dwellers. Civic organizations that were prevalent in rural areas—from evangelical churches to Right to Life groups to gun clubs—became effective in mobilizing people to participate in politics, supporting Republicans. Barbara Jones, a Democratic county chair in rural Missouri, put it in stark terms: "The evangelical right has pretty much taken over this area. They base their politics and the education of their children on their faith." Evangelical churches, several county chairs in different states noted, helped get the vote out.

A Republican Party county chair in southeastern Ohio, Tom Reynolds, explained that when Democrats went "after the NRA," it was a "game-changer for a lot of people here," because it "alienates a lot of Democrats . . . who are gun owners." He mentioned shooting clubs for kids, including Annie Oakley Competitions for girls, and noted, "It gives kids that may not be in other sports a chance to participate." Such groups are typically affiliated with the NRA, which in recent decades has connected people to politics, specifically as supporters of the Republican Party.

Already we have seen two sweeping forces, the rise of place-based economic inequality and perceived overreach by urban elites, that spurred a massive change in rural voting patterns. To these, we add a third: an organizational dynamic, by which we mean the role played—or not played—by political parties and other political groups, churches, and civic associations.[1] Scholars have demonstrated that several organizational developments in recent decades have aided the rise of conservatives in politics and the rightward shift of the Republican

Party.[2] As we show in this chapter, these changes in associational activity have not been distributed equally across place; rather, those aligned with the Republican Party have been disproportionately concentrated in rural areas. The organizational dynamics worked in tandem with the other two processes, effectively cementing the rural-urban divide and place-based polarization.

How Parties and Other Organizations Politicize and Mobilize Voters

In politics, rarely do facts, events, or changed circumstances simply "speak for themselves," conveying their meaning directly to voters, and voters often do not respond entirely of their own volition. To the contrary, political elites—broadly construed as elected officials, party leaders, and organizational actors—typically intervene and play a crucial role in making sense of developments for their constituents, supporters, or members. In so doing, political parties and other organizations try to raise the salience of some issues or identities at the expense of others (e.g., the economy as opposed to gun rights; religion as opposed to class); cultivate and crystalize particular identities; and mobilize voters accordingly.[3] To the extent they succeed, political parties—and often the organizations that work alongside them—shape the electorate.

Political scientist V. O. Key in the early 1960s dispelled the idea that "public opinion" emerges organically from citizens themselves. To the contrary, he wrote, "The voice of the people is but an echo. The output of an echo chamber bears an inevitable and invariable relation to the input. As candidates and parties clamor for attention and vie for popular support, the people's verdict can be no more than a selective reflection from among the alternatives and outlooks presented to them."[4] Political leaders engage in "framing," meaning they promote an "organizing idea or story line that provides meaning to an unfolding strip of events, weaving a connection among them."[5] This helps citizens confront complex issues and understand them, using a particular lens that focuses their attention on some dimensions while permitting them to ignore others.[6]

As jobs disappeared in the Kentucky coal industry in the 1990s and early 2000s, for example, plausible culprits abounded. These included technological change, which had reduced mining jobs since the 1940s, competition from coal-producing states in the American West and abroad, and the abundance of natural gas. But Republican leaders effectively pinned the blame on Democrats, saying they had instigated environmental laws that decimated the industry. This framing simplified the issue and spotlighted particular culprits while obscuring others.[7]

As national partisan leaders promote their candidates and encourage Americans to support them, they often focus on the media, seeking to effectively frame and communicate their message through it.[8] Many assume that political polarization is primarily driven by media consumption. Certainly public relations efforts can strengthen the political commitment and views of citizens who are already devoted to the party, the "base."[9] Yet partisan media outlets and the framing of stories rarely change people's views, and in instances when they do, those effects tend to be short-lived.[10] In other words, partisan conversion through exposure to the media is fairly atypical. By the same token, neither does the media do much to politically engage citizens who would otherwise be disengaged.[11]

More consequential, we argue, are political parties and affiliated organizations. Here we examine the role they can play in engaging people in politics and channeling their support. Scholars have long argued that parties at the organizational level are vital for democracy. When strong, they can connect citizens to the governing process, engage them in taking an interest in politics, help them to learn about issues, and ultimately encourage them to participate, electing candidates and holding them accountable. In these ways, they help make representative government work effectively.[12]

People's social group affiliations more generally—their ties not just to political parties, but also to churches, civic organizations, and other membership groups—provide important sources of meaning and connection, and strongly influence their partisan identity.[13] Such organizations can dramatically shape the fortune and character of parties by connecting their members with them. They engage people in politics more effectively than if individuals are just left to themselves to assess which party best represents them on the issues.[14] Rather, through repeated interactions over the long term, such groups can shape the very identities and capacities of voters, including how they interpret the world and their ability to act on it. They may highlight economic and social conditions such as those discussed in the previous chapters, creating a narrative that assigns credit or blame for such trends. They can also socialize voters in ways that provide a rationale for their political choices and motivate them to participate in elections.[15] As a result, they serve as particularly powerful sources of mobilization, and they forge enduring linkages among voters and parties. Organizational bonds not only help ensure that citizens actually vote and participate; they also strengthen citizens' partisanship.[16] We turn attention, therefore, to the ties between political parties and such organizations—and how they have changed over time—in order to understand how they shape politics today.

Changes in Political Parties and their Organizational Ties over Time

Political parties are weak in the United States today, relative to the past. This might sound surprising, since we are in an age of strong partisanship—both at the elite level (meaning among elected officials) and also at the mass level (meaning among many ordinary citizens).[17] But parties actually peaked in strength as organizations, with a strong presence at both the state and county levels, in the mid-nineteenth century. Parties then began a long period of deterioration. Progressive Era reforms deliberately aimed to weaken parties and give voters themselves—as individuals—more direct influence on the political system.[18] Beginning in the 1960s, furthermore, the United States' largest voluntary organizations—such as the Elks, the Masons, the Order of the Eastern Star, and the Grange, each of which had members active in local chapters across the nation—faced precipitous declines in membership. They were replaced by advocacy organizations, which lack members and do their work though paid staff operating primarily out of

Washington, DC, or New York City.[19] Political parties were no exception to this trend, as their membership rates declined sharply from the 1970s on.[20] Several developments hastened the process, such as the rise of direct primaries for candidate nomination and candidate-centered campaigns. The shift from labor-intensive to capital-intensive campaigning hurt as well, as parties' traditional reliance on armies of volunteers to get out the vote was replaced by the use of polling, television advertising, and calls to carefully chosen groups of voters.[21]

The two parties have not suffered equally from organizational decline. Political scientist Daniel J. Galvin argues that Republican presidents, as leaders of the party that was out of power throughout the middle of the twentieth century, worked hard to "cut into the Democratic Coalition, tap new sources of support, and awaken their 'silent' majority." Meanwhile, because the Democratic Party's long-running success since the New Deal appeared to be deep and durable, Democratic "presidents simply saw no urgent need to make long-term investments in their party."[22] Democratic candidates viewed campaigns as requiring them only to mobilize their base, whereas Republicans sought to attract new groups of voters, and they were more willing to invest in party organization in order to do so. "Repeated over time," writes Galvin, "this dynamic stunted the growth of the Democratic Party organization" well into the twenty-first century.[23]

As parties changed, so did the organizations that supported and acted in coalition with them. As political scientist Daniel Schlozman argues, from the Civil War to the present, social movements and the organizations that fueled them created alliances with parties, serving as "anchoring groups" between them and their key constituencies. Given the organizational capacity of these face-to-face groups, it is invaluable for parties to secure access to them and their resources and time. In exchange, parties offer these organizations the opportunity to gain political influence so they can achieve their policy goals, even if that means moving away from what the typical voter desires.[24]

While Democrats particularly benefited electorally from such group affiliations in the mid-twentieth century, Republicans have been the primary beneficiaries in more recent decades—a time when the

challenges parties faced made forging organizational coalitions especially valuable. Labor unions long served as the organizational backbone for the Democratic Party, particularly from the mid-1930s through
the 1960s.[25] Yet several political, economic, and legal shifts eroded those
ties considerably, especially in Midwestern states that have been pivotal
in recent elections. Meanwhile, the Republican Party developed new
ties with conservative groups, which, unlike most civic organizations,
have been ascendant and highly politicized. These groups helped buoy
the party at the ballot box while at the same time shaping its agenda and
character. This process began with the Christian right, and it continued
with the NRA and gun groups loosely connected to it, the Koch-
affiliated organizations such as Americans for Prosperity, and chapters
of the Fraternal Order of Police.[26]

How might these organizational developments aid the emergence of
a new political divide? Once a potential cleavage has opened up,
organizations can effectively help cement or crystalize it by strengthening the ties between voters and parties.[27] The strong social attachments
that group members associate with their political party means they are
likely to experience challenges to it, or instances when it loses elections,
as personal attacks on their identity, as we discussed in chapter 1.[28] This
results in greater negative partisanship and social polarization, generating hostility toward those in the other party. The activist orientation of
such groups, furthermore, prompts members to play an outsized role in
contemporary party politics, for example by participating in primary
elections and drafting platforms. They tend to hold positions that are
more extreme than the average voter.[29] To be sure, depending on the
incentives they face, some groups can mitigate polarization by bringing
together a diverse group of people and diffusing differences.[30] Yet on
net, through the means mentioned, such organizations often do more
to foster polarization than reduce it.[31]

Organizational shifts in recent decades have unfolded in ways that
harmed the Democratic Party nationwide and aided the electoral fortunes of the Republican Party, yet their effects have not been geographically neutral. The core organizations bolstering the Republican Party
coalition are disproportionately located in rural areas. They hastened

the two processes we've already examined, fueling the dramatic shift of rural voters to become stalwart GOP supporters. In the process, they shaped the party in ways that made it more extreme.

Organizational Atrophy Compounds
the Challenges for the Democratic Party

Does the Democratic Party itself deserve blame for losing the support of residents in rural areas where it had competed successfully for decades?[32] As we saw in chapter 3, some highly visible Democratic officials in the 1990s and early 2000s embraced more conservative economic policies that proved detrimental to rural areas, prompting many to lose faith in the party. Yet in recent years, the party has pursued more progressive economic policies, and key officials have continued to advocate for other policies that aided rural dwellers. Republicans, meanwhile, have remained less likely to do so. Political scientists find that although the Democratic Party today does include many affluent voters among its cross-class, multiracial alliance, it remains committed to a relatively progressive economic agenda, as evidenced by both its messaging and its policy goals.[33] Nonetheless, once voters lose faith in a party, it can be difficult to regain their trust, especially once a political cleavage has been formed and other actors and organizations are vying for their attention and votes. For most Americans, furthermore, arguments they hear from candidates or via the news media are not by themselves enough to sway them to change long-standing partisan allegiances. Rather, individuals are more likely to alter their behavior if others with whom they socialize and participate in community events—those with whom they are connected socially and emotionally—are so convinced.

For decades, labor unions had provided such connectivity among many working-class Americans, and while their members were likely to be far more concentrated in urban areas, they included rural dwellers, particularly in some Midwestern states. As we saw in chapter 3, manufacturing played an important role in rural economies, even more so than in urban

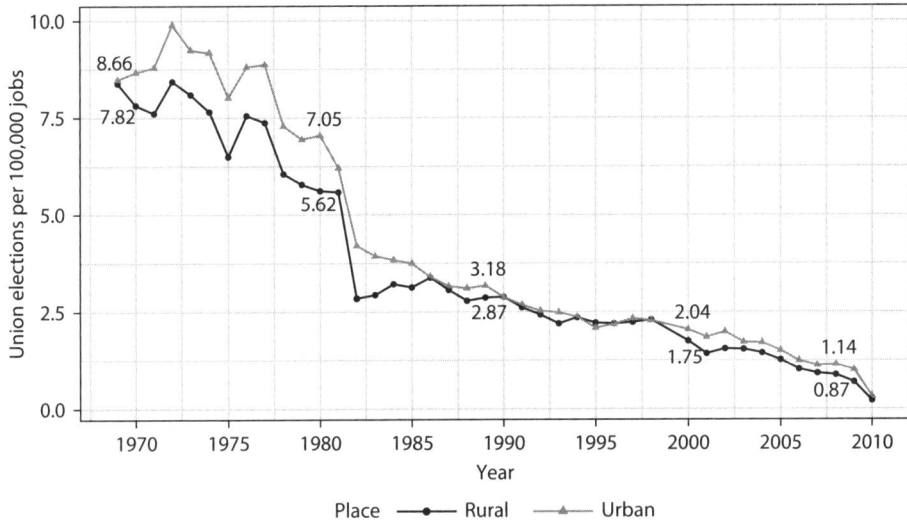

FIGURE 5.1. Union activity as measured by elections, rural and urban counties, 1969–2010
Source: Union data come from John-Paul Ferguson; measure of rural from OMB

areas. Using local union election data, a limited but nevertheless telling indicator of organizational presence, we find that as unions have declined in the number of people they cover, their activity has declined precipitously in both rural and urban counties (figure 5.1; see appendixes).

While certainly unions primarily improved workers' economic well-being through collective bargaining and benefits provided to members, they did far more: They also increased their members' political knowledge, civic skills, and rate of political participation.[34] These effects were particularly impactful among members with lower levels of education, who were otherwise less likely to be involved in politics. To the extent that unions influenced members to support the Democratic Party, that effect seems to have been most pronounced among non-Hispanic whites, who were often appealed to by the Republican Party, and thus cross-pressured.[35] Unions stress solidarity among workers and against bosses, and they forge identities that organize politics around economic issues. In many small industrial towns, they, along with other civic organizations, served as "vital hubs and underlying social infrastructures," creating a rich fabric of social life.[36]

Through the middle decades of the twentieth century, unions strongly supported the Democratic Party and cultivated ties with their members that promoted grassroots support for it.[37]

Yet those powerful bonds were not to last. As unions faced challenges over the latter decades of the twentieth century, private-sector union membership fell precipitously.[38] Although the size of public-sector unions remained relatively steady, their members tended to be more highly educated and already within the Democratic Party's fold.[39] Overall, private-sector union membership fell to roughly 6 percent of the workforce nationwide by 2019.[40] The demise of these unions directly harmed Democratic vote margins. Political scientist David Macdonald shows that union decay harmed the party's ability to "educate, inform, and socialize [its] members," which undercut support for Democratic candidates among white people.[41] In so-called right-to-work states—or states that have scaled back workers' organizing rights—unions raised less in campaign dollars and contacted voters less often. This in turn harmed Democratic vote share in presidential, congressional, and state elections.[42] Efforts in recent decades by conservative political leaders to claw back collective bargaining rights sharply curtailed unions' already-limited geographic reach. Indeed, as of 2023, three in ten union members were located in just two states: New York and California.[43] With this previously important source of sustenance for the Democratic Party badly depleted and geographically constrained, workers' allegiances were up for grabs. But just as the organizations that helped buttress the Democratic Party decayed, the Republican Party found itself the beneficiary of newly invigorated groups.

Organizations Fuel the Rural Transition to Voting for Republicans

In the decades prior to the divide's emergence, Republicans purposefully tried to recruit various groups as supporters, but rural voters nationwide did not appear to be among their explicit targets.[44] From at least Richard Nixon's campaign onward, leaders pursued a "Southern strategy," appealing to Southern whites by focusing overtly on law and order issues and opposition to school busing but in the process attracting those who were antagonistic to civil rights. Certainly the South up until then had been predominantly rural, so this approach implicitly included rural residents, but it did not single them out specifically. In fact, Republicans meanwhile courted suburban voters, and not only in Sunbelt areas such as Arizona and Orange County, California, but also in cities such as Atlanta, where "white flight" was underway. In time, these strands combined to aid Reagan's ascendance in the party.[45] Then Congressman Newt Gingrich and his allies sought to distinguish the GOP from the Democrats by embracing a combative approach. They promoted unyielding positions on issues and launched persistent verbal attacks on Democrats, demonizing them as a permanent majority that had grown bloated and corrupt.[46] Republicans' efforts to improve their electoral fortunes bore fruit in the 1994 elections when the GOP won control of the U.S. House of Representatives, in part by flipping many rural seats, as we will show in the next chapter. Subsequently, in the years that followed, rural areas would become increasingly important to the party's success.

One strategy that Republican Party leaders pursued that helped change its status in more rural states was the adoption of term limits. A movement to enact these took off in the early 1990s, and they gained a prominent mention in the party's 1994 "Contract with America" campaign manifesto.[47] Proponents argued that term limits would increase the number of citizens who served, make legislatures more responsive to voters' preferences, and cut down on the power of incumbent politicians and interest groups.[48] A few national groups promoted these reforms, including Citizens for Congressional Reform, founded by the conservative billionaire brothers David and Charles Koch.[49] Although the U.S. Supreme Court in 2005 declared terms limits for members of Congress to be unconstitutional—and eventually some state courts did the same to limits pertaining to state legislatures—sixteen states have permitted them to remain in place. Many of these are disproportionately rural, including our case study states of Michigan, Missouri, and Ohio, and also Nebraska, South Dakota, and Montana.[50]

Term limits dislodged many Democratic incumbents who had served for a long time and managed to stay in office even when their party became unpopular among local voters. As political scientist Andrew B. Hall explains, "Term limits have caused a significant reallocation of power away from the Democratic Party and toward the Republican Party, at least in part because [they] erode the Democrats' typically large advantage in legislative seniority."[51] After term limits were adopted, many long-serving rural Democrats who had seemed familiar and safe to residents—immune to their negative associations with the national "party brand"—lost their seats to Republicans. As Brent Jackson, a Democratic Party organizer told us, term limits "are the worst thing ever to have happened to Missouri politics. . . . People might think they don't like Democrats, but they like the [elected official] known in their community, they know Bob, their neighbor. Even if they don't agree, they know they can talk with that person, things can be done. Leadership is a rare set of skills, but term limits tosses them to the side."[52]

Yet while term limits may have helped Republicans gain seats in state legislatures, they cannot account for the immense partisan shift in presidential or congressional voting that occurred over these decades. Rather, we find that the Republican Party benefited electorally from the vibrancy and assistance of other organizations that helped promote political engagement generally and voting in particular. Nationwide, such organizations had been on the rise for decades and working assiduously to develop ties with and influence the Republican Party. By the 2000s, they produced results that have been concentrated in rural areas.

Christian Conservatives

The Christian right began to emerge as a political force in the 1970s. At the time, states were quickly ratifying the Equal Rights Amendment (ERA), which Congress had approved in 1972. Phyllis Schlafly, a lawyer, conservative political activist, author, and former vice president of the National Federation of Republican Women, began to criticize the ERA, heaping particular scorn on the Republican leaders who endorsed it. Schlafly organized a group called the National Committee to Stop ERA, which aimed to terminate ratification. Proponents used as their symbol a red stop sign in which "STOP" was an acronym for "Stop Taking Our Privileges." By 1973, Schlafly and her lieutenants had organized chapters in twenty-six states, particularly in the Midwest and South, bringing ratification to a halt in most of those states. Although the anti-ERA forces originated with Schlafly's associates who had also supported Barry Goldwater in his presidential run in 1964, as well as members of the John Birch Society and other anticommunist groups, soon conservative religious women joined in and became the foot soldiers of the movement, dramatically increasing its grassroots power.[53]

Later in the decade, several other conservative Christian political organizations emerged. They enabled thirty new Republican U.S. House candidates—including Gingrich—to trounce Democrats in Southern districts long held by their party and helped Ronald Reagan win the presidency in his surprise 1980 landslide election. The Moral Majority was formed, and its leader, Rev. Jerry Falwell, announced that a "sleeping giant" had been awakened in American politics in the form of the religious right. James Dobson founded Focus on the Family, which features a daily radio program and advocates for conservative family values. Paul Weyrich, Richard Viguerie, and others established Christian Voice, a group that explicitly aimed to involve evangelical Christians in elections.[54] Some of the momentum for these organizations came from the battle forced by segregated religious schools to maintain their tax-exempt status. Soon they coalesced with groups that had opposed the ERA and expanded their focus to defending school prayer, opposing abortion and gay rights, and promoting the appointment of conservative judges.[55] In 1989, Pat Robertson formed the Christian Coalition, aided by Ralph Reed, and it sought a closer relationship with the Republican Party than its predecessors.[56]

Most of these organizations did not endure. Nonetheless, the Christian right has had staying power across the decades because, as political scientist Daniel Schlozman notes, "person-to-person networks rooted in churches and linkages between elites and masses rooted in direct-mail lists survived the organizational tumult." Evangelicals played a major role in the transformative 1994 elections by registering and contacting voters and getting them to the polls. It was not until the twenty-first century that religious polarization peaked among Americans generally.[57]

The 2004 election in particular showcased the role of Christian conservatives. That year, thirteen states—a group that skewed rural and includes our case study states of Georgia, Michigan, Missouri, North Carolina, and Ohio, among others—voted on ballot initiatives regarding whether their constitution should be amended to ban gay marriage. The prior year, numerous conservative Christian organizations had combined in the Arlington Group to "pool resources and [to] come up with a combined strategy for fighting the forces of secularism," beginning with banning same-sex marriage.[58] The member organizations promoted the bans by talking about them on their weekly radio broadcasts, sending materials to churches to share in their bulletins, and sending speakers around the country. High-profile members such as Dobson of Focus on the Family also spoke about the issue.[59] A coordinated effort between these groups and the George W. Bush campaign was evident, presumably motivated by the hope that voting on the bans would spur more votes for Bush himself. Bush's campaign strategist Karl Rove often remarked that "four million evangelicals" had failed to vote in the 2000 election—an election so close that the final result still remained unclear weeks later, when the Supreme Court stepped in and effectively permitted Bush to be declared the winner. Bush's reelection, Rove explained, depended on evangelicals' greater involvement.[60] Notably, Rove coordinated weekly calls to evangelical pastors in the Arlington Group, and the Republican National Committee inundated evangelicals with direct mail.[61] In the end, the bans were enacted in all thirteen states, with support by large majorities.

The key question for us is whether the rise of Christian conservatives in politics helped to drive the rural-urban divide. Examining the presence of evangelical churches in rural and urban communities, we find that, consistently since the 1970s, they have been concentrated disproportionately in rural areas by a ratio of nearly three to one, after adjusting for population differences.[62] When it comes to how the presence of evangelical congregations in rural and urban areas relates to partisan voting, we find that they interacted with place in significant but different

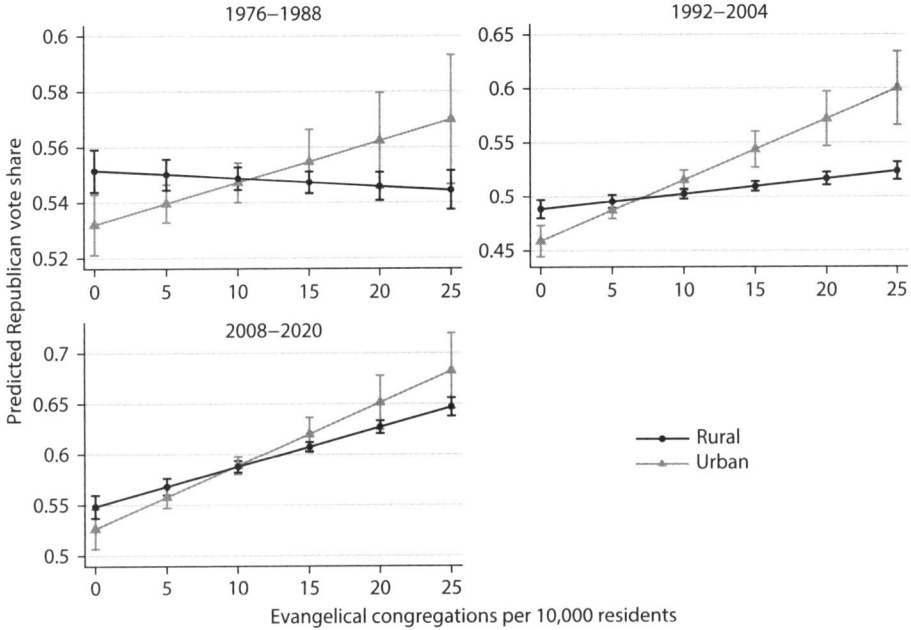

FIGURE 5.2. Evangelical congregations and Republican vote share, rural and urban counties
Note: Estimates were generated using multivariate regressions, including county-level controls for job growth, racial and ethnic demographics, and age, among other factors. Full results, model specifications, and sources are in appendixes.

ways in each period (figure 5.2; see appendixes). In the first period, 1976 to 1988, it was chiefly in urban areas that evangelical congregations served as a mobilizing force for the Republican Party. In the second period and third periods, 1992 to 2004 and 2008 to 2020, however, a marked change occurred: A greater presence of evangelical congregations in either rural or urban counties was related to supporting Republican candidates.[63] Rural areas, furthermore, feature many more congregations per resident than urban ones; in 2010, for example, rural counties had roughly thirteen congregations per ten thousand people, while urban counties had just five. The relationship between congregation density and Republican vote share has also grown over time in rural areas (for full results, see table A5.1 in appendixes).

The timing of these relationships indicates that evangelical churches played a crucial role in facilitating rural voters' transition to supporting the Republican Party, especially since 2008. The churches mobilized rural communities, particularly non-Hispanic white people, prompting them to vote for the GOP. This happened only after the political economy changed, causing rural residents to feel left behind. Rural areas with more evangelical congregations then became a stronghold in the GOP. Rural congregations, given their prevalence, have been able to deliver a particularly large impact and cement the rural-urban divide.

In addition to evangelical churches, in many states the organization Right to Life (RTL)—a national antiabortion group—also worked to mobilize voters to support Republican candidates. The organization was founded by the Catholic church in 1968, but in the wake of *Roe v. Wade* in 1973, it separated from the church in order to appeal to more constituencies, not only Catholics.[64] Its website announces that it is the nation's "oldest and largest grassroots pro-life organization," and that it has affiliates in all fifty states.[65] Some RTL state affiliates in our case study states make clear on their websites their explicit ties with the Republican Party. In Texas, for example, the webpage announced its "2020 Republican Primary Endorsements," listing numerous congressional and state house candidates. The Georgia affiliate did the same and made its director available as a speaker for several county-level Republican Party groups. In other states, the RTL groups posted voting guides, engaged in lobbying of elected officials, and provided information to citizens about the issues.

A classic federated organization, Right to Life also claims to have over three thousand local chapters nationwide, and through them it asks members to call their elected officials, write letters to the editor, and volunteer on political campaigns for prolife candidates.[66] To probe the geographical distribution of such groups, we homed in on Michigan, a state useful for our purposes because the locations of its chapters are available online, along with their Facebook pages.[67] This allows us to classify each as existing in a rural or urban county while conducting an inventory of their activities over the past year.[68] Among the eighty-three counties in Michigan, fifty-seven are considered by our measure as rural. Overall there are thirty-eight RTL groups in rural counties, and thirty-seven in urban counties. Taking into account population size differences, we find that the RTL groups are much more prevalent in rural counties, which have five times as many chapters per person as the state's urban counties. Throughout Michigan, the local groups often convene monthly meetings, hold live events, circulate materials to inform the public about issues, and participate in prolife marches or rallies, among other activities. On a per capita basis, the rural RTL groups are almost five times as active as urban groups, with about four times as many web-based activities (e.g., maintaining live Facebook pages) and five times as many in-person activities (e.g., holding public events, participating in marches and rallies, etc.). In fact, even if we don't adjust for population size, we still find that the rural RTL groups are, in aggregate, just as active as urban ones.

How might the larger presence of RTL groups in rural areas encourage Republican voting? It is often assumed that "beliefs precede action," implying that an individual would only become active in a Right to Life organization if they already felt strongly that abortion was wrong, but research by sociologist Ziad Munson turns that idea on its head. Studying the prolife movement, he found that people often held ambiguous views on abortion when they first became involved, and only developed a firm prolife position later on, as the result of their engagement. "Individuals stumble into contact with different pro-life organizations in the course of their daily lives," he observes, attending meetings because a friend invites them, for example, or because they have some free time and are looking for a way to get involved in the community.[69] That engagement in turn spurs their commitment to the issue. Political scientists find, furthermore, that individuals may begin to affiliate with a political party on the basis of one issue, and then, in turn, adjust their other policy views as they develop a commitment to that party.[70] Through such dynamics, RTL groups in rural Michigan are likely to aid Republican outcomes in elections.

Gun Groups

It is well known that the National Rifle Association today ardently defends the right to bear arms and opposes gun control legislation, but the source of its power is less widely understood.[71] Two Civil War veterans initiated the organization in 1871, in an effort to promote good marks-manship skills and related sportsman's activities. Though it established headquarters in Washington, DC, in 1907 and played a role in shaping the nation's first laws regulating guns in the 1930s, its involvement in politics remained modest until the 1960s, when it began to do more.[72] At an annual meeting in 1977, a new guard of leaders who were more allied with the ascendant conservative movement wrested control of the organization and sought the means to dramatically reduce gun con-trol.[73] From that point onward, the NRA became closely aligned with the Republican Party and highly influential in blocking gun control leg-islation, especially after the 1990s. The organization's power is not, how-ever, derived primarily from a handful of lobbyists in Washington, DC.

Rather, the NRA has cultivated massive grassroots support among citizens, particularly white men, who promote its political agenda. As political scientist Matthew Lacombe demonstrates, the organization has successfully "created a distinct social identity built around gun owner-ship" and connected it to politics, making support for gun rights crucial to the contemporary conservative coalition.[74] The NRA did this in part through its communication materials. Furthermore, as sociologist Jennifer Carlson shows, it worked at the state level for the enactment of "shall issue" laws, which permit ordinary citizens to carry concealed guns. In 1976, only four states had such laws, but over the ensuing years, nearly all states adopted them. As a result, "more Americans in every region of the United States are now licensed to carry guns than at any other time in history." Now the NRA plays a crucial role in making concealed carry a reality by providing the required firearms training to some 750,000 Americans annually, and in the process the organization inculcates this model of citizenship and social identity.[75]

We build on these analyses of the NRA's grassroots power by probing its organizational strength at the local level, comparing rural and urban places.[76] In 1921, the organization's membership remained small, with just about thirty-five hundred members. That year, the national promo-tions manager instigated a crucial change, affiliating the organization with two thousand sporting clubs, and membership quickly soared.[77] Today, the NRA claims affiliations with ten thousand local clubs and associations, a vast network of like-minded citizens that it mobilizes to

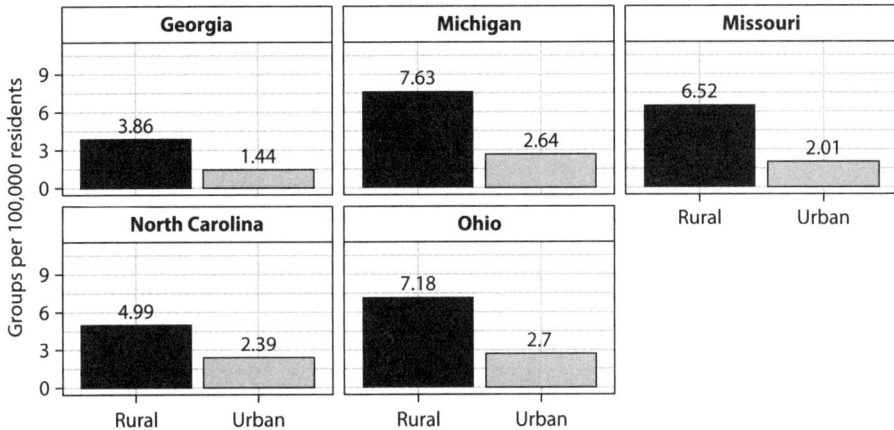

FIGURE 5.3. NRA-affiliated gun clubs, rural and urban counties, by state
Source: NRA website (2022); measure of rural from OMB

participate in politics. Some five thousand other groups affiliate with
the NRA as well, with categories that include Places to Shoot, encompassing both public and private ranges; Hunters for the Hungry, a program through which hunters can donate meat to supply meals for the
community, generally through butcher shops and other meat-processing
facilities; and Second Amendment Activist Centers, which seek to involve people in legislative and political issues related to firearms.
Through all these groups, people develop and maintain social connections with others in their community, forging bonds that can in turn be
politicized and activated by elites.

We found that in each of our case study states, the per capita presence
of NRA groups in rural areas vastly outnumbers their presence in urban
areas (figure 5.3; see appendixes). The dense presence of these NRA-
affiliated groups in rural areas likely plays some role in mobilizing people
to vote for Republican candidates.[78] The social networks that the NRA
fosters in connection with gun ownership provides individuals affiliations that powerfully shape political identity. The national organization,
meanwhile, has tightly aligned itself with the GOP over the past four
decades and regularly communicates with its members.[79]

Republican officials have clearly stated, time and again, their intent
to protect gun rights. The strong social ties fostered at the local level by
the NRA, combined with its unambiguous positions on gun issues, can

fuel voting for the Republican Party even in the absence of an overt campaign to promote it.

In sum, although the Republican Party itself lacks the internal strength it had in earlier times, organizations such as evangelical churches, Right to Life groups, sportsman's groups, and others associated with the National Rifle Association have stepped in to serve as mobilizing forces, particularly in elections. In the process, they have pulled the Republican Party to the right and helped increase its vote share.[80] They have done so in a geographically uneven way, bolstering support for Republicans particularly in rural areas. They have raised the salience of some issues—such as abortion, gay marriage, and gun rights—at the expense of others. In all these ways, organizations have crystalized the rural-urban political divide.

A New Organizational Landscape

Elaine Murphy is the Republican chair in a county in southwestern Georgia. When we were communicating with her to set up the date and time for our interview, she mentioned, "Usually I go to church on Wednesday night as is common in rural counties, but I will be glad to meet with you." Indeed, as we drove through miles of countryside for our meetings, we passed churches with remarkable frequency.

Contrary to conventional wisdom, the rural-urban political divide was not inevitable: It did not emerge automatically or inexorably. For decades, the Democratic Party in rural areas had been sustained by the goodwill it had gained in the New Deal and beyond and by long-standing incumbents, locally elected officials who were able both to maintain the trust of constituents and to manage campaigns in their regions.[81] Yet those relationships began to fray.

Starting in the 1990s, policy-induced shifts that ravaged rural economies helped open up a potent place-based cleavage. After the economy bottomed out in rural areas and boomed in many urban ones, white rural dwellers came to perceive highly educated, seemingly well-off urban elites as imposing policies on them without their consent. This process deepened the cleavage, but it did not cement it.

Rather, organizations played crucial roles in the processes of sequential polarization. Although both political parties have grown weaker as organizations over time, the Republican Party has been aided electorally by the politicization of groups that ally themselves with it. These associations happen to be particularly prevalent in rural areas. There, they have helped to make meaning of changing circumstances for their members, in ways that help orient many toward supporting Republican candidates and making sure they vote. Meanwhile, the Democratic Party suffered from the weakening of its organizational apparatus. The dense social networks forged by labor organizations that had long helped it had largely dissipated. Other organizations did not come to its aid.

Now we will turn to studying the consequences of this place-based political transformation.

PART III

Consequences

6

Polarizing Congress by Place

THE IMPLICATIONS FOR GOVERNANCE

IN 1976, Democrat Dan Glickman beat an incumbent Republican to become the representative of the fourth district of Kansas in the U.S. House. Though he lost narrowly in Wichita, his hometown, he managed to win all the rural counties in the district. "I couldn't possibly have won that race today," he marveled. Glickman prevailed by going door to door and talking with people. He connected well with farmers, whose work he deeply respected, and "so there was a kind of empathy that caught on," he explained. For the next many years, he spent "a disproportionate amount of [his] time in rural and small town parts of Kansas and became an advocate for farm issues."

Fast forward eighteen years, when Glickman was serving in the 103rd Congress, and he voted for the federal assault weapons ban, which was signed into law by President Bill Clinton. That vote met with wide resistance in his district. Glickman remembers canvassing in a precinct soon after he had cast a vote that would save some one thousand jobs in airplane manufacturing. At one home, a resident who worked in that industry said to him, "I can't vote for you, because of your stand on guns." Glickman responded, "Why? I saved your job!" The man responded, "Mr. Glickman, you come from a wealthy family; you have all the things in life that you can enjoy. All I have is my recreation and my guns—and you are trying to take that away from me."

Glickman lost his seat that fall, due largely to diminished support in typically Democratic precincts. He believes that many constituents abandoned him because they felt that gun control was, as that one constituent conveyed to him, "taking away my lifestyle, my joy, what makes me a man, a human being." In other words, they felt pushed around on key issues—by outsiders.

Glickman thinks of that conversation as a preview of what eventually became a growing rural-urban political divide. He reflected, "That was the beginning of an era when you saw very few Democrats [elected] from rural America." Explaining why, he said that many rural Americans today "feel nobody cares about them."

In this chapter we explore how place matters for rising polarization in the U.S. Congress, particularly the House of Representatives. Are Americans in particular locales sending different types of members to Congress than they did in the past? If so, has it affected how the House operates and the policymaking process? As divisive partisanship grew in the U.S. political system in recent decades, it also emerged in Congress.[1] Many scholars have charted its timing, elaborated on what drives it, and considered how it is shaping behavior among lawmakers.[2] When it comes to place, researchers of American politics have shown how the gradual political transformation of one region, the South, affected this pattern as it shifted from electing almost entirely Democrats to almost entirely Republicans to Congress.[3] Political scientists M. V. Hood III and Seth C. McKee trace this shift in the South specifically as it occurred in rural places.[4] This begs the question of whether the rural-urban divide that we have seen manifested in presidential elections has spread to other parts of the U.S. government as well.[5] To the extent it has, how is it affecting governance?

It turns out that the place-based divide has spread far and wide. It runs deep through the halls of Congress, the judiciary, and public policy. In this chapter, we consider its emergence especially in the U.S. House of Representatives, and how it has shaped some of the major policies of the last three decades.

As recently as the early 1990s, rural districts were roughly as likely to be represented by Democrats as Republicans. They typically elected representatives who were relatively moderate, who focused on their constituents' economic concerns, and who helped to forge compromises that permitted the enactment of major legislation. Not so today. Rural areas now reliably send among the most conservative, extreme Republicans to Congress, members who have been willing to override basic democratic norms.

Before the Rural-Urban Divide Emerged in Congress

In the late 1980s and early 1990s, American government appeared to be functioning quite well—even when different parties controlled the White House and Congress. During the presidency of Republican President George H. W. Bush, the Democratic-controlled Congress passed several major pieces of legislation and the president signed them into law. In retrospect, lawmakers racked up an impressive number of major policy achievements. How did these occur?

In some instances, laws passed with strong support from both parties, among rural and urban members alike. This broad bipartisanship characterized the Clean Air Act Amendments of 1990, the Americans with Disabilities Act of 1990 (ADA), and the Civil Rights Act of 1991.[6] Among those three, the ADA—which outlawed discrimination against people with disabilities by employers and in public services and accommodations—enjoyed overwhelming support. Bush had campaigned on it in 1988, and it had strong proponents in both parties in Congress. On final passage, members of both parties shared emotional stories of family members with disabilities before casting affirmative votes.[7]

In the case of the Civil Rights Act, the process was more complicated. Though Bush initially vetoed it, he would eventually change his mind, particularly in the wake of Anita Hill's charges of sexual harassment by Supreme Court nominee Clarence Thomas, along with the spectacle of former Ku Klux Klansman David Duke running on the GOP ticket in the race for the governorship of Louisiana. An earlier version of the 1991 bill would have permitted women, religious minorities, and people with disabilities to collect larger financial damages from employers, as people of color were already permitted to do. It proved divisive and passed in the House by 273–158, largely along partisan lines.[8] The compromise bill that passed both chambers put restrictions on money damages that workers could win in job discrimination lawsuits, but it was nevertheless significant, pushing back on decisions by the Rehnquist Court that denied such awards. Despite the tumult that characterized the process, on final passage in the House only 33 Republicans and 5 Democrats opposed it.[9] As in the case of the ADA, furthermore, no rural-urban divide was present in lawmakers' stances on it.

Of the three laws, the Clean Air Act Amendments encountered the most trying process of enactment, and in this case the divide was not partisan so much as regional. It faced the greatest opposition from Midwestern lawmakers, concerned that the costs of reducing acid rain would affect their states in particular, and those from Gulf Coast states who feared the economic impact of controls on offshore oil drilling. Yet it enjoyed strong support within both parties. President Bush led the Republican effort himself; he parted ways with Reagan by not only promoting the environmental legislation but even proposing a version of it during his first year in the presidency. Democrats also backed it more than they had in the past, since former Senate Majority Leader Robert Byrd of West Virginia, who had feared it would cause coal miners to lose jobs, was replaced as leader by George Mitchell of Maine, a proponent of the legislation. In the House, even leaders who were adversaries with respect to the bill—for example, Energy Committee Chairman John Dingell, who advocated for people in the auto industry, versus Health and Environment Subcommittee Chairman Henry Waxman, both Democrats—worked long and hard to arrive at compromises that permitted most rank-and-file members to get on board in support of it.[10] As a result, it ultimately passed in the House with only twenty-one votes against it, sixteen Republican and five Democratic. Once again, neither partisanship generally nor a rural-urban divide in particular stymied enactment.

In retrospect, this period amounted to the calm before the storm—a period of productive, bipartisan lawmaking prior to the emergence of the rural-urban divide. That's not to say that the policymaking process

was smooth; the nation's institutional complexities and the proliferation of organized interests typically ensured a fair amount of drama.
Nonetheless, in enacting major laws, policymakers managed to navigate the inevitable obstacles while working across partisan divides and
regional differences. Notably, some of these laws are now long overdue for updating and policy maintenance, having languished as partisan divides in Congress have intensified, exacerbated by growing
place-based divisions.[11]

Tough Votes for Rural Representatives: On the Cusp of Division

In 1992, for the first time since 1976, the Democratic Party won back a
trifecta—control of the presidency, Senate, and House—and yet the
next two years would prove to be tumultuous for governing. President
Bill Clinton won only a plurality, not a majority, of the popular vote—
43 percent—because independent candidate Ross Perot took
18.9 percent, leaving incumbent Bush with only 37.5 percent. Although
Clinton did win the Electoral College votes of thirty-two states, Republicans would soon benefit from the party's vulnerability, particularly in
rural places. Ensuing legislative battles further imperiled rural lawmakers, Democrats in particular, by presenting them with challenging votes.

As Clinton sought to make good on his campaign promises, three
policies proved to be particularly contentious in Congress, not only between the parties but also within them. These included the Omnibus
Reconciliation Bill, signed by the president in August 1993, and its proposed energy or BTU (short for British thermal unit) tax that was eventually dropped; the ratification of the North American Free Trade
Agreement (NAFTA) in December 1993; and the assault weapons ban,
which ultimately became part of the large crime bill enacted in August 1994. Ironically, in retrospect, NAFTA was not characterized by a
strong rural-urban divide; rural lawmakers were themselves divided in
ways that seemed related to which agricultural and manufacturing sectors were prevalent in their local economies. The budget bill and assault

weapons ban, however, forced rural lawmakers—particularly Democrats—to take a stand on contentious issues.

Given rising concern about the national debt, spurred in part by Perot's campaign, Clinton was determined both to slash deficits and to make good on his campaign promises to invest in education, health care, and science and technology. All these goals became entwined in the Omnibus Reconciliation Bill, otherwise known as the "budget bill." The version that was ultimately enacted extended the life of the Medicare Trust Fund by three years, expanded the Earned Income Tax Credit (and thus greatly enlarged the number of Americans lifted out of poverty by it), and reduced subsidies to bankers by creating the Direct Student Loan program.[12] In order to pay for its investments, the bill increased taxes on the wealthiest Americans, raising the top marginal tax rates to 36 percent and 39.6 percent, respectively, cut various tax expenditures, and imposed a higher top marginal tax rate of 35 percent on corporations with income in excess of $10 million. The Congressional Budget Office analyzed the bill and predicted that it would reduce the deficit by $433 billion over five years.[13]

Fractious battles ensued as the bill proceeded through Congress, particularly over the BTU tax. Vice President Al Gore and environmental groups had encouraged Clinton to promote this broad-based energy tax, which would affect industry and consumers, as a means both to raise revenues and to encourage energy conservation and the transition toward more renewable sources.[14] Once the House Ways and Means Committee began work on the bill, it quickly became clear that Republicans generally opposed the BTU tax—arguing that it would harm business—and many Democrats from rural places in particular feared it. As we were told by Thomas Wright, a senior staff member for Lloyd Bentsen, who had served in both the House and Senate for decades and was then secretary of treasury, "I can tell you that the outrage in rural areas was huge, due to the increase it would cause in prices." Remote, rural areas are particularly sensitive to energy costs. This owes not only to the long distances that residents drive for work and other activities, but also to the impact on high-energy-consuming types of agriculture and extractive industries. Some modifications were made to the BTU tax proposal for those involved in agriculture, but meanwhile a bipartisan group of senators—including Democrats from energy-producing states, such as David Boren from Oklahoma and Bennett Johnston from Louisiana—came out in favor of an alternate plan that eliminated the tax. House Democratic leaders retained it, though, and continued to push their cross-pressured members to support the bill, and it passed by a razor-thin margin of 219–213. In the upper chamber, however, Democratic senators from rural states pressed harder, and the BTU tax was dropped, replaced by a 4.3 cent per gallon increase in the federal gasoline tax. Ultimately the bill passed with the increased gasoline tax in place of the BTU tax, but with only Democrats in favor of it and without a single vote to spare in either chamber.[15]

Examining Congress as a whole, political scientists have found that controlling for several factors, House Democrats who supported the budget bill were penalized in the 1994 election, and among them, those from districts where Clinton had netted less than 40 percent of the vote share in 1992 were especially likely to lose their seats.[16] Members who had taken the tough vote early on and supported the BTU tax before the Senate dropped that feature found that it came back to haunt them during their campaigns, when Republicans running against them made it clear that they had voted for tax increases. As Congressman David Obey, Democrat of Wisconsin, wrote, "The GOP demagogued the BTU tax and made it sound as though it would result in a huge hit on the middle class."[17] The expression "getting BTU'd" endured on Capitol Hill as a reference to high-pressure votes that required members to "walk the plank," risking that they might later be punished by voters.[18] Indeed, the tax would have disproportionately affected rural areas, and as we will see in the next section, rural members of Congress were especially likely to lose their seats in the next election.

The other issue that proved particularly contentious for lawmakers from rural areas was the assault weapons ban, which became part of a massive crime bill that was signed into law in August 1994 by President Clinton. When the Senate had first considered the bill in November 1993, Democrat Dianne Feinstein managed to work out a compromise with her partisan colleagues Dennis DeConcini of Arizona and

Howard Metzenbaum of Ohio: a bill that would prohibit the manufacture, sale, or possession of nineteen particular weapons. They offered it as an amendment, and it passed 56–43, with five Republicans supporting it. The House moved more slowly on the crime bill, though, and the year ended with no major legislation advanced.[19] The next spring, the House was ready to move forward, but the assault weapons ban was not popular among rural members, and its inclusion risked jeopardizing the entire bill. At this point, however, President Clinton decided it should be part of the package. He instructed Treasury Secretary Lloyd Bentsen and Attorney General Janet Reno that they needed to marshal support for the ban.[20] Bentsen was a gun owner from Texas who was known for saying, "My idea of gun control is a steady hand."

Wright recalls that he was riding in a car with Bentsen on the way from the White House to the Capitol after learning about the president's request that Bentsen rally support for the ban. Wright reiterated the request and said to the secretary, "We need a strategy." Says Wright, "Bentsen was a very controlled man. Usually if he did as much as raise an eyebrow, that might mean he was angry. But at that moment he slammed his arm down and said, 'We're going to lose twenty-five seats over this in the House! For what?'" Wright pointed out to the secretary that the president wanted the provision passed, and Bentsen was best poised to make the case on the Hill. "So you will need to do so," Wright said to him. Bentsen had already voted in favor of the ban when he was still in the Senate, and had received loads of angry mail from constituents in response. So Wright said to him, "Here's what you have to do. Go to every police department in the country, go out on the range with the police chief and shoot, and then ask the chief to make a 'man in blue' argument," meaning that an assault weapons ban would help protect the safety of police officers. "We did that, and it passed," Wright told us.

High drama surrounded the legislation in the House right up to the final moments before the vote, when it still seemed at least fifteen votes shy of the number needed to pass. Members reported being inundated by phone calls from opponents of the ban. Representative Charles Wilson, a Democrat from Texas, said, "If I voted for it, I wouldn't be physically safe when I go home this weekend." Many other members—including some from each party—explained their support for it as a vote of conscience, but predicted that it would hurt them politically.[21] Some members decided to vote in favor just before casting their votes. Ultimately it squeaked by with a two-vote margin, 216–214; among Democrats, the votes ran 177 in favor and 77 opposed, and among Republicans, 38 to 137. Examining the vote, we find that while rural Democrats tended to oppose the bill at a greater rate than their urban copartisans, nonetheless a few dozen rural Democrats proved pivotal for its passage. Several more "near-death" moments occurred between that vote and the legislation's successful final passage in both chambers as part of the crime bill. Throughout the process, the National Rifle Association intensively pressured members to drop the ban.[22] Ultimately, Bentsen's prediction that the ban would cost the Democratic Party many seats proved auspicious, as many rural supporters of the bill from moderate districts lost their seats in the 1994 election.[23]

In sum, rural representatives, especially Democrats, played a crucial role in the 1980s and early 1990s in helping to enact major legislation. Significant achievements occurred on numerous issues that enjoyed the support of a majority of Americans, thanks to their support. Yet during Clinton's first two years in office, such votes became more difficult. This was particularly the case when they faced an organized opposition, whether it was companies that produce fossil fuels, the NRA, or the Republican Party. After the 1994 election, many of these rural members would find themselves out of office.

The Rise of Rural Republicans and the Demise of Rural Democrats in Congress

In the 1994 midterm elections, the Republican Party, after having languished in the minority for the better part of sixty years, took Congress by storm. Ever since the election of President Franklin D. Roosevelt in 1932 had swept in large Democratic majorities, the GOP had controlled both chambers of Congress for a grand total of only four years. In the Senate, the Republicans had been victorious as recently as the 1980s, when they gained the majority on President Ronald Reagan's coattails and held it from 1981 to 1987. In the House, however, the GOP had been completely shut out of power since 1952. The party's 1994 gains in both chambers were huge: Whereas historically the party that loses the presidential election rebounds in the midterm to gain an average of four Senate seats and twenty-eight House seats, in that year the Republicans picked up eight Senate seats and a whopping fifty-four House seats.[24] Since making those gains, furthermore, Republicans have held power more often than not: They have controlled the House in twenty-four of the past thirty years, and the Senate for eighteen of those years. What role did rural and urban areas across the nation play in this Republican Revolution, both at its inception and as the years progressed?

Of the seats Republicans flipped in the Senate in 1994, four were located in relatively rural states, namely Maine, Michigan, Ohio, and Oklahoma. Senator Bob Dole, poised to become the majority leader in the Senate, triumphantly announced to the crowd gathered at the Republican National Committee headquarters in Washington, DC, "I've never known a better night in electoral politics for the Republican Party, and the best is yet to come."[25]

In the House, the Republican Party gains in 1994 occurred particularly in rural districts, amounting to a "rural wave" (figure 6.1). Organizing all congressional districts into five equally sized buckets (or quintiles), from the most urban (1) to the most rural (5), we find that the greatest number of flipped seats occurred in the two most rural quintiles. The flipped rural seats were to be found across the nation, with fifteen in the South, eight in the Midwest, seven in the West, and three in the Northeast.

We examined the partisan composition of each Congress from 1982 to 2020 by the degree of how rural or urban each district is. Here we show a few years that demonstrate long-term patterns and when and how they changed (figure 6.2; see appendixes for full series). The partisan affiliation of members by place in 1992 closely resembles that for the preceding Congresses. The most urban districts were consistently dominated by Democrats, as they had been since the New Deal. What is so striking, though, is how well Democrats did in more rural districts up

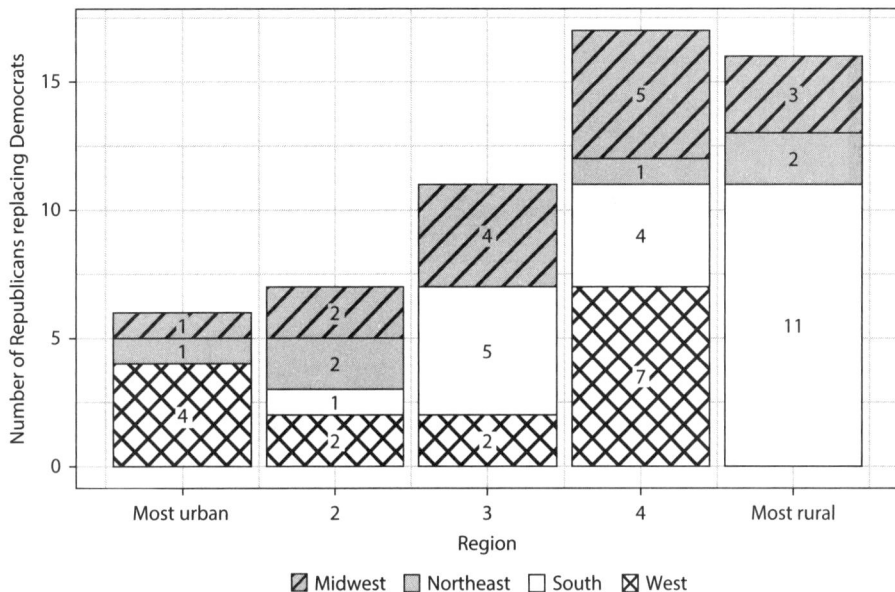

FIGURE 6.1. U.S. House seats gained by Republicans, 1994 election, rural and urban districts, by region
Source: Voteview; measure of rural from U.S. Census Bureau

until the early 1990s. Indeed, they typically did as well as, if not better than, their Republican counterparts.

The 1994 elections altered this pattern, however, as Republicans picked up seats particularly in more rural places. While the party managed to flip a handful of urban districts, its victories were far more impressive in the less densely populated ones. Democrats' long-standing ability to compete in the most rural districts was undercut as Republicans claimed seats in forty-nine of them, compared to thirty-nine by Democrats, and they won an even larger share in the next most rural districts. Over the next decade, congressional elections produced similar outcomes, with Republicans winning dozens more seats in the more rural districts compared to Democrats.

In 2006 and 2008, Democrats did manage to claw their way back in many rural places. In fact, in 2008, Democrats took the majority of the most rural districts, for the first time since 1992 (figure 6.2). What might explain it? Certainly President George W. Bush had grown unpopular,

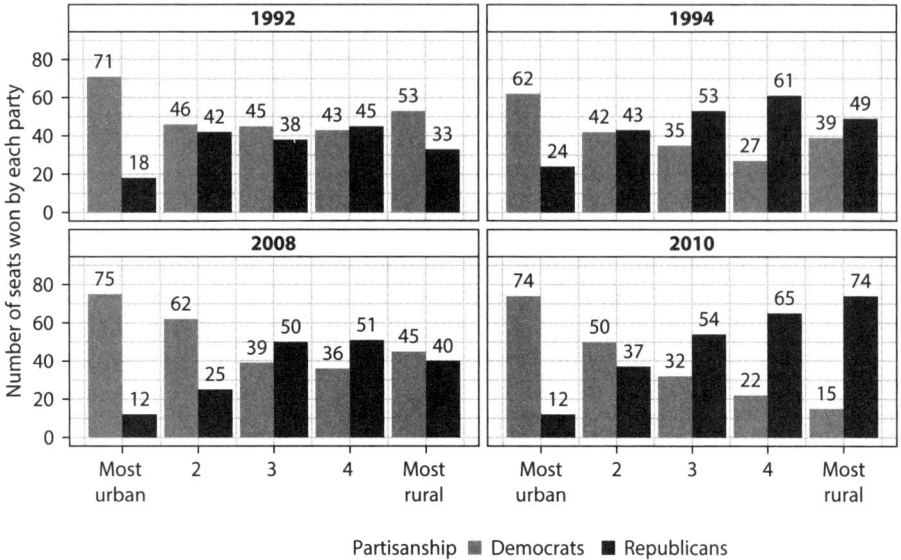

FIGURE 6.2. The rise of rural Republicans in the U.S. House
Source: Voteview; measure of rural from U.S. Census Bureau

owing to the war in Iraq and what was widely viewed as a failed response to Hurricane Katrina. Some suggestive evidence, described in chapter 9, points to the organizing and, crucially, party-building strategies employed by Democratic National Committee Chair Howard Dean and by the 2008 Obama campaign.[26]

But the Democratic resurgence would not last. In 2010, Republicans, energized by the Tea Party and organizations discussed in chapter 5, came roaring back and made overwhelming gains (figure 6.2). In fact, that election exacerbated the trend that had been in place from 1994 to 2006, making partisanship and rurality more tightly linked. The pronounced place-based divide that emerged has endured ever since. By 2020, nearly all the most rural districts were represented by Republicans, and the most urban by Democrats.

In short, an immense transformation occurred in the relationship between members' party and the places they represented. Kicked off by the 1994 Republican Revolution and deepened by the 2010 Tea Party ascendance, the Republican caucus became a rural caucus and the Democratic caucus an urban one. In 1992, less than half the Republican delegation came from the most rural districts; by 2020, more than two-thirds did. Conversely, among the Democrats, in 1992, 37 percent of their delegation hailed from rural places—but by 2020, that figure had plummeted to just 13 percent. Congress had become polarized by place.

The Rural-Urban Divide Increases Polarization

As the House of Representatives became divided by partisanship along rural and urban lines, how would it matter for public policy and governance? On the one hand, it might be reasonable to assume that it would make little substantive difference. Many rural Democratic lawmakers have belonged to the "Blue Dog Coalition," a congressional caucus formed in 1995 with a reputation for being more fiscally and socially conservative than their Democratic colleagues. It could simply be that such Democrats were replaced by moderate Republicans, a group of lawmakers with similar position stances but a different party label, such that this development matters little for polarization.

In fact, Blue Dog Democrats defy easy categorization. Although the group originated with conservative Southern white men, more recently its members have come from rural districts in all regions of the country, and they include women, immigrants, and African Americans. Ideologically, some have been described as "pragmatic progressives," such as Jared Golden of Maine and Marie Gluesenkamp Perez of Washington State, and recent members of the group have generally been less conservative than earlier members, who were typically center-right.[27] The Blue Dogs peaked in 2009 with fifty-four members, but as of 2023—given the demise of rural Democrats—membership had dwindled to ten.[28]

We examine if the demise of rural Democrats in Congress mattered by exploring how the ideology of all representatives—organized by the places that elected them—changed from 1982 to 2020 (figure 6.3; see appendixes). As noted earlier, as polarization has risen, members of both parties have grown more ideologically extreme, especially Republicans, who became much more conservative. Using multivariate regression that accounts for other factors (see appendixes for more details),

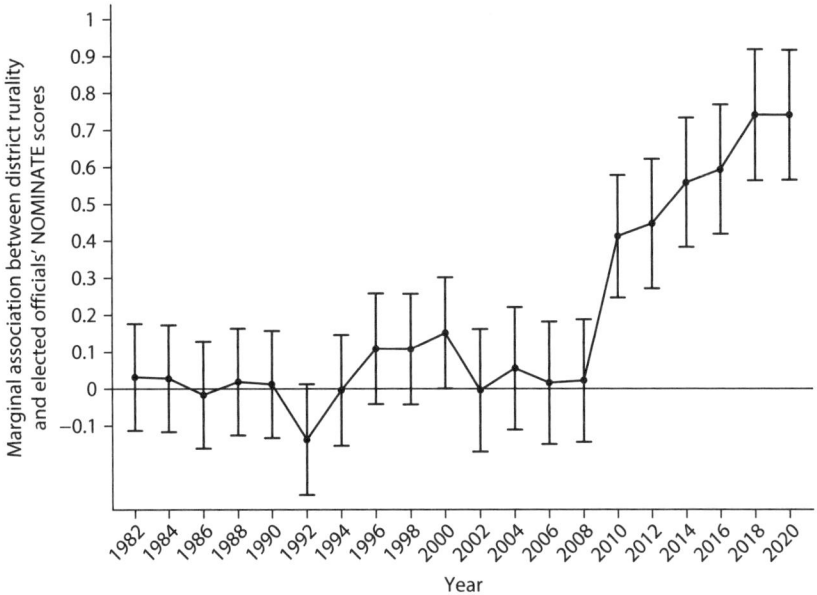

FIGURE 6.3. The growing relationship between rurality and ideological conservatism in the U.S. House
Note: Line represents the relationship between the share of a district considered rural and House members' ideology; positive scores indicate more conservative, and negative more liberal. Estimates were generated using multivariate regressions, including controls for other characteristics of congressional districts, such as age, education level, and racial and ethnic demographics. See appendixes for full model specification and sources.

we test if the share of people in a district that is considered rural is related to how members of the U.S. House vote. From the 1980s through the early 2000s, there was little relationship between the ruralness of districts and ideology. Voters from most districts sent a relatively diverse ideological group to Congress, with only those in the most urban districts sending more liberal members. Yet starting in the 1990s and dramatically since 2010, districts became polarized by place, with the more rural districts typically electing the most conservative Republicans. By 2020, shifting from the least to the most rural district is associated with a remarkable increase in conservatism, even after accounting for other district-level characteristics—such as education level, age, and race and ethnicity. In the 117th Congress, it would have been the equivalent—in terms of ideology and voting patterns—of a moderate Democrat, such as Jared Golden of Maine, being replaced by arch-conservative Republican Virginia Foxx of North Carolina, or a liberal Democrat, such as Katie Porter of California, being replaced by conservative Republican Steve Scalise of Louisiana. In other words, our findings suggest that place has become a major driver not only of party identification, but also of ideological polarization in the contemporary Congress.

Reforms Achieved Owing to Crucial Rural Support

From 1995 to 2004, Republicans represented many more rural House districts than Democrats; in the wake of the 2004 election, the GOP seat advantage was around two to one in such districts. Perhaps the most consequential bills enacted during this time period were the tax cuts of 2001 and 2003, both of which helped primarily the wealthiest Americans. They were enacted entirely along party lines and lacked the backing of the majority of Americans. Both severely reduced the federal government's revenues, harming its capacity to support popular programs.[29]

In the 2006 elections, Democrats came storming back and regained the House majority, retaking some rural districts, and they made even greater gains in 2008, when President Barack Obama was elected. That year they picked up 21 seats to gain a majority of 257 seats to Republicans' 178—on par with their numbers prior to the 1994 election. Notably, Democrats now outnumbered Republicans in representing the most rural districts. The party scored wins in rural places at a nationwide rate that it has not matched since then, gaining seats in Alabama, Idaho, Indiana, Iowa, Mississippi, Ohio, and Wisconsin. That same year, Democrats also won the largest margin they'd had in the Senate since 1977: 60 to 40.[30] What difference would the return of rural Democrats make for lawmaking?

Health Care Reform

Obama chose to make the expansion of health care coverage to working-age Americans his top priority in his first term, but it was a daunting goal. For over seventy years, Democratic lawmakers had aspired to extend health coverage to all Americans, yet successes had been piecemeal and hard won at that. The United States remained an outlier among affluent nations for failing to grant health care to so many of its citizens. President Franklin D. Roosevelt, confronted with opposition from the American Medical Association (AMA), had chosen against including health coverage in the package of programs included in the Social Security Act of 1935.[31] President Harry S. Truman made national health coverage for all Americans his cause, but he encountered virulent opposition and cries of "socialized medicine" not only from the AMA but also from conservatives in Congress, Republicans and Democrats alike.[32] Subsequently, lawmakers sought more incremental approaches to extending health coverage, and it would be President Lyndon Johnson who in 1965 would sign into law Medicare, for senior citizens, and Medicaid, for low-income people. This still left all other Americans without coverage, unless they were among those whose employers granted it, and even members of the latter group were in danger of becoming uninsured if they lost their job or had a preexisting medical condition. President Bill Clinton hoped to make health reform the hallmark of his presidency, but by the time his plan reached Capitol Hill, it was dead on arrival. As of 2008, although health care consumed 16.2 percent of the nation's economy, 14.7 percent of Americans lacked health coverage, and a large share of the public was just a job loss away from being uninsured.[33]

Obama would succeed where others had failed, and the Affordable Care Act—which he signed into law on March 30, 2010—remains the most significant legislative accomplishment of his presidency. The process of enacting it involved pitched battles in both chambers, not only between the parties but within them as well, as numerous potential features of the law were considered. Meanwhile, the Tea Party emerged and tried to stop the advance of the bill, objecting to it vociferously at town hall meetings held by members of Congress in their districts in the summer of 2009.[34] That November, the House passed its version by 220 to 215, with only one Republican voting in favor. On Christmas Eve, the Senate followed with its own bill; there, all 60 Democrats in the chamber allied in a filibuster-proof majority just large enough to support passage, but not a single Republican joined them. Members adjourned for the holidays, planning to reconvene in late January 2010 to reconcile the differences in the bills and to hold final votes. But on January 19, a special election to fill the late Ted Kennedy's Senate seat destroyed their plans: Republican Scott Brown, supported by the Tea Party, won in an upset, undermining the bill's ability to withstand a fili-buster in the next round of voting.[35]

All seemed to be lost, and it appeared that Obama might join the list of presidents whose health care reform plans had been foiled. Demo-cratic Congressman Barney Frank declared, "It's dead," and Obama's advisors recommended a replacement "skinny bill," perhaps featuring just coverage for children. House Speaker Nancy Pelosi, however, re-fused to accept that verdict. She persuaded President Obama and Senate Majority Leader Howard Reid of another way forward: via the budget reconciliation process.[36] If the new health law was rolled into a budget bill that was deficit reducing, it would only require 51 votes in the Senate, not a full 60. Proceeding in this way, the bill passed in the House on March 21, by 219–212, and in the Senate on March 26, by 56–43.

How did Obama and Congress succeed in getting health care reform across the finish line in 2009–2010, when so many others had failed previously? Certainly Obama had learned crucial lessons from previous failed efforts. Unlike Clinton, he was willing to lead with broad outlines while leaving it to Congress to work out the specifics of the bill and to build the necessary coalitions to pass it, and he was game to find ways to make deals with key stakeholders, such as insurance companies and the pharmaceutical industry, to win their support.[37] Pelosi and others offered invaluable leadership as well. What has not been acknowledged elsewhere, however, is the ACA's indispensable support among many rural lawmakers in Congress. Their votes proved essential to the law's passage, and they worked—in both the House and Senate—to arrive at key compromises that allowed enough of them to support the act that it could became law. In the House especially, Pelosi needed every vote she could find to secure final passage.

Rural Democrats in the House were likely to be swing voters on the ACA, uncertain throughout the process whether they would support it or not, and not all would find their way to doing so. One member who ultimately voted against it was Heath Shuler, who represented the large rural district in the western North Carolina Smoky Mountains region where he was born and grew up before playing professional football. At Bill Clinton's urging, Shuler had run in 2006 and beat a Republican who had been in office since 1990. Shuler did his best to communicate with his constituents about all major votes before they came up; he voted with the majority of each party about 50 percent of the time, and he enjoyed a high approval rating of over 70 percent in his district.

Shuler served as the whip of the Blue Dogs, who had several ideas for how to design health care reform. President Obama met with them at the White House and listed seven objectives he wanted in health reform. Sometime later, Shuler recalls, the president "called me into his office a few days before the vote. He said, 'Heath, I need your vote.' . . . I said, 'Sir, with all due respect, you only got three of the objectives you wanted, and as a quarterback, I know that if I only complete three passes out of seven, that will get me benched. We Blue Dogs know that health care needs to be fixed.'" Shuler explained that they thought the current design would not help bring down health care costs, and they felt shut out of the process. He voted against the ACA, and he did get re-elected for another term before he chose to retire. His district has been held by conservative Republicans since then. Those Republicans include Mark Meadows, who started the right-wing Freedom Caucus in the House and then served as Trump's chief of staff, and the bombastic young firebrand Madison Cawthorn.

Unlike Shuler, Bart Stupak—who represented a large rural district in northern Michigan—ultimately voted for the ACA, though his decision was also in question until very late in the process. He consistently espoused both a prolife stance on abortion and progressive approaches to curtailing corporate power and supporting labor, civil rights, and the environment.[38] He had sought health care reform since being elected in 1992, but he was concerned that the bill under consideration in 2009 would provide funds for abortion.[39] Just before the House vote in November, Pelosi permitted Stupak and his allies to allow a vote on strict abortion restrictions on private plans that would be part of the health exchanges. Acknowledging this compromise as the price of getting the bill passed, prochoice Democrats were willing to support it. When the House voted on the Senate version of the bill in March 2010, the issue came up again, as Stupak and about a half dozen other members remained concerned that ACA subsidies might be used to pay for abortion. Pelosi knew that their votes would be necessary for the bill to pass. President Obama assisted by promising to issue an executive order after the House vote to bolster the prohibition on abortion funding that was part of the legislation.[40] Stupak ultimately provided one of the key votes that secured the bill's enactment. Subsequently, however, he received a barrage of threats and vitriol from those on either side of the abortion debate, and within a few weeks he announced his plans to retire.[41] His seat has been held by Republicans ever since.

Many other rural members fully embraced the Affordable Care Act, including some long-serving progressives. David Obey, who represented the most rural district in Wisconsin, in the state's northwest corner, had first entered Congress in 1969. He rose to become the powerful chair of the Appropriations Committee and was known as a "die-hard liberal."[42] He attributed his values to Catholic social teachings as well as the social justice and workers' rights traditions of progressive Robert La Follette of Wisconsin. He was also protective of gun rights and some abortion restrictions.[43] Like Stupak, he viewed health care reform as the legislation that had been his goal ever since he was first elected. Just weeks after voting for it, though, he announced that he planned to retire from Congress. His district flipped after he stepped down, and it has been held by conservative Republicans ever since.[44]

Across the border, in the Iron Range area of Minnesota, Democrat Jim Oberstar represented the vast rural eighth district from 1975 to 2011, with a voting record that was among the most liberal in the House. The son of a United Steelworkers member, he strongly supported organized labor and workers' rights, and he was also renowned for his pro-environmental voting record and support for progressive taxes. Like some other rural Democrats, he favored some restrictions on abortion (though he supported it in the case of rape, incest, or if the life of the mother was endangered), and was against gun control. Oberstar voted

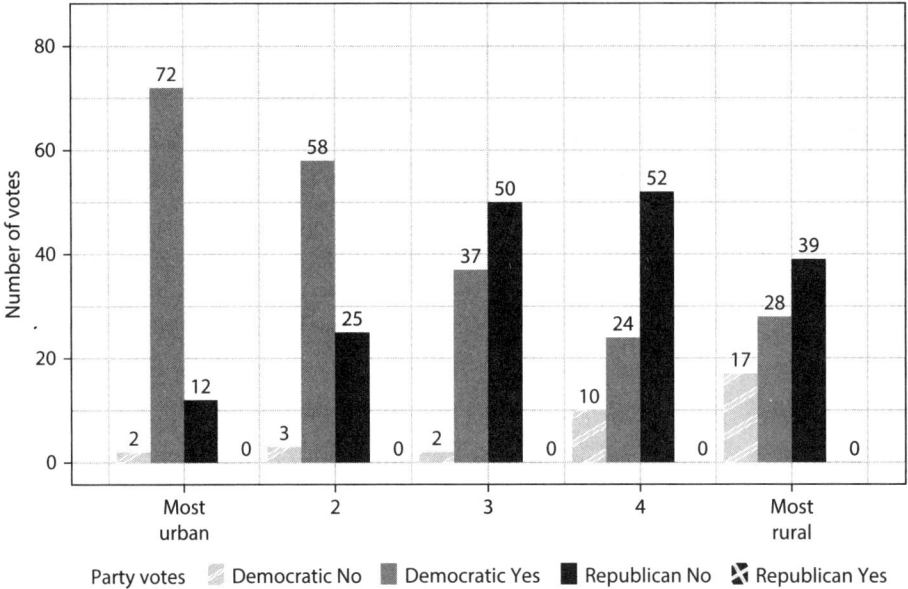

FIGURE: 6.4. U.S. House votes on passage of the Affordable Care Act, by district, rurality, and party
Source: Voteview; measure of rural from U.S. Census Bureau

for the Affordable Care Act. In the next election, he lost by five thousand votes to Republican Chip Cravaack, a Tea Party candidate. Since then, the district has flip-flopped between the parties.

Rural Democrats provided the crucial swing votes that ultimately ensured the enactment of the ACA (figure 6.4; see appendixes). While several of them, such as Shuler, decided they had to vote against it, far more, almost two-thirds, voted in favor. The law could not have passed without their support. Many of them voted for the law even as it grew more evident that they could face a backlash in the upcoming election from the insurgent Tea Party movement.

Viewed in historical perspective, the ACA was an immense achievement, on par with the nation's most significant laws ever passed. From the outset, it meant that insurance companies could no longer refuse to cover anyone due to pre-existing conditions, or charge them more for health insurance if they were ill. As more states expanded Medicaid under the law, year by year, health coverage rates grew. The uninsured rate was 17.8 percent in 2010 when Obama signed the law; by 2022, it was down to 9.6 percent.[45] Owing to the ACA, young adults can stay on their parents' coverage up to age twenty-six, prescription costs for seniors were lowered, and Americans' out-of-pocket health costs were reduced.[46]

Earl Pomeroy, who represented North Dakota in the U.S. House of Representatives from 1993 to 2011, is one of several rural Democrats who were ousted in the 2010 elections following their votes in favor of the Affordable Care Act. Nonetheless, Pomeroy calls the ACA "the crowning achievement of my time in public service." The Catholic bishops in his state tried to pressure him to oppose it, claiming that the bill would support abortion, an argument that he considered "stretched" and which failed to acknowledge the significance of extending health coverage to tens of millions of people. Opponents of the bill spent millions running ads against it in North Dakota, and a poll showed that he would be defeated soundly for reelection if he voted for it. In Washington, protesters who wanted him to vote against it "were coming by my office, in a physically intimidating way." But according to Pomeroy, "I was never here for tenure; I was here to do stuff. This is the moment you've been waiting for." Having served as an insurance commissioner for the state for years, he knew that the bill—while imperfect—would be good for his constituents and for the nation as a whole. He recalled that when it was time for the vote, his entire office staff went to the chamber to watch. He was one of the final representatives to vote, securing the act's passage. "It was a moment of great joy," he said. Yet Pomeroy lost his seat. After forty years in Democratic hands, it has been held by Republicans ever since.

From Reforms for the Many to Benefits for the Few

Besides the ACA, rural members' support proved crucial to other major accomplishments of Obama's presidency. One was the student aid bill, which terminated bank-based student lending, a program that had long generated profits for bankers at the expense of students and taxpayers, and replaced it with 100 percent direct lending from the federal government. It also increased Pell Grants for low-income students and mandated that they must increase with inflation.[47] Another achievement was the Dodd-Frank Wall Street Reform and Consumer Protection Act, which aimed to hold financial firms accountable for the kind of risk-taking that had led to the 2008 financial crisis. It also introduced new regulations aimed to protect Americans from unfair financial practices and established the Consumer Financial Protection Bureau.[48]

Despite these accomplishments, Democrats were vulnerable in the 2010 elections. In the lead-up to November, the well-organized Tea Party energized conservatives. Many voters who had supported Obama in 2008, by contrast, seemed largely unaware of or unimpressed by the policy accomplishments.[49] Democratic leaders, meanwhile, soft-pedaled their achievements. The result was another wave election like the one in 1994 in which many rural Democrats lost their seats to Republicans, but this time they—along with some moderate Republicans—were replaced by far more conservative members than in the earlier wave. As the years proceeded, this pattern continued.

Once Trump was elected president, the more conservative and rural-skewed House Republican majority threw its support behind many key pillars of his agenda. This included passing the 2017 tax cuts that aided extremely wealthy Americans and corporations, and rolling back numerous regulations, including some of those included in Dodd-Frank. In short, many of the districts that had been key to bipartisan and even progressive lawmaking in the not-so-distant past are now home to lawmakers pressing to roll back such efforts—including deregulating the economy—and, as we discuss next, threatening democracy itself. The change in rural districts from being represented by moderate Democrats to conservative Republicans has swung policymaking in the U.S. Congress from reforms for the many to benefits for the few.

The Rural-Urban Divide and Democracy

In recent years, the Republican Party in the U.S. House has increasingly sought power at all costs, never mind democracy. This came to a head in the efforts, led by President Donald Trump, to overturn the 2020

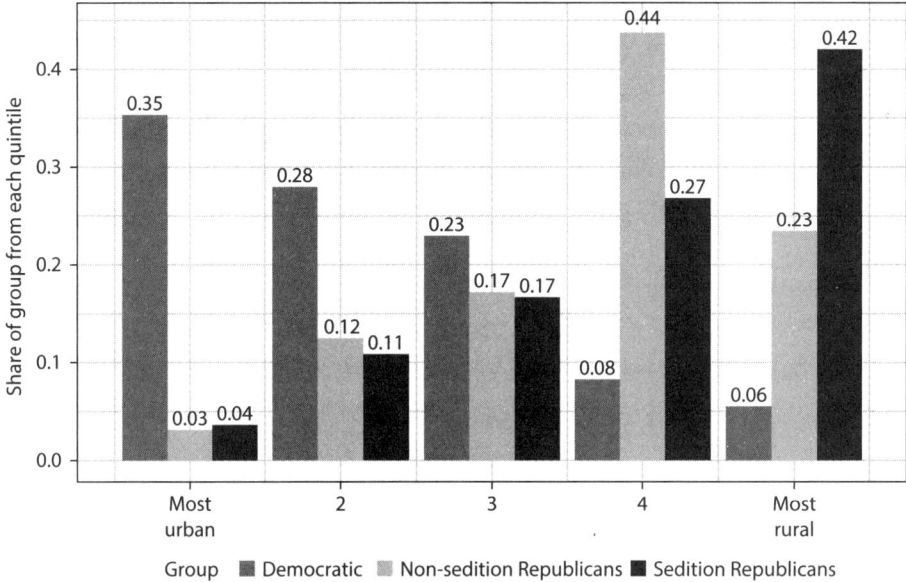

FIGURE 6.5. U.S. House votes on certifying the 2020 election, by district, rurality, and party
Source: Voteview; measure of rural from U.S. Census Bureau

presidential election. When Congress reconvened in the evening after the January 6, 2021, insurrection at the Capitol, 139 Republican House members—known as the Sedition Caucus—sided with Trump in his claims that the election was fraudulent, defying state and federal election officials from both parties who stood by the results, and dozens of court decisions.[50] These representatives—each of whom rejected the Electoral College votes from at least one of the two contested states, Arizona and Pennsylvania—hailed from districts where Trump won by particularly large margins. Analyzing the congressional districts of Sedition Caucus members in terms of rurality (using the same categorization scheme as the one described above), we find that more than two-thirds of them came from the most rural districts in the country (figure 6.5). They included Marjorie Taylor Greene, of Georgia, and Elise Stefanik, from the Adirondacks region of New York. Only 4 percent of seditionists came from the most urban districts.

The Republicans who defied the president and accepted the election results, by contrast, represented more densely populated places on average than their seditionist colleagues, though their districts still tended to be more rural than those won by Democrats. They included Representative Adam Kinziger of Illinois and John Katko of central New York, both of whom were vocal in their denunciations of Trump's behavior in inciting the riot and voted for impeachment in January 2021. The Sedition Caucus did not consist of representatives from just one region of the nation: While more than half hailed from the South, 43 percent were elected in states across other regions, including Democratic strongholds.

Beyond members of Congress, Republican state officials from more rural states also backed efforts to overturn the election results. In December 2020, the (relatively urban) state of Texas filed a lawsuit asking the Supreme Court to discard millions of votes in key battleground states that had made voting by mail easier due to COVID-19 related concerns. Just one day after the lawsuit was filed, Republican attorneys general from seventeen states threw their weight behind it, with the majority coming from states with relatively high shares of rural populations, such as West Virginia, Mississippi, and Montana. These examples suggest that the rural-urban divide has helped foster a politics within the Republican Party that threatens key tenets of American democracy.

The Politics of Place Transformed

Democrat Bob Kerrey thought he understood how to win a statewide election in his home state of Nebraska. In 1982, he'd been elected governor, and in 1988 he'd won a U.S. Senate seat. In 1994, he defied the political winds and was reelected to the Senate, cornering 55 percent of the vote. After completing that term, he presided over a university for a decade, but when Democrats recruited him to run again for the Senate in 2012, he threw his hat in the ring.

As it turned out, the election that year was a rude awakening about how much Nebraska's politics had changed in the meanwhile. Kerrey lost by a wide margin, winning only the state's two most populated counties, those containing the cities of Omaha and Lincoln, and just three others. He was trounced in rural areas. "Oh yes," he explains, now "it's nearly impossible for a Democrat to win statewide."

"I think the breaking point was the 2011 election and the rise of the Tea Party. That was a game changer." He blames the Tea Party for demonizing the Affordable Care Act, and believes the organization had the effect of undermining support for Democrats, particularly in rural areas. He noted that when he was campaigning in 2012, Nebraskans were highly focused on the ACA. "They knew how it had gotten passed; they knew that my predecessor [Democrat] Ben Nelson had been the deciding vote to allow cloture to occur. They knew about cloture! They'd come up to me and say, 'What do you think about cloture?' That was not a question I had in the 1980s or 1990s."

Considering the nation as a whole, Kerrey is struck by the transformation of the Republican Party. "When I arrived in the Senate in 1989, here are the Republicans who were there, and not a single one of them could win a primary in their state today." He proceeded to tick off the names of moderate Republican senators—Bob Dole and Nancy Kassebaum, both of Kansas; Alan Simpson of Wyoming; Jack Danforth of Missouri; Warren Rudman of New Hampshire; Mark Hatfield of Oregon; and John Heinz of Pennsylvania—each of whom except Rudman and Hatfield had represented heavily rural populations. "If there was a weakening of a civil rights [policy] from a court decision, Danforth would be rushing down there [to the chamber] trying to change the law. Heinz may have been the forerunner of concern about the environment. Simpson and Rudman were valiantly prochoice. Those are really good examples of what's changed about American politics." Indeed, the mostly conservative Republicans representing rural states today typically oppose such initiatives.

Thinking back to his own elections in Nebraska, Kerrey comments that in the first three, "I never got less than 20 percent of the Republican vote." But in 2012, only 2 percent of Republicans voted for him. "Voters are not splitting their ticket," he explains.

The consequences for public policy were profound. Whereas Democrat Ben Nelson had ultimately supported the Affordable Care

Act and Kerrey promised to do the same, Republican Deb Fischer—who defeated Kerrey—favored its repeal, repeatedly. Once Trump was elected, Fischer voted for the 2017 tax cuts that favored the wealthy and the bill that undermined parts of the Dodd-Frank regulations. She joined a Congress that had become increasingly dominated by a Republican Party elected from rural America, but one that represented the country very differently than elected officials of not many years earlier had done.

Contemporary partisan polarization in Congress is fundamentally organized by place. Representation of rural areas has changed dramatically over just a few decades, as districts that not long ago sent Democrats to Washington, DC, have been transformed into Republican bastions. Meanwhile, more urban districts have become more reliably Democratic strongholds. This place-based divide makes it more difficult for Congress to pass major legislation that meets broad public needs and addresses the concerns of ordinary Americans. It has also imperiled basic procedures that uphold democratic norms.

How has the rural-urban divide affected the distribution of governing power and the vibrancy of democratic well-being in other parts of government? We explore that question in the next chapter.

7

How the Rural-Urban Divide
Shapes Political Power

RICK SWENSON, the chair of the local Republican Party, and Mary Bowers, one of the officers in the group, met with us at a restaurant in the center of their small town in the Lower Peninsula of northern Michigan. Bowers explained to us their shared skepticism about election returns in the state. "There are [fifty-eight] rural counties in Michigan and only [twenty-five] urban ones, but somehow they [the urban counties] win," she says in disbelief.[1] "The numbers don't compute." Referring to the state's most populated county, the one containing Detroit, she says, "We realized that Wayne County is always the last to turn in their numbers, and we started joking that they were waiting to see how much they needed to cheat by to win the election." Swenson explained that he favored adopting an Electoral College–style system for elections within the state of Michigan, so that rural counties would each have a larger voice—and would gain more clout. It is not just in Michigan that rural voters feel disenfranchised and marginalized; these views have been reported widely.[2]

This raises the question of what difference the rural-urban political cleavage makes for the distribution of political power in the United States today. To use two classic formulations of the central question in the study of politics, how does the shift of white rural dwellers nationwide into the Republican Party affect "who governs" and "who gets what, when, and how"?[3] We contend that the transformation of rural politics matters so much in part because it has been channeled through institutions that amplify its power. Several features of U.S. political institutions set forth in the Constitution have always given disproportionate influence to less-populated places. Yet now as never before, these advantages are consolidated in one party. That party is the beneficiary of this extra leverage, which—particularly in the context of highly competitive elections—can permit it to gain control over several sources of political power without the support of the majority of Americans.

Take the Electoral College, for example, which decides presidential elections: By giving each state as many votes as it has U.S. Senators and Representatives, it offers a boost to the most sparsely populated states, which each receive at least three votes. It is not new for scholars to point out the impact of these arrangements on political inequality.[4] Yet as seen in chapter 2, the effect of such features has been diffused by the fact that historically, small-population states did not behave as a bloc; they typically varied from one another in their partisan leanings, and some featured competitive parties that often traded hands or shared governance. But now that nearly all such places have consolidated in a single party, we aim to evaluate this question anew. Returning to the Electoral College example, just since the rural-urban divide widened in American politics, the winner of the popular vote has lost the presidential election on two occasions.[5] How might this place-based cleavage be shaping the distribution of power across other institutions?

In this chapter, we show how the rural-urban divide has been channeled through many governing institutions to empower the Republican Party. It is important to note that U.S. elections are structured by the Constitution such that voters have a say primarily through the political geographic units in which they live: Their state of residence influences their impact on presidential and Senate elections, and their congressional district is the basis of their representation in the House. In other words, the size and distribution of the population—rural versus urban—within these units provide crucial filters on individuals' political voice. To be clear, we are not arguing that rural people themselves are empowered by these arrangements. Rather, their consolidation nationwide into one political party has enabled all elected officials in that party to gain and wield more power than they would otherwise. This place-based advantage is especially dangerous when it is combined with a party that takes extremist positions, pursuing policy goals that lack the support of a majority of Americans, and is willing to violate basic checks and balances. The United States' uniquely place-biased electoral institutions, combined with the rural-urban divide, are converging to imperil democracy.

Countermajoritarianism and the U.S. Senate

We start by examining one of the most obvious instances of small-state and rural bias—the U.S. Senate. As is well known, the framers of the Constitution included the Senate as part of the Connecticut Compromise as a way to ensure that small states were not dominated by the interests of larger ones. Because each state is allotted only two seats, in effect smaller, less densely populated states are, by design, given relatively more weight. What is perhaps less appreciated is that, since the nation's founding, the U.S. population has both grown tremendously and become far more urban. In 1790, when the Senate first convened, roughly 95 percent of the population lived in rural places as defined by the census; in 1900, just 60 percent did; by 2020, that figure had dropped to 20 percent.[6] Since the Senate apportionment rules have stood still in those years, the maldistribution of power to small states has increased dramatically over time. In 1790, Rhode Island, among the least populated states, had a population of 68,825, while Pennsylvania, among the most densely populated ones, boasted a population of 434,373.[7] This granted Rhode Islanders roughly six times as much power as Pennsylvanians in the Senate during the legislative body's first session. As the United States population has grown, however, and further urbanized, this representational gap has increased dramatically. As of 2020, California, the least rural state in the country as measured by the Census Bureau, had a population of more than thirty-nine million.[8] Meanwhile, Wyoming—among the most rural and least populated states— contained a population of just over 576,000. That means the residents of Wyoming wield much greater power in the Senate than Californians—sixty-eight times as much.

Researchers who study politics and democracy worldwide have suggested that the U.S. Senate is among the most malapportioned—or
poorly representative—legislative bodies in advanced democracies.[9] This
has vast implications for everything ranging from budgetary policy—for
which Senators from small-population states are able to garner far more
for their residents—to judicial appointments, as we will see below.[10]

Why does using states as the basis for choosing senators foster, on net,
inequality in representation? After all, just because a state has a small
population does not necessarily mean its residents are disproportionately
rural. Rhode Island and Delaware, for example, are highly urban, and each
contains around one million residents.[11] Yet it turns out that how rural a
state is and its population size are fairly well correlated; indeed, smaller-
population states tend to be more rural, even if the relationship is not
perfect.[12] Moreover, *within most states*, rural people tend to be more
prevalent relative to their presence in the U.S. population. In other words,
most states tend to be more rural than the United States at large. As of
2020, thirty-two states had a higher percentage of rural residents than the
national aggregate share of 20 percent. As a result, despite the growth of
the nation's urban population over the last century and more recently,
rural people have been a disproportionate share of the population *in more
than half of all states over the last four decades*.[13] At a minimum, this gives
rural people in those states an outsized, though certainly not overwhelming, voice in the election of the president and the Senate.

Conceivably, however, even a growing divergence between the states
in terms of their urban and rural populations need not necessarily present a problem for democratic governance. If some rural states gravi-
tated to one political party and other rural states to the other party, they
would in effect neutralize each other, and the extra institutional leverage
granted them collectively by the Constitution would not matter for
political power. Similarly, if their partisanship was not rigidly fixed but
vacillated over the course of several elections, we need not be concerned. In the contemporary United States, however, the consolidation
of rural voters into one party means that the institutional levers of
power—in this case the malapportionment of the Senate—accrues almost entirely to one party. The fact that this pattern has endured and

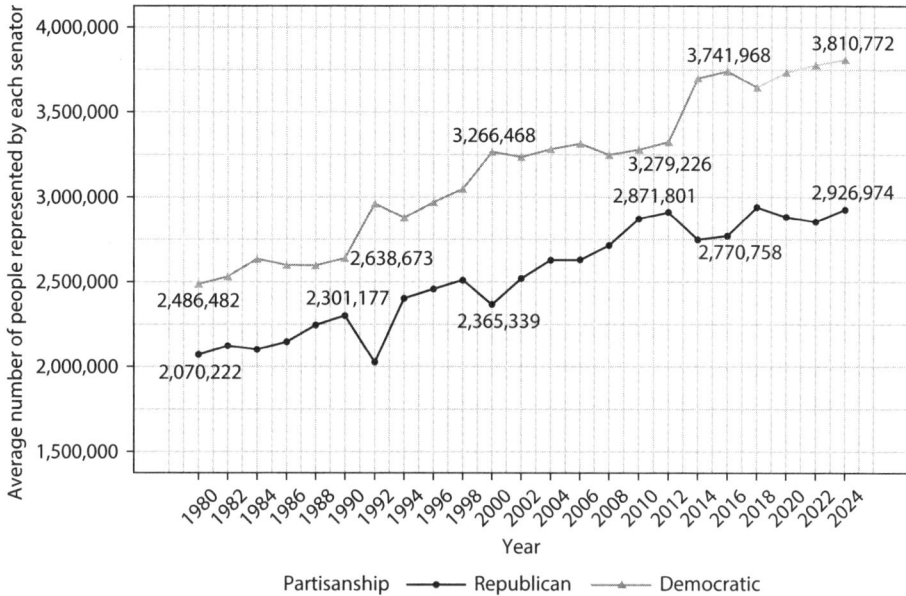

FIGURE 7.1. The growth of the partisan representation gap in the U.S. Senate, 1980–2024
Source: Voteview and U.S. Census Bureau

deepened over many years exacerbates the problem, as we will see in our analysis of the judiciary below.

Figure 7.1 sheds light on how, as the rural-urban divide has grown, the Senate's small-state bias has resulted in significant representational gaps between the parties. For every Congress since 1980, we tally up the total number of people represented by a senator of each party, using the population of each senator's state. We then divide the total population represented by each party by the number of senators it has in office (see appendixes). (We do so without considering who controls the chamber, a topic we examine below.) As is displayed, as late as 1980, Republican and Democratic senators represented fairly similar numbers of Americans. The average Democrat represented just under 2.5 million people, while the typical Republican represented just under 2.1 million people. This in part reflects the fact that Democrats were able to run and win Senate seats in smaller-population, more rural states—for example,

George S. McGovern of South Dakota, Tom Harkin of Iowa, and Max Baucus of Montana. In recent decades, however, a striking divergence has emerged. As the rural-urban divide has widened and the overall urban population has grown in many states, Democrats increasingly represent far more people than their Republican counterparts. The gap grew especially large beginning in the late 1990s and, for the most part, has accelerated since then. By 2024, the typical Democratic senator represented 3.8 million people, 31 percent more than the average Republican, who had 2.9 million constituents. In short, the representational gap between the two parties has more than doubled since 1980.

How might this gap matter for who governs the Senate? After all, by itself it indicates nothing about who actually controls the chamber and wields political power. If Republicans are representing fewer and fewer people over time—but also controlling the Senate less often—perhaps we should not be concerned with the small-state and rural bias of the institution. This, it turns out, is not the case. In the twenty-three Congresses running from 1980 through 2024, Republicans controlled the Senate twelve times (figure 7.2; see appendixes). Over that stretch, Republicans represented the majority of the population just two times, and by very slim margins. The last time Republicans held control of the Senate and represented a majority of the population was in the late 1990s—around the time when the rural-urban political divide began opening up. Across this period, when Republicans controlled the Senate, on average they held roughly 53 percent of seats yet represented just 48 percent of the population. Meanwhile, each time Democrats have controlled the Senate, they have safely represented a majority of the United States population: They held a similar amount of seats (fifty-four) as when Republicans held control, but they represented 59 percent of the population. Finally, as time has gone on, Republicans when controlling the Senate have increasingly represented a smaller and smaller share of the American population. Indeed, the Republican-controlled Senate during the first two years of the first Trump administration—which helped enact far-reaching policy changes—represented only 44 to 46 percent of the U.S. population.

Of course, the figures above raise normative concerns about the fairness of the U.S. Senate. In *nearly half* the Congresses over the past two

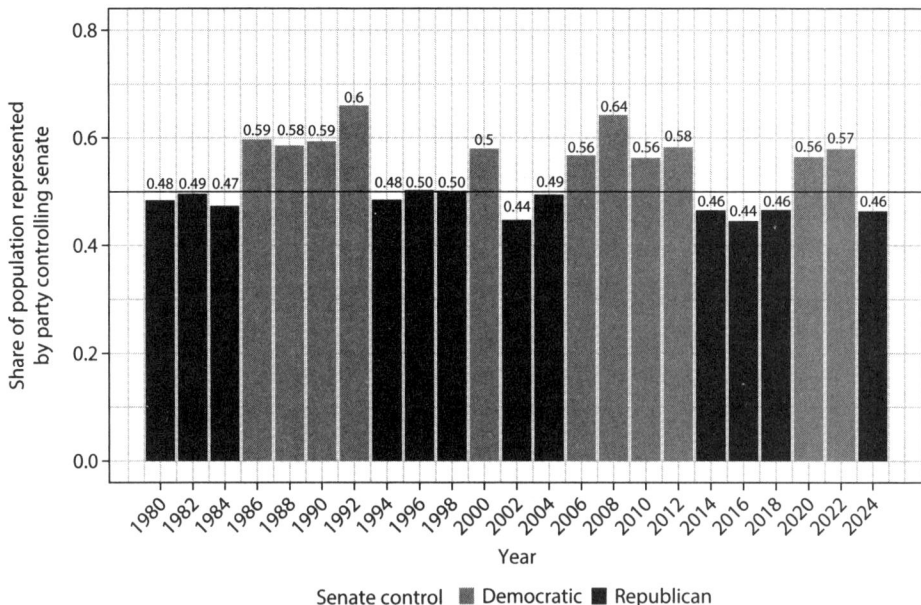

FIGURE 7.2. Minority control of the Senate by Republicans, 1980–2024
Source: Voteview

decades, the controlling party has represented just a minority of Americans. Several scholars have shown that, in addition to overrepresenting rural areas, the Senate's malapportionment tends to underrepresent African Americans, Latinos, and ideological liberals, who tend to live in states with larger populations.[14] This poses deep concerns about the Senate's representational adequacy. But the trends shown above ultimately matter for who wields power and what policies are produced. And the Senate is not only among the most malapportioned legislative bodies in the world; it is also one of the most powerful. In many countries featuring bicameralism, or two legislative chambers, the so-called upper chamber has little say over lawmaking.[15] Such is not the case in the United States, where the Senate is just as powerful as, if not more powerful than, the House.

How, then, might the malapportionment of the Senate shape policymaking? While we do not undertake a systematic analysis here, several scholars have begun to address that question in sophisticated ways. In their analysis of votes on several key policy issues from 1961 to 2019, Richard Johnson and Lisa L. Miller show that the Senate has had a distinctively conservative bias, particularly over the last three decades.[16] By reapportioning the Senate and making it more representative of the population size in each state, the scholars were able to generate counterfactual votes—or scenarios that could have happened—if the legislative body were more representative. They find that if the Senate were apportioned more equally, votes on issues such as gun control, abortion, and health care would have all been decided in ways that are more in line with the public's views, which in these cases are more liberal.

Furthermore, power in the Senate influences not only the content of the laws that are enacted; it is also crucial for *stopping* legislation. Indeed, among scholars, lawmakers, and advocates alike, the institution is regularly described as the "graveyard of legislation." This is, in part, because of the U.S. Senate's filibuster rule. Highly unique in Western democracies and created by accident, the rule allows lawmakers to delay legislation indefinitely if they oppose it.[17] When a minority of forty Senators act in unison, they can prevent legislation from coming to the floor. Filibusters can be overcome with a sixty-vote margin, but as partisan polarization has increased along with what political scientist Frances Lee has called "teamsmanship"—whereby parties increasingly act as coherent teams or blocs, regardless of their ideological commitments—those sixty votes have become harder to come by.

The filibuster power, while negative in orientation, is highly consequential. Sometimes the ability to say no in politics is just as important as advancing one's own policy agenda. Consider policymaking during the Obama administration. Obama won the White House with 53 percent of the vote—a higher percentage than any Democrat since Lyndon Johnson—and Democrats won both the House and Senate for the first time since 1992, featuring ample margins at that. Nonetheless, Obama's agenda faced a precarious landscape for policymaking. Despite strong efforts at bipartisan policymaking, Senate Democrats enjoyed a filibuster-proof sixty-vote majority for only four short months of the Obama administration's first term. As one headline memorably put it when Republicans landed a surprise victory in the special election to

fill the Senate seat vacated when Ted Kennedy died, "Scott Brown
Wins Mass. Race, Giving GOP 41–59 Majority in the Senate."[18] Republican Minority Leader Mitch McConnell (R-Kentucky) gained the
forty votes needed to construct a political strategy of obstructionism
by continually threatening to invoke the filibuster. Indeed, according
to our analysis of Senate data, the filibuster was invoked in 2009 and
2010—when Republican senators represented just 39 percent of the
population—more times than during the twenty-nine Congresses in
the years running from 1917 to 1974.[19]

To be sure, as discussed in the previous chapter, Democrats in Congress were able to advance significant legislation in President Obama's
first term, including health care reform that expanded coverage to millions of Americans, student aid, financial reform, and policies to help
address the Great Recession. Yet the Republican Party, acting in unity,
imposed minority rule by blocking other significant—and
popular—reforms. These included, among other things, legislation that
would make it easier for private sector workers to join unions, immigration reform, cap-and-trade rules to mitigate climate change, and a Supreme Court replacement following Justice Antonin Scalia's death.[20]

The Senate has produced obstructionism well beyond the Obama administration. In recent decades economic inequality has grown tremendously in the United States, far outpacing its rise in other countries.[21] As
we have seen, it has had a particular geographic bias, advantaging urban
counties at the expense of rural areas. Political scientist Peter Enns and
his collaborators have demonstrated that the institutional design of the
Senate itself has facilitated the growth of economic inequality. Using data
that stretches over six decades, they find that growing polarization in the
chamber—and the resulting reduced legislative output due in large part
to the filibuster—has generated such outcomes.[22]

Of course, now that Democrats find themselves in the minority in the
Senate—and may continue to do so for the foreseeable future—they too
will rely on the filibuster to prevent the enactment of legislation to which
they object. Democrats have been less inclined than Republicans, however, to use this tool to block legislative action. When faced with a choice
of permitting a vote on a budget bill they dislike versus facing a

government shutdown, for example, Democrats' desire to enable the government to keep functioning generally inclines them to avoid a filibuster. Whichever party uses the filibuster, it shrouds responsibility and stymies responsive government by permitting a minority to prevent action.

How Place Shapes the Judicial Branch

Beyond its malapportionment and power over lawmaking, the Senate is unique in another way: in its responsibility to approve federal judicial appointments. In theory, the separation of powers is supposed to ensure that the judicial, legislative, and executive branches all remain relatively independent. As partisan polarization has increased in recent decades, however, this has seemingly become less tenable. Presidents—particularly Republican presidents—have come to nominate more and more ideological and extreme judges, and for the most part presidents' copartisans in the Senate have tended to act in coordination with the executive branch to approve such nominees. Republicans have been especially aided in these endeavors by extraparty organizations, through dynamics similar to those discussed in chapter 5. As political scientist Steven Teles has shown, starting in the 1970s, right-wing donors and foundations began to invest substantially in the production of a pipeline of conservative jurists, through the creation of think tanks, journals, formal organizations, and informal networks.[23] The most notable instance is the Federalist Society, an organization with chapters at an estimated two hundred law schools in the United States. These efforts have proven highly successful: At least four of the six conservative justices on the Supreme Court are either current or former members of the society.[24]

The significance of such judicial appointments should not be understated. As legal scholar K. Sabeel Rahman and political scientist Kathleen Thelen have persuasively argued, "Compared to other rich democracies, the American judiciary is more powerful, more politicized, and more directly involved in shaping [policy] outcomes."[25] Furthermore, the United States is among just a handful of countries that grants its federal judges lifetime tenure.[26] This raises the stakes of not only who is appointed but also *when*. Parties have sought to confirm as many judges as possible, knowing they will serve as a durable source of influence.

As the rural-urban divide has grown and Republican senators have come to represent a smaller portion of the citizenry, how might this have shaped the highest and most powerful court in the land? We examine Senate confirmation votes for each successful judicial nomination running back to 1980, and analyze the percentage of the U.S. population represented by the senators who voted in favor of each successful nominee (figure 7.3). Several trends stand out. First, over time, as partisan teamsmanship has increased, Supreme Court nominees are being confirmed by senators representing smaller and smaller shares of the U.S. population. The trend started with the controversial appointment of Clarence Thomas, but it has accelerated in recent years. Second, and relatedly, justices have received diminishing numbers of votes from members of the opposing party. When President Bill Clinton nominated Ruth Bader Ginsburg in 1993, she was confirmed ninety-six to three, with only three Republicans voting against her. This stands in sharp contrast to when President Obama nominated Elena Kagan in 2010, and she received just five votes from Republicans. Finally, and most important, the partisan and geographic skew of justices' support has tended to overlap. When a Democratic-controlled Senate has approved a judicial nomination, senators voting in favor of confirmation have tended to represent well over a majority of the U.S. population. In stark contrast, when a Republican-controlled Senate has successfully confirmed a nominee, supporting votes have relied increasingly on senators representing a *minority* of the population. Justice Alito was confirmed by Senators representing just 50.2 percent of the U.S. population. Meanwhile, Justices Clarence Thomas, Neil Gorsuch, Brett Kavanaugh, and Amy Concy Barrett were all confirmed by senators representing less than half of the U.S. population. And while the trend of more conservative justices securing nomination with only minority support escalated with the first Trump presidency, as figure 7.3 makes clear, this pattern has been decades in the making.

The current Supreme Court is remarkable in its antimajoritarian status. Five of the current conservative justices were confirmed by senators

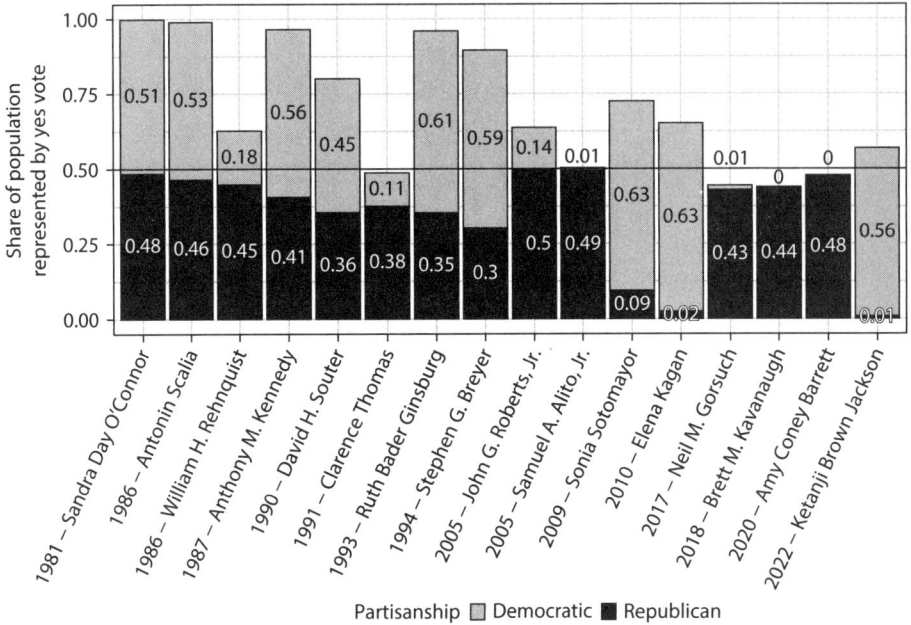

FIGURE 7.3. Share of U.S. population represented in confirmations of Supreme Court justices
Source: Voteview and U.S. Census Bureau

representing barely half of Americans or fewer. We take a deeper dive into specific decisions with the discussion of the first Trump administration below, but it is worth noting that the contemporary court is the most conservative one in almost a century, according to analysis by legal scholars Lee Epstein and Steven Quan.[27] And this conservative bent is not in line with public opinion on many important issues, among either rural or urban dwellers.

The House of the People? Finding Rural Bias Where We Would Least Expect It

What about the House of Representatives? In many respects, the House is the most small-*d* democratic institution in the country. Often described as the "House of the People" or as the embodiment of "one person, one vote," we might expect it to reflect little, if any, geographical bias. In the early 1960s, moreover, the Warren Court handed down a series of decisions making the House as well as state legislative districts more fair and electorally representative. Before those decisions, dozens of states—particularly in the South—had not redistricted in decades, thus granting rural people a disproportionate amount of representation. The court upended that lopsidedness. In one of the cases, Chief Justice Earl Warren, delivering the majority opinion, declared, "Legislators represent people, not trees or acres. Legislators are elected by voters, not farms or cities or economic interests. As long as ours is a representative form of government, and our legislatures are those instruments of government elected directly by and directly representative of the people, the right to elect legislators in a free and unimpaired fashion is a bedrock of our political system."[28] As a result of these court cases, states were forced to redraw districts so that each contained roughly the same number of residents. This decision is regarded by scholars to have "revolutionized representation," and ultimately led to congressional maps that rewarded rurality less than before.[29] Consider two examples from the maps constructed following the 2020 redistricting cycle. Kentucky's congressional district five, among the most rural districts in the nation, with 75 percent of its population considered rural by the Census's definition, contains roughly the same number of people as California's district thirty-four, an entirely urban district in Los Angeles that includes no rural residents.

Given the equal distribution of representatives across districts, in many ways the House of Representatives is what social scientists refer to as a "tough test" for our argument. Yet despite the Warren Court's proclamation that such plans would result in equal legislative representation regardless of place, the growth of the rural-urban divide has in many ways challenged this, as we will see.

In recent years, many Americans have come to assume that unfairness in representation emanates primarily from one particular type of geographical bias: partisan gerrymandering.[30] Because state legislatures have the authority to draw U.S. congressional districts, this privilege has always offered partisans the ability to draw ones that are favorable to their party, and the likelihood of doing so has grown with contemporary polarization. Lawmakers can favor their own party by "packing" supporters of the opposing party in some districts, so that they are inefficiently distributed and win fewer seats than they otherwise might have, or by "cracking" particular constituencies, so they are scattered across several districts and their votes are diluted. Following the ascendancy of the Republican Party at the state level in 2010 and a subsequent round of redistricting that appeared to feature highly partisan or gerrymandered maps (the so-called Great Gerrymander of 2012), a growing literature drew attention to how state lawmakers were stacking the deck in favor of their party.[31]

Yet the concern with gerrymandering is not so much wrong as it is incomplete. Republicans have certainly benefited from gerrymandering in recent election cycles, but its impact pales compared to the substantial advantages the party currently enjoys owing to the particular geographic distribution of its supporters.

For starters, consider the electoral rules of U.S. House elections. Most House elections are governed by "winner-take-all," "first-past-the-post" rules, meaning that the single candidate who wins the most votes wins the seat. No matter how many votes are secured by losing candidates, they receive no seats. This is in contrast to other electoral systems in democracies around the world—particularly those featuring proportional representation—that award seats based on the overall share of votes a party wins. In the U.S. system, as a rule roughly 50 percent of all votes for U.S. House seats are "wasted" each election, meaning they either go to a losing candidate or merely pad the margin of victory for the winning candidate. Consider, furthermore, that a common norm in drawing congressional districts is to privilege a "community of interest" to ensure that population centers are adequately represented. For this reason, state lawmakers, with some important exceptions, are reluctant to break up cities or counties when drawing districts, on the assumption that doing so might dilute their representation.[32]

All of this means that the distribution of partisans—where they live and vote—matters greatly in U.S. House elections. If one party's voters become "packed" into a city, as many Democrats have come to be, that party can "waste" a lot of votes. As an example, take Detroit, Michigan, a city from one of our case study states. Detroit includes a few of the most urban districts in the country. Indeed, as defined by the Census Bureau, several of its districts feature a completely urban population—in other words, not a single person living in the district is considered rural. In 2010, for example, in district thirteen, Democrat Hansen Clarke beat his Republican challenger John Hauler 100,885 votes to 23,462—a roughly four-to-one margin.[33] Yet while netting Clarke a seat, this skew (along with the skewed results from several other urban Detroit house seats), was relatively inefficient, at least by America's electoral rules. He only needed roughly 63,000 votes to win the seat, meaning Democrats effectively "wasted" around 37,000 votes. Those surplus votes could have been put to much better use in Michigan district seven, with a population that is far more rural—46 percent—than most of the rest of Michigan's districts, and far more rural than the rest of the districts in the House more broadly.[34] In Michigan's seventh, Republican Tim Walberg unseated Democratic incumbent Mark Schauer by a rather thin margin of just 10,783 votes.

The "efficiency gap" is a useful concept that quantifies how efficiently a party translates the number of votes it receives into seats, and thus it provides a systematic measure of the circumstances we've described above. We examine the efficiency gap over time for Michigan and our other case study states—Georgia, North Carolina, Ohio, and Missouri (figure 7.4; see appendixes). The efficiency gap was first constructed to detect gerrymandering.[35] Yet the measure can also be used to consider how efficiently partisan support is distributed across place.[36]

In each case study state, Democrats were fairly well distributed across districts throughout the 1980s. This in part reflects their ability to win seats not only in densely compact urban areas, but also in rural ones, as we saw in the previous chapter. Yet as the rural-urban divide has opened up, this trend has reversed. Democrats continue to run up vote margins in urban areas, but as Republicans have made inroads in rural areas, they have become far more efficiently located geographically,

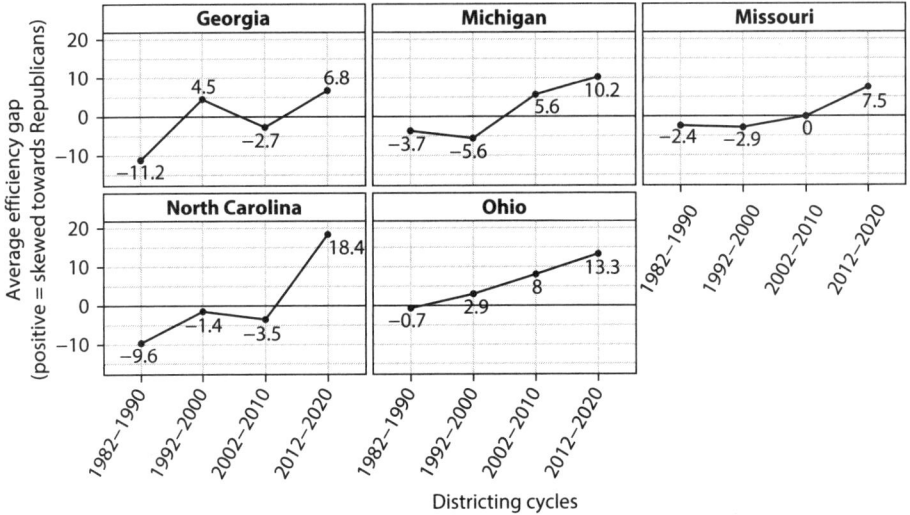

FIGURE 7.4. Growing Republican geographic advantage in the U.S. House, by state
Source: MIT Election Lab
Note: Results depict how Democrats increasingly "waste" votes in more urban areas.

and as a result, as figure 7.4 shows, they have been able to convert more votes into seats.

For the nation as a whole, we see trends similar to those in our case study states (figure 7.5). In the 1980s, Democrats were well distributed across place, owing to the fact that they were able to win and compete in many rural districts. Yet as the rural-urban divide grew and partisan competition heightened, Democrats lost their advantage. Conversely, as Republicans became ascendant in rural areas, they more efficiently translated their votes into seats. By the 2000s, Republicans had a slight advantage, and by the 2010s, a strong one.

The large pro-Republican efficiency gap scores after the 2010 redistricting cycle suggest that Republicans were able to build on their growing geographic bias and stack the deck in their favor. Michigan and North Carolina, with their very high scores of 10 and 18 respectively, have been called out by observers and researchers as especially egregious examples.[37] North Carolina's congressional redistricting practices

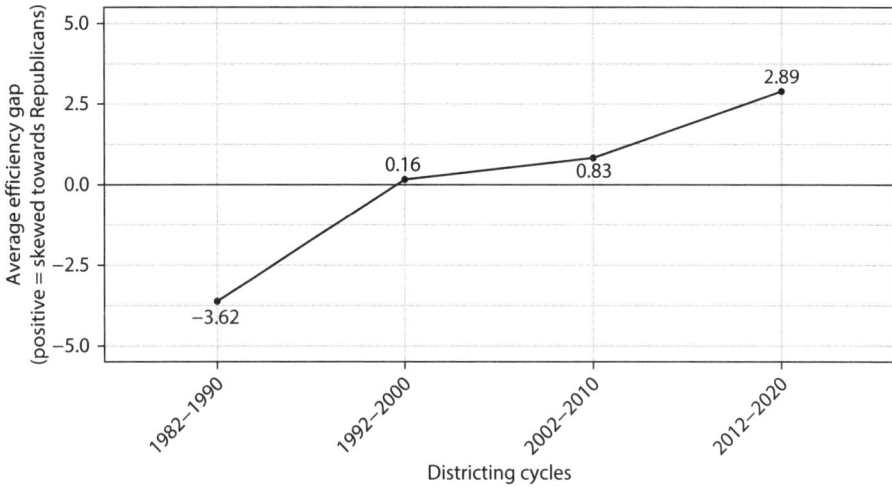

FIGURE 7.5. Growing Republican geographic advantage in the U.S. House, nationwide
Source: MIT Election Lab
Note: Results depict how Democrats increasingly "waste" votes in more urban areas.

in particular have been legally challenged on the basis that they dilute the votes not only of Democrats, but also of Black voters.

While we cannot disentangle the pro-Republican bias of recent gerrymandering from the more fundamental advantage of dominating sparsely populated areas, our research aligns with analyses suggesting that gerrymandering alone cannot account for all the Republicans' recent success. Using sophisticated software to simulate hundreds of district plans for each state, political scientists Jonathan Rodden and Jowei Chen have found that even if maps were drawn impartially, Republicans would still have a net advantage due to Democrats' inefficient distribution.[38] This is the case both in the U.S. House and in several state legislatures.[39] In short, while gerrymandering is certainly a problem, it cannot explain all or even most of Republicans' geographic advantage in the House. Instead, Republicans have used it to build on an advantage they already had thanks to the nation's growing rural-urban cleavage. The consequences have been significant, as we will see.

The Rural Bias and the First Trump Presidency:
A Case Study in Minority Rule

Now we examine how the rural biases discussed above advantaged the Republican Party during the first Trump administration. We focus on it in particular because it illustrates the various dangers of the following factors in combination: (1) the malapportionment of electoral institutions, (2) the consolidation of rural support for one party, and (3) high levels of extremism in one party.[40]

Consider first that Trump won the presidency in 2016 owing to his Electoral College victory, but he lost the popular vote. By scoring victories in several relatively rural and Rust Belt states, including Ohio, Michigan, and Georgia, he defeated Secretary Hillary Clinton by seventy-seven electoral votes, while losing the popular vote by nearly three million. He became one of only five presidents in American history to have lost the popular vote, with George W. Bush as the only other modern president to have done so. Following the 2016 election, Republicans also held control of the Senate, with a slim majority of fifty-two seats. Yet those Senators represented states containing just 44 percent of the American population. In other words, the Republican Party gained control of two of the most powerful institutions in the world without receiving support from a majority of the American population in either case.

Once in power, what did the Trump administration and congressional Republicans attempt to achieve? Among their top priorities were repealing the Affordable Care Act (ACA) and, relatedly, gutting federal funding for Medicaid, the publicly funded insurance program that covers low-wage workers, people with disabilities, and many senior citizens living in nursing homes. While the ACA was initially unpopular, when pollsters asked Americans about individual provisions—especially the expansion of Medicaid to low-wage workers and protections for preexisting conditions—the majority actually approved of them.[41] By the time Congress began attempting to repeal the ACA in 2017, with Trump poised to sign the change into law, more Americans viewed it favorably than unfavorably.[42] Medicaid, meanwhile, has enjoyed broad public support for decades.

Nevertheless, more than a week before his inauguration, then–President Elect Trump encouraged Congress to repeal the ACA and replace it "very quickly."[43] Within hours of being sworn in, he signed an executive order aimed at undermining the ACA.[44] For several months the administration and Republican congressional leaders sought to repeal the act and gut Medicaid. According to estimates from the Congressional Budget Office, the legislation would have resulted in twenty-three million people losing health insurance.[45] Several third-party, nonpartisan analyses showed that repealing the ACA and cutting Medicaid would have disproportionately harmed rural areas.[46]

The GOP efforts to "repeal and replace" the ACA were also extremely unpopular. According to analysis from political scientist Christopher Warshaw, the Republican health bill was arguably one of the most unpopular pieces of major legislation in modern history; it received support from just over 20 percent of those polled.[47] Though the Trump administration and congressional Republicans ultimately failed in dramatic fashion, their repeated attempts to roll back an increasingly popular policy indicates how untethered their agenda was from the mass public's preferences.

Arguably the Republicans' most significant legislative achievement during 2017–2018, when they controlled the presidency and both chambers of Congress, was the 2017 Tax Cuts and Jobs Act. One of the most regressive tax cuts of all time, the bill slashed the corporate tax rate from 36 to 21 percent, reduced rates on the highest-earning individual taxpayers, and doubled exemptions for the estate tax—a tax that disproportionately affects the wealthy. According to public opinion polling from Gallup, the law was remarkably unpopular, with 55 percent of Americans disapproving of it before it passed and 56 disfavoring it after it was signed into law.[48] It ranked among the most unpopular pieces of major legislation in modern history. In the Senate, it was passed on a straight party-line vote, meaning it was approved by lawmakers representing only a minority of Americans.

Beyond these highly skewed tax policy changes, the first Trump administration's most lasting success was the appointment and Senate confirmation of three conservative Supreme Court justices—Neil M.

Gorsuch, Brett M. Kavanaugh, and Amy Coney Barrett. Together with Justices Thomas and Alito, these Trump-appointed justices have overturned extremely popular laws and judicial precedents. Most notably, the *Dobbs* decision undermined the legal right to abortion, long established by *Roe v. Wade*—which, as we saw, was supported by a majority not only of Americans but also of rural dwellers.

In addition, the conservative justices appointed by Trump have been pivotal in rulings with far-reaching consequences for the distribution of social, economic, and political power in the United States. These include those that have undercut labor unions' ability to organize (*Janus v. AFSCME*), struck down affirmative action policies at universities (*Students for Fair Admissions, Inc. v. President & Fellows of Harvard College*), and curtailed the enforcement of environmental regulations (*West Virginia v. EPA*). More recently, they have issued rulings that weaken federal agencies' authority to interpret the law, significantly limiting the government's ability to enforce regulations that protect the environment, ensure economic fairness, and promote equity across society (*Loper Bright Enterprises v. Raimondo*).[49] Perhaps most shockingly, they have ruled in favor of presidential immunity from criminal prosecution for crimes committed while in office (*Trump v. United States*). In short, the ultraconservative justices on the Roberts Court are likely to shape government policy for decades—despite having acquired their authority through procedures that did not reflect the will of the majority of Americans.

Rural Overrepresentation and American Democracy

American political institutions have always granted extra power to rural, sparsely populated areas. It might stand to reason, therefore, that rural overrepresentation does not pose an especially dangerous problem for American democracy. Yet as we have shown in this chapter, those institutional biases have been exacerbated by the emergence of the rural-urban political divide, particularly since the late 1990s. Now that one party—the GOP—has for the first time in history consolidated the support of rural dwellers, it can count on an important electoral bonus that spans across several institutions. These circumstances permit the party to remain electorally competitive while imposing unpopular policies and, as we saw in the last chapter, fostering obstructionism.

The first Trump presidency illustrated several of these dangers. While the rural slant in American political institutions did not begin in 2016, President Trump and the Republican Party exploited it to enact several policies and make important appointments that will have long-lasting consequences. Their crowning legislative achievement—highly regressive tax cuts—undercuts the federal government's ability to make investments in pressing public priorities, such as economic inequality, climate change, and physical infrastructure. Furthermore, the three conservative justices who were confirmed by a Senate that did not represent a majority of Americans are likely to entrench a jurisprudence that will make it more difficult for the federal government to address the needs of all Americans, including rural dwellers. The consequences, in short, will be both long-lasting and harmful to democracy in the United States.

How can the rural-urban divide be mended? Many rural people, such as Mary Bowers and Rick Swenson, feel underrepresented in American politics. While we have shown in this chapter that the situation is far more complicated—indeed, American political institutions have historically granted rural areas more power over time—many rural people still rightfully feel that the government is unresponsive to their needs. Having examined the consequences of the rural-urban divide, we turn to potential solutions. Can public policy make a difference in reducing place-based polarization? That is our next question.

PART IV

Solutions

8

Does Public Policy Help
Mend the Divide?

AS THE CONVERSATION continued with Republican county chair Rick Swenson and officer Mary Bowers in northern Michigan, we asked, "What are the biggest challenges faced by the local area?" "Jobs," Swenson responded without hesitation. "Especially for younger people. It's desolate for jobs here if you want to raise a family." His description echoed answers to this question that we heard in counties in each of our case study states: Republican and Democratic county chairs alike answered—as if in unison—that employment opportunities were slim. Just as noteworthy, though, was what Swenson said next: "If you can't find a job working for the state, the county, or the gas company, you've got to move." Government employment, it seemed, kept the local economy afloat. "Or you can get pregnant and get on welfare," added Bowers, with an eyeroll. It's not that government has been absent in rural communities in recent decades; rather, if noticed at all, the help that it provides is often deemed to be a suboptimal solution, if not the last resort.

Now that we have examined the sources of the rural-urban divide, its development over time, and its consequences for lawmaking and political power, what about solutions? What might mitigate this cleavage that is tearing at the United States' social fabric, making government so dysfunctional, and threatening democracy? We consider the question in this chapter and the next, beginning by examining whether public policy provides an answer.

In theory, public policy could allay the problems mentioned above and, in turn, reduce polarization. At its core, democracy involves a relationship in which citizens can hold their representatives accountable through elections: reelecting them if they are responsive to citizens by enacting policies they favor, and voting them out of office if they fail to do so.[1] Whether policies can serve these democratic ends, however, is contingent on several things. It hinges in part on the visibility of public policies' design and their traceability to government, as well as on whether public officials, civic organizations, or media shine a spotlight on them.[2] Further, policies can influence whether citizens bother to participate in politics or not, by spurring engagement or disengagement. Policies produce such feedback effects through various pathways, in particular by bestowing resources, conveying messages about government, or empowering groups that in turn mobilize citizens. For example, if policies grant valuable resources to communities or the citizens living in them, making them better off, that might motivate citizens to reelect officials who are responsible for creating or sustaining them. In addition, if policies make people aware that government officials are responsive to people like them, such messages could promote similar outcomes.[3] Conversely, policies that are stigmatizing, difficult to access, or hidden from view by their design may yield either negative effects— for example, they may weaken confidence in government or discourage participation—or have no impact at all.[4]

As we saw in chapter 2, the federal government has long nurtured rural areas though a wide array of policies, ranging from regulatory policies that ensured fairness in the political economy to agricultural policies, social welfare policies, and infrastructure policies, among others. These policies did not go unnoticed by rural dwellers. For a half century after the New Deal, many of them continued to support the Democratic Party, appreciative that it had taken care of their parents' and grandparents' generations and confident that it stood on the side of everyday people. Here we will examine what has become of government's role over the past few decades, as the rural-urban divide has emerged and intensified. Rural dwellers have certainly felt left behind in many respects; have they in fact been neglected by the federal government as well, excluded from its public policies? Moreover, to the extent that federal policies do incorporate rural areas, do they help to mitigate the growing partisan divide?

Fading Political Will to Strengthen the Rural Economy

As recently as the 1980s, a wide array of federal policies—many of them dating back to the New Deal—supported the rural economy. Perhaps the most important were those that regulated how the market operated, including antitrust policies that regulated the fair terms of competition between businesses and those that governed behavior in the financial sector in particular. As we saw in chapter 3, by the late twentieth century policymakers had shifted away from strict enforcement of those laws and even reversed some of them, such as Glass-Steagall. In combination with technological changes, these policy changes weakened the rural economy.

We asked former Democratic Senator Tom Daschle, who represented South Dakota from 1987 to 2005 and served as minority leader, about the impact of deregulation on rural places. He replied, "I think that accelerated the outmigration in rural America, in many ways. The regulatory framework we'd had was designed in part to ensure that regardless of where you lived, you had access to many economic opportunities. With deregulation, you further accelerated the disadvantages that there were in living in rural America . . . whether it was aviation or banking, or any one of a number of other contexts. It made it much harder for smaller entities to compete." Summing up, Daschle explained, "The more we deregulated, the greater leverage larger entities had, and the more leverage they had, the harder it was to create the kind of level playing field necessary for smaller entities to stay in the room and at the table."

As the economy changed, other policies that in the past had bene-fited rural dwellers grew narrower in scope and reached fewer of them. New Deal–era rural policies had aided farmers in particular, but as agricultural consolidation led to the demise of family farms, the percentage of rural people who benefited from such policies declined sharply. As the United States liberalized trade, particularly through NAFTA and with East Asia, deindustrialization intensified and factories in many rural areas either downsized dramatically or went out of business altogether. All told, policies that had long helped to ensure job opportunities and decent pay deteriorated or became increasingly irrelevant to rural Americans. What would take their place?

Social Welfare Policies on the Rise

With few exceptions, federal social welfare policies created during the New Deal and the Great Society remained intact. In fact, from the 1980s through the 2000s, policymakers expanded the reach of several of them and created new ones. Most of these policies—called "social transfers"—targeted individuals or households, whether by supplementing their income or providing them with assistance to cover the costs of health care, education, or other services. Overall, the amount of resources flowing from government to citizens through social transfers has grown nationwide.[5] As we show below, these benefits have increased in rural areas in particular, which is not surprising given that a higher proportion of the rural population qualifies for many of them, whether due to age or lower income level. In short, as other sources of income vanished in rural places, federal social welfare policies took up some of the slack.

We use data from the federal government to show the amount of federal social transfers per capita received by rural and urban counties from 1970 to 2019, adjusted for inflation (figure 8.1). We include a wide array of policies, namely Social Security, Medicare, Medicaid, SNAP (Supplemental Nutrition Assistance Program, previously called Food Stamps), Unemployment Insurance, EITC (Earned Income Tax Credit), and several others (see appendixes). While rural and urban counties relied on such transfers at similar rates in the 1970s and 1980s, they diverged from the 1990s onward as rural places faced economic tumult and residents came to rely more on government benefits. By 2019, on the eve of the pandemic, rural people benefited from social transfers by $1,749 more per person per year than their urban peers.[6]

Now we examine rural versus urban reliance on particular social welfare policies. Social Security, established in 1935, is the nation's most

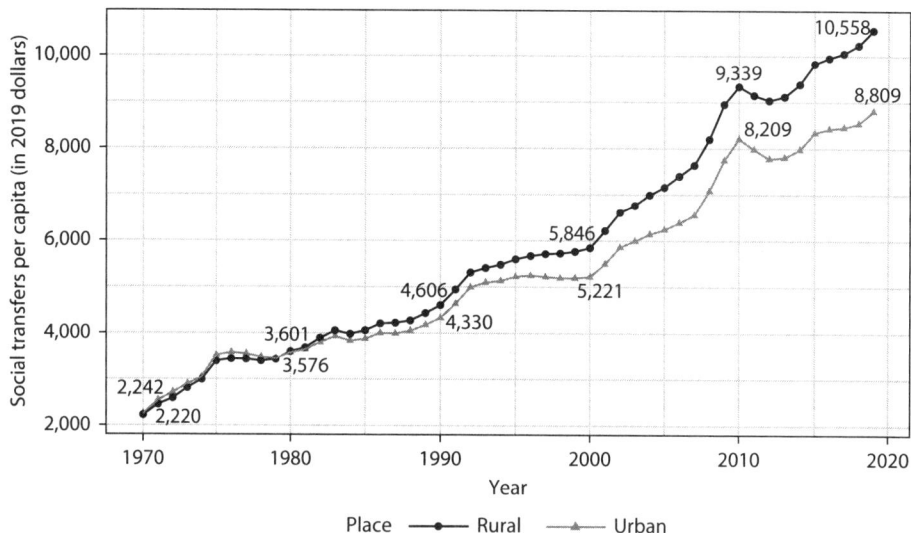

FIGURE 8.1. The rise of federal social transfers in rural and urban counties, 1970–2019
Source: BEA; measure of rural from OMB

generous and inclusive social program, providing benefits to nearly all retired workers and their spouses or survivors, as well as to younger workers who are disabled. Since 1971, benefit rates have been subject to annual cost of living adjustments; in 2022, for example, beneficiaries received an increase of 5.9 percent in their payments. Established in 1965, Medicare provides health coverage to most of the same population, and spending in the program has grown over time, with the cost of health care. While these two policies combined have long disproportionately benefited rural areas relative to urban ones, this gap has widened, particularly in the twenty-first century (figure 8.2, top panel).

Medicaid, also established in 1965, has transformed dramatically since it was enacted, evolving into the nation's most widespread social policy, providing health coverage to more than one in five Americans.[7] Originally, it targeted those who benefited from other programs but did not qualify for Medicare; this included poor aged, blind, or disabled adults, as well as those in single-parent families covered by Aid to

Medicare + Social Security

6,000
5,000
4,000
3,000
2,000
1,000

5,312   6,540
5,165
3,597   4,286
2,932
2,658   3,115
2,156
1,322   2,056
1,202

1970   1980   1990   2000   2010   2020

Medicaid

2,000
1,500
1,000
500

2,039
1,637   1,837
1,512
1,124
1,049
608
363   588
199   288
109

1970   1980   1990   2000   2010   2020

Social transfers per capita (2019 dollars)

SNAP (formerly Food Stamps)

300
200
100

276
240   176
159
126   138   88
52   105   107   72
31

1970   1980   1990   2000   2010   2020

Earned Income Tax Credit (EITC)

250
200
150
100
50

248   220
183   215   197
150
63
23   38   45

1980   1990   2000   2010   2020

Place   ● Rural   ▲ Urban

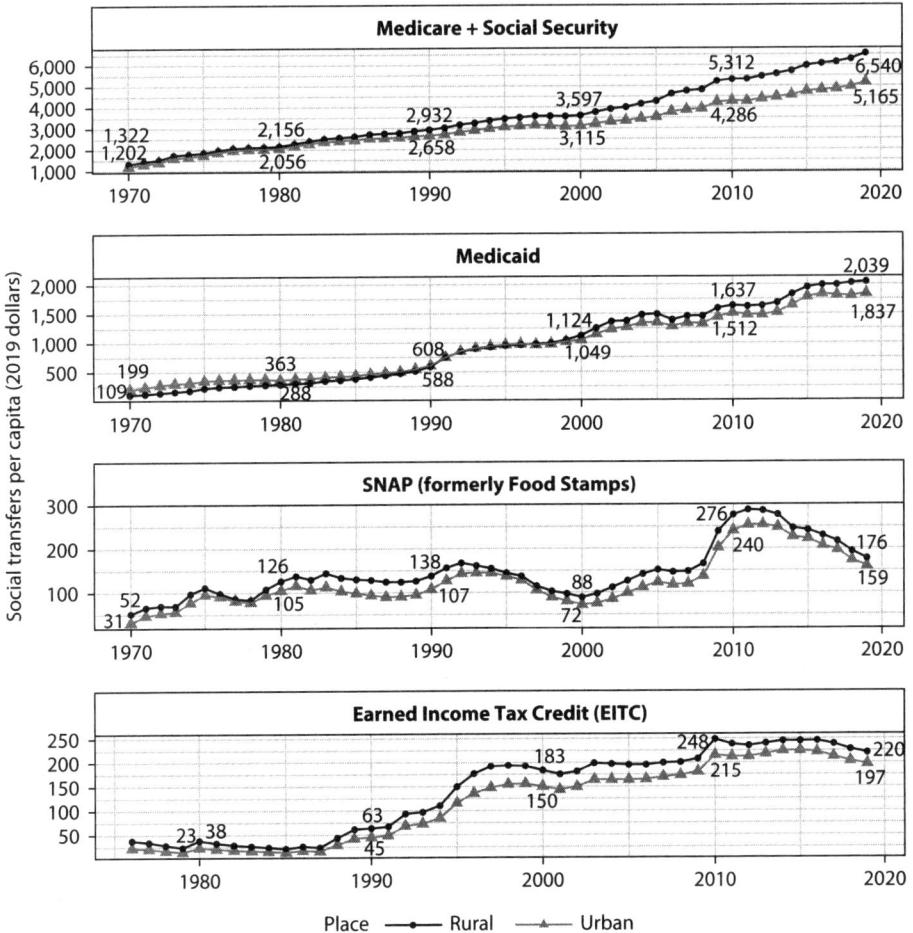

FIGURE 8.2. Selected social transfers in rural and urban counties, 1970–2019
Source: BEA; measure of rural from OMB

Families with Dependent Children (known as "cash welfare"). At that point, it provided an indistinguishable amount of aid to rural and urban counties (figure 8.2, second panel). In the 1980s, Congress expanded its coverage to reach more low-income children, and by 1990 it covered all under age eighteen who lived in poverty.[8] It was not until the early 2000s that rural areas began relying on Medicaid at higher rates than urban areas. This gap increased slightly more after 2010, when President Barack Obama signed into law the Affordable Care Act (ACA), with provisions that further enlarged Medicaid to cover families up to 133 percent of the poverty level. At present all but ten states have expanded Medicaid under the ACA.[9] While the gap between rural and urban areas is noticeably smaller than for Social Security and Medicare, it is worth noting that it would likely be somewhat larger had more states adopted Medicaid expansion. Most of the states that have refused to adopt expansion have a more rural population than the nation generally, and if they had accepted the increased coverage, rural people likely would have benefited disproportionately.

We also considered other federal social transfers, most of which boost the incomes of nonseniors and a few that facilitate educational opportunity or assist with housing costs. Collectively, until the late 1990s, these policies did not exhibit a noticeable gap between rural and urban areas. Separately, we examined the two policies with the broadest coverage, the EITC, which has grown into the nation's largest poverty-reduction policy, and SNAP. Each of these distributes slightly greater benefits in rural counties (figure 8.2, third and fourth panels).

As we learned in chapter 1, it does not appear that rural white people are especially less supportive of government spending than their urban peers; rather, like most Americans, they would prefer for themselves and their fellow citizens to make a living by gainful employment. Political theorist Judith Shklar famously observed that along with the right to vote, the right to a job is considered fundamental to Americans, as a source of the dignity bestowed on those considered to be full and equal citizens.[10] It is therefore no surprise that many rural dwellers often express antipathy to social welfare programs, particularly those for which deservingness is not tied to workplace participation.[11] In part, these attitudes revolve around others' use of such policies. For example, political scientist Katherine Cramer, in her ethnographic research in rural Wisconsin, found that residents there felt that urbanites relied more than themselves on government benefits and paid less in taxes.[12] But rural dwellers also expressed reluctance to use such policies themselves. Sociologist Jennifer Sherman, who did similar research in the

Pacific Northwest, observed that rural people placed a high value on self-reliance and hard work, which they perceived as indicators of morality, and they viewed use of government programs as less respectable. When they themselves needed to use such benefits, they experienced a deep sense of stigma and shame. They drove to stores far away to use SNAP benefits, hoping to avoid the gaze of their neighbors and community members.[13] Barbara Jones, a county party chair in Missouri, explained to us that antigovernment attitudes run deep in her remote region, where people pride themselves on their independence. She told of a friend who lived with her husband and six children in a trailer with no running water. Given the expensive copayments on the insurance the husband had from his job in a mine, Jones suggested that Medicaid could be helpful to them. Her friend flatly rejected the idea, explaining, "Then people would think we were poor." Of course, urban dwellers also prize work and self-reliance, and face stigma when using government benefits.[14] Nevertheless, it is clear that the increased prevalence of social transfers in rural areas has not helped reduce the rural-urban divide.

Declining Public Support for College Attendance

The fact that some social welfare policies disproportionately benefit rural areas would be of little solace to many rural dwellers who would prefer greater job opportunities instead.[15] Increasingly, decent-paying jobs require advanced education, yet the growing educational gap that separates rural and urban places impedes opportunities to attain them. As our analysis in chapter 4 showed, as of 2019, while a full 35 percent of urban adults aged twenty-five and older had a four-year college degree, just one in five rural dwellers did.[16] This begs the question, do local institutions of higher education allow rural people to extend their education?

We considered the prevalence in rural counties of community colleges, which tend to be the most affordable institutions of higher education (see appendixes). By offering job training for employment in the local area, community colleges can enable residents to acquire new skills, particularly when jobs in long-established local industries decline. They can also provide other crucial resources, such as mental health

counseling, food banks, and internet access.[17] We find that while unsur-
prisingly there are more community colleges in urban areas overall, in
fact rural areas have seven times more such institutions per person.

In the past, these rural community colleges played a key role in fostering human capital development. Sociologists Andrew Crookston and
Gregory Hooks found that in the period from 1990 to 1997, established
rural community colleges made a "positive and significant contribution
to employment growth," but in the period 1997 to 2004, areas with such
institutions actually experienced a loss of jobs. Probing further, they
found that this occurred particularly in states in which funding for community colleges had recently diminished.[18] Generally, after decades in
which states had invested in such institutions, these revenue sources
declined in the late twentieth and early twenty-first centuries. That's
because most states operate under relatively strict balanced budget
amendments, and funding for community colleges in state budgets
therefore had to compete with growing costs for other priorities, namely
Medicaid, K–12 education, and prisons.[19] According to Crookston and
Hooks's estimates, in the period from 1960 to 1980, roughly three new
community colleges were built in rural counties for every prison; in
1980 to 2000, by contrast, fourteen new rural prisons were built for
every new community college.[20] In response to the budget shortfall,
community colleges had to raise tuition to make up the difference. Students attending such institutions in rural areas are especially likely to be
first-generation college students and to have low incomes, so increased
tuition can deter enrollment.[21] In sum, despite the greater presence of
community colleges in rural areas, in the 2000s these institutions have
faced considerable challenges in meeting local needs.

More broadly, public funding for U.S. higher education has fallen
behind in recent decades, even as tuition has increased more quickly
than inflation. As a result, between 1993–1994 and 2023–2024, adjusting
for inflation, tuition at public two-year colleges grew from $2,650 to
$3,990 per year, and at public four-year colleges from $5,380 to $11,260
per year.[22] These soaring costs, at a time of rising economic inequality
between American households, have made it extremely difficult for students from low- and middle-income households to enroll in college

and, once enrolled, to remain in school long enough to graduate.[23] While investing in college education is no guarantee of reduced polarization in the near term, it would nevertheless be an important way to promote access to more skills and better-paying jobs for those struggling, in both rural and urban areas. Furthermore, greater investments in colleges in earlier periods of economic decay, when the rural-urban divide began to emerge, likely could have softened the blow for many rural dwellers.

Rural Public Employment on the Rise

Another way for government to aid rural economies is by offering jobs to local residents, and this raises the question of how public employment might be distributed across rural and urban areas. Historically and in democracies around the world, public-sector jobs have been an important source of economic opportunity for otherwise disadvantaged groups.[24] In Cramer's research in Wisconsin, however, she found that rural residents were often resentful of government workers, perceiving them to have comfortable, well-paying positions that seemed like a waste of tax money. They thought of government employees as lazy, out-of-touch with the needs of rural people, and disproportionately concentrated in urban areas.[25] Yet we find that in the nation as a whole, rural residents themselves increasingly rely on public-sector employment.

We calculated the number of public jobs in rural and urban areas, including all state, local, and federal employees in each county, excluding those in military service (see appendixes). We found that urban areas were home to a larger number of public jobs per capita from the 1970s into the 1990s. Starting then and until the present, the public sector became a significantly more prevalent source of employment in rural relative to urban areas (figure 8.3). As private-sector jobs have diminished in rural areas, the public sector has provided a partial economic backstop. Public employment typically offers greater pay and stability for those with lower levels of education than jobs available in the private sector, and it has become especially important in rural areas in the wake of job losses in industries that previously employed those with modest

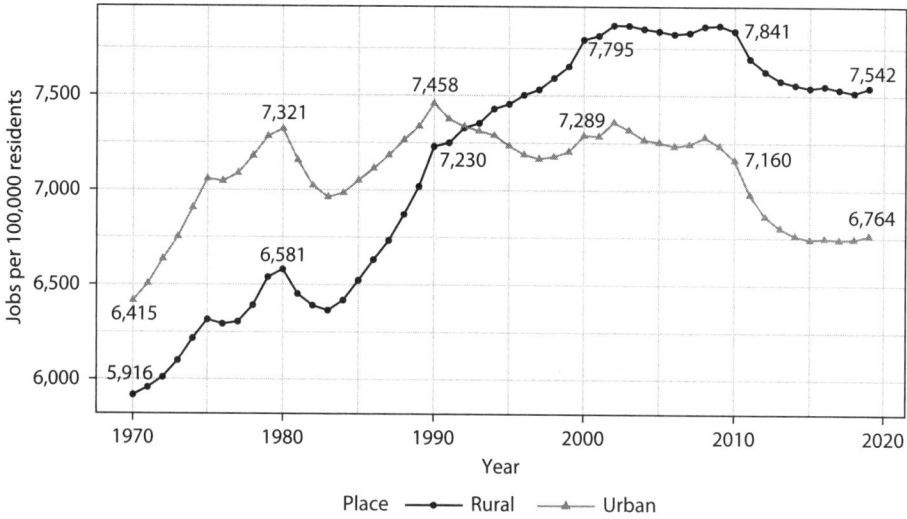

FIGURE 8.3. The rise of public-sector employment in rural counties, 1970–2019
Source: BEA; measure of rural from OMB

levels of education, as discussed in chapter 3. Rural areas, despite their growing support for the party that most consistently criticizes the role and size of government, have become more reliant on it to provide employment.

One way that politicians brought more jobs to rural areas in the late twentieth and early twenty-first centuries involved the prison boom. As incarceration rates soared, prisons were built particularly in rural areas, providing a source of employment there. According to sociologist Jason Eason, as of 2010 roughly 70 percent of all 1,663 prisons were located in rural counties.[26] As Eason finds, prison construction tends to have a short boom effect, promoting local economies and helping them weather decline, though only for a brief period of time.

Military Service and Its Rural Toll

We now turn to military service, which alongside its role in national security, represents another means through which government provides employment opportunities. Scholars find that military recruits come disproportionately from places that have suffered job losses due to free trade.[27]

Of course, military service, different from most other jobs aside from protective services, entails the willingness to put oneself in harm's way—and for some, it may mean making the ultimate sacrifice. Throughout the first two decades of the twenty-first century, the United States engaged in a number of drawn-out wars and military interventions abroad, most notably in Iraq and Afghanistan. How might military service relate to place? Scholars have found that since the conclusion of World War II, communities at the lower end of the socioeconomic ladder have borne a disproportionate share of the costs of war.[28] Yet no research to our knowledge examines how the socioeconomic and place-based inequalities of war might intersect with rurality.

We calculated the number of military-related deaths per one hundred thousand residents in rural and urban communities respectively, since 2001 (details in appendixes). Rural areas have disproportionately paid the price of recent wars (figure 8.4). Overall, from 2001 to 2020, deaths during military service were about one and a half times as many among residents of rural places as among residents of urban places, adjusting for population. In short, while military service has provided employment opportunities that help compensate for lost jobs in rural areas, it has come with a very heavy price, as these same communities have suffered far higher mortality rates than others in the United States. We suspect that this imposes a greater sense of collective loss on rural places and may compound the sense of being subject to the policy choices of an overbearing elite, as described in chapter 4.

How Might Rural Policy Benefits Affect Partisan Support?

The higher use of social welfare programs in rural counties raises the question of why these areas are not more supportive of Democratic candidates in elections. After all, the Democratic Party has shepherded such policies and sought opportunities to fortify them, whereas Republican candidates in recent decades have often campaigned on

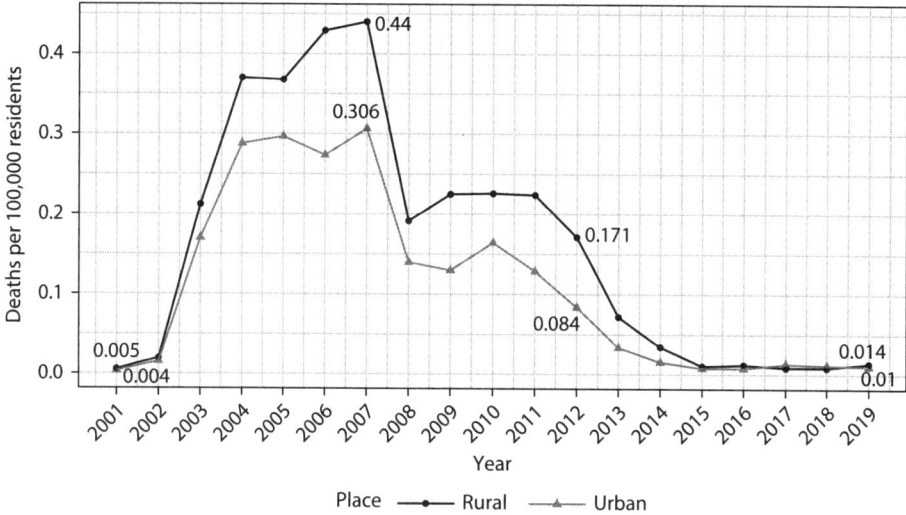

FIGURE 8.4. Deaths that occurred during military service, among residents of rural and urban counties, 2001–2019
Source: Department of Defense's Defense Casualty Analysis, "Names of the Fallen"; measure of rural from OMB

curtailing benefits or restricting access to them, and aimed to do so once in office.[29]

How, then, might we make sense of these trends? Before speculating based on what we know from existing research, we should caution that our data do not permit us to identify the precise relationship between policy trends and voting patterns.[30] Lacking data linking individual receipt of social welfare benefits and voting choices to location, we are limited in the conclusions we can draw.[31] Nevertheless, existing research does offer us some clues.

Intense partisanship may weaken a policy's effects.[32] Rather than responding to the resources and messages conveyed through policies, citizens—even if they personally benefit from such policies—may instead follow cues from their fellow partisans, who may oppose the policies or the officials or party that advanced them. Political scientist Michael E. Shepherd has examined how rural Americans assigned attribution following hospital closures in their counties in recent years, a phenomenon that has been particularly common in states that refused expanded Medicaid under the ACA. Shepherd found that ironically, in counties that lost hospitals, independents were particularly likely to switch from supporting Obama in 2012 to voting for Donald Trump in 2016.[33] It is possible for policy effects to overcome the intensity of partisan forces, but it requires an event or organizational effort that makes the value of the policies overwhelmingly apparent. In the case of the ACA, partisanship blocked its effects until it faced the very real threat of repeal, at which point various groups of beneficiaries and others in their communities either shifted away from virulent opposition or shifted toward greater support.[34]

As for public employment, it could be that rural people do not find that such jobs confer the type of standing or value that private employment does. Possibly these patterns reflect the sentiments of the Republican Party officers in rural Michigan, mentioned at the beginning of this chapter, who viewed public-sector employment as an unsatisfactory solution to economic deterioration. It might also be that particular types of public employment—in the form of law enforcement and employment in prisons and jails—might foster ties in rural areas between residents and the Republican Party, to the extent that the GOP is seen as the protector of these aspects of governance.

To be sure, many policies have been important to the *material* well-being of rural dwellers. Rigorous empirical studies have shown that several of the social programs described above improve the life outcomes of recipients.[35] Nevertheless, broadly speaking, government's involvement in rural communities in recent decades seems to have done little—at best—to bolster *political* confidence in government or in the party that has typically championed and protected these policies. To the contrary, policies have in many instances fostered a sense of resentment toward government and reinforced rural dwellers' sense that Democrats in particular—and perhaps also more traditional Republicans—fail to understand their needs. This became evident in some of the policies discussed in chapter 4, such as the renewable energy sitings that failed to take rural perspectives into account. It is not that government has failed to show up in rural places, but either it has provided help that was different from what rural dwellers themselves wanted, or the policy process failed to include input from them.

Rural Investments by the Federal Government During the Biden Administration

After decades during which the federal government refrained from the New Deal approach of promoting economic development in rural places, during the Biden administration lawmakers changed course. Several of the major policies that President Biden signed into law made concerted efforts to respond to rural needs, particularly by trying to spur the development of jobs and economic growth in specific places, including rural ones.

The American Rescue Plan Act, the pandemic relief package President Biden signed in March 2021, did this in various ways. It included a competitive grant program for regional development, the Build Back Better Regional Challenge, that stressed the importance of rural communities. More importantly, its State and Local Fiscal Recovery Funds were allocated on a noncompetitive basis to every unit of local government, rural and urban alike.[36] Rural areas, owing to their lower levels of government capacity and their relative lack of access to capital, are inherently disadvantaged in competitive grant programs as well as in programs that require matching funds. For this reason, the State and Local Fiscal Recovery Funds were particularly helpful to rural places.

In 2021 and 2022, Biden signed three major laws—the Infrastructure Investment and Jobs Act (hereafter called the Investment Act), the CHIPS and Science Act (CHIPS), and the Inflation Reduction Act (IRA). Each of them included significant funds that could be used to invest in rural areas, whether through infrastructure, clean energy, climate resilience, or industrial policy. According to Brookings analysts Anthony F. Pipa and Elise Pietro, "$464 billion, or 45% of the combined appropriations in these three laws, present a significant opportunity for rural America," although they caution that the matching requirements in many of the programs, along with other aspects of their design, reporting requirements, and other procedures may introduce obstacles to local governments.[37] Nonetheless, subsequent analysis found that 59 percent of strategic-sector investments in employment-distressed counties made under these laws went to rural counties.[38]

The "digital divide" that has limited access to the internet in rural places was addressed through one program that aimed to bring broadband to undeserved areas and another that provided subsidies to low-income households to help them afford it.[39] The latter, the Affordable Connectivity Program, spurred the enrollment of 20.6 million households in its first two years, with the greatest percentage increases occurring in relatively rural states, including North and South Dakota, Wyoming, and Maine.[40] Such subsidies are found to boost local residents' employment rates and earnings substantially, and to lower costs for government, for example by permitting patients to attend nonurgent health care appointments virtually rather than in person.[41]

In brief, under the Biden administration the federal government made more funds available to rural areas for economic development than they had received in many decades. Could these policies foster a coalition between rural and urban dwellers, similar to that of the New Deal? Because policy feedback effects often take time to set in, we will need to wait for a definitive answer.[42] We suspect, however, that this scenario is unlikely. Aside from some of the particular challenges to implementation discussed above, contemporary policies for rural places run headlong into entrenched anger with the federal government in general and with policy initiatives associated with Democratic leaders in particular. As a result, these Biden-era policy initiatives likely garnered little appreciation, even if they produced effects that benefit local areas. What is clear is that in the 2024 election, rural counties shifted even more toward supporting Trump than they had previously.

Rural residents may be largely unaware of such policies unless local organizations and political leaders help to make them and their impact visible. As Margaret Simpson, a Democratic county chair in Marjorie Taylor Greene's district in northwestern Georgia, told us in 2023, local residents there seemed incognizant of policies that helped the district during the Biden presidency: "We've got roads being fixed. We've got money coming in to hire new public servants, police, firemen, teachers, from the bills that were passed—and [Greene] voted against them, because they had one little thing in them that she didn't like, or just because Joe Biden [supported them]." She noted that local officials themselves weren't making the connections between those resources and federal policies, and neither was conservative media. Without a stronger presence of the Democratic Party, or other organizations such as labor unions that could highlight policies, even an infusion of federal resources can go largely unnoticed by local residents. In short, despite serving crucial needs for rural areas, in a highly polarized environment, public policies appear ill equipped to do the work that politics must. We will now turn to that topic, investigating the role of political organizing in rural areas.

9

Party Building

A PATH FORWARD

ELSIE TASSLER first got involved in politics in North Dakota through the women's movement in the 1970s. The Great Plains had long been progressive on women's issues, with several states permitting women to vote even before the ratification of the Nineteenth Amendment. In North Dakota, that spirit still prevailed, and Democratic and Republican women alike, particularly in rural areas, supported the Equal Rights Amendment, which aimed to incorporate Americans as equal citizens regardless of sex. "It wasn't even controversial to be involved in those issues" at that time, recalls Tassler. In February 1975, the state became the thirty-fourth in the nation to ratify the ERA, putting it just four states away from the threshold needed to become part of the U.S. Constitution. Then the backlash movement spearheaded by Phyllis Schlafly gained momentum in the states that had not yet acted, and only one more state—Indiana—ratified it before the deadline in 1979. Although Congress granted a three-year extension, no additional states took action. The quest for legal equality had failed, and it has not been pursued again since.[1]

Meanwhile, Tassler became involved in Democratic Party politics as a means to support the progressive ideas that had such a rich history in North Dakota. The state's Democratic party—formally known as the Democratic-Nonpartisan League (Democratic-NPL) Party—has roots in the Progressive Era. It embodies the merger of two parties in 1956, one of which, the NPL, boasted a long tradition of promoting public ownership of a state bank and other entities. Party leaders enlisted Tassler to organize in rural areas, where the party had deep roots that it liked to nourish. She traveled to remote towns, where on each visit she was met by a local resident—always a woman—who would put her up in their home. "I would help them to organize phone banks, and we'd go together to farms and towns, and I'd give speeches. We [the Democratic Party] won and we won big," dramatically increasing its numbers in the state legislature. "It was always the women" who were the backbone of the party, she remembers.

Several Republicans in the state triumphed on Ronald Reagan's coattails in the 1980 elections, but Democrats in the state organized intensely in response, particularly in rural areas. "Because back then, rural America was very much Democratic!" says Tassler. They staged a comeback, and for several years thereafter, the "momentum was going our way."

Then the farm depression hit and brought "incredible change" that eventually left the Democratic Party severely weakened. Two-thirds of family farms in North Dakota went out of business. Suicide rates increased, domestic violence became more prevalent, and antisemitic literature circulated. Farmers moved to Minneapolis, Minnesota, to get jobs. In North Dakota, the city of Fargo flourished, acquiring a more highly educated population and greater prosperity. And politics changed as a result, says Tassler: "I saw that women who had been the heart and soul of Democratic Party politics—they organized it—now that wasn't happening much anymore because those women were working outside of the home." In addition, associational life in the state changed as evangelical churches were on the rise, and they promoted political conservatism.

Although the state routinely supported Republican presidential candidates (the last Democrat who won the state was Lyndon Johnson), residents kept reelecting Democratic Senators Kent Conrad and Byron Dorgan and Representative Earl Pomeroy. All three stressed economic issues first and foremost, taking action on them at the national level, and voters responded. "People still believed there were answers in the Democratic Party," Tassler explains. But since the 1990s, something has shifted in the state's politics, as Democrats came to be viewed as urban elites who were determined to impose their policies on rural places. The party still gained support as recently as 2008 when Obama ran for president, and "thousands of people as far as you can see" showed up at a rural rally for him, Tassler notes. Though McCain won the state, Obama took a respectable 45 percent of the popular vote.

Soon after Obama's election, residents worried that he threatened to bring in "socialism" in the form of health coverage. Tassler comments, "There was a time when it wasn't a problem to be a socialist in North Dakota!" Then the Tea Party surged in the state. She recalls town meetings that became "frightening," with people screaming in anger at the congressperson in attendance. At one meeting, a nun spoke up in support of the Affordable Care Act, and others in attendance "shouted her down." In 2016, Democratic nominee Hillary Clinton won only 27 percent of the vote, Libertarian Party candidate Gary Johnson claimed 6 percent, and Donald Trump trounced both with 63 percent. By 2018, the last Democrat serving the state in the U.S. Congress, Senator Heidi Heitkamp, lost her seat. Tassler reflected with incredulity at how dramatically the state's politics had changed from the days when residents broadly supported the ERA and grassroots organizers fueled the Democratic Party in their local rural communities.

———

Over the past three decades, white rural Americans have developed growing antipathy to the Democratic Party and have elected increasingly conservative Republicans—not just in North Dakota but nationwide. As politics has changed in these areas, residents of all partisan stripes have lost opportunities to hear about politics from anyone in their district who sees things differently. As a result, even when Democrats in Washington, DC, planned generous and valuable policies for rural areas, as the Biden administration did, most rural members of Congress—who are now Republicans, as we've seen—joined the rest of their party in voting against them. Once the new broadband benefits and infrastructure policies rolled out, these officials refrained from highlighting their existence, showcasing their successes to constituents, or crediting them to the Biden administration.

A few decades ago, labor unions and nonpartisan civic organizations might have performed these roles of "connecting the dots" for citizens. They might also have shown how residents could take advantage of valuable programs and pushed lawmakers to improve them. Few such organizations exist in rural places today. While certainly policies are necessary to address the need for economic development and alleviation of poverty in rural areas, by themselves even the best ones are currently not sufficient to mitigate growing political division, as we showed in the last chapter.

Our research suggests that mending today's fractured polity requires something deeper and more profound: Americans need to rebuild relationships across places, as Elsie Tassler and her fellow Democrats tried to do in North Dakota decades ago. As we have seen, the rural-urban divide is not the result of a single presidential candidate or rural dwellers' attitudes on a particular set of policy issues. To the contrary, it has developed over about thirty years, through widespread and sequential political developments that have interacted with one another, deepening Republican dominance. It can only be mitigated now, we argue, if party officials on the other side of the political cleavage establish a meaningful presence in rural communities, listen to local residents, work to foster understanding, and organize.

Here we focus on party building, which means, as political scientist Daniel J. Galvin puts it, "investing in new organizational capacities to expand the party's reach and enhance its electoral competitiveness," making it a "stronger, more durable, and more capable organization."[2] Parties typically spend most of their efforts on supporting specific candidates in particular elections, but party building involves longer-term goals. Through our interviews with rural party chairs, we have learned about a variety of approaches to organizational activity in both parties.

On the ground in rural areas, local party leaders exhibit resiliency and ingenuity as they participate in democracy and try to enable their communities to do so as well. Certainly, the strategies employed by Republicans in some places reflect the deeply polarized politics that is fostered by the rural-urban divide, though elsewhere the party itself contains divergent factions that local leaders struggle to unite. Democrats face greater obstacles to organizing but demonstrate fortitude and often creativity in facing them. What becomes clear is that many rural people are working against the odds in trying to bridge the divide. Reinvigorating two-party government at the local level would be a crucial step toward fostering healthier politics.

Rural Parties and County Chairs in the Twenty-First Century

Each of the nation's two major political parties aims to recruit a volunteer leader in every county, to organize and lead local grassroots members. The responsibilities of these county chairs vary somewhat between states and between parties, but generally speaking they seek to send delegates to the county and state conventions, recruit candidates to run for local office, and raise money to help support their campaigns. Some set up informational booths at local events, or in other ways try to be visible as a presence in the community and to attract more supporters. They may also engage in voter registration efforts. Yet while these duties add up to the basic job description, our interviews revealed that chairs approach the job in different ways depending on the political context in which they operate.

The county chairs that we interviewed, both Republicans and Democrats, have a great deal in common. Our conversations revolved around how they approached their jobs, focusing on organizational strategies rather than party positions or ideology. Local leaders in both parties confront similar challenges and try many of the same things to address them. Yet in the political climate in rural areas in recent decades—born of economic deterioration, fueled by the perception that Democratic elites are imposing policies from afar, and mobilized by active grassroots groups that work with the GOP—Republicans generally have enjoyed more opportunities while the Democrats have faced greater obstacles. To illustrate, we zoom in on a few counties, most of them in the Lower Peninsula of Northern Michigan, which are part of the first congressional district. As described in chapter 6, this is the district that Democrat Bart Stupak represented from 1993 until he stepped down after his 2010 vote in support of the ACA. The district has since been represented by Republicans.

Mobilized Republicans

Matthew Novak, a young Republican county chair, began with an explanation that we heard from several chairs in both parties: "I was asked to be chair. No one else wanted it. I didn't know what the heck I was doing." That was early in the Obama presidency, though, and since then the GOP's fortunes have improved in the area. Novak explained that the Tea Party, which emerged on the national scene in 2009, became active in many counties throughout the years that followed. In some communities, it took over the party, elsewhere it blended with it, and in still others, "the old establishment held strong and defeated Tea Party candidates." He felt that the Tea Party, being more "principles-based, mad about spending and taxes," helped to "infuse new blood into the party and was good for the party." Novak continued, "I would contrast that with Trump. He activated a group of people who hadn't been involved but who are different from the Tea Party: They are fixated on him, a person," rather than on principles. "They are not really policy based. A party is not supposed to have fealty to an individual. It's the moderate parts of the party versus the extreme wings of the party." Some party members challenged Novak for the chair position, wishing for a leader who was more loyal to Trump, but he held on to the post.

It's worth noting that these internal divisions among Republicans have strained county organizations elsewhere as well. Bob Hopkins in southern Ohio credited the Tea Party with reenergizing the party, creating "an awakening" of sorts. Yet he also criticized several of its proponents as "firebrand extremists" who failed to respect the party's core values in favor of "normal, common sense" principles. Some became "disruptive," adopting a "shut it all down" stance toward government and "browbeating" other members by citing specific parts of the Constitution that they believed justified their views. Others, recoiling from such conduct, stopped attending meetings. At that point, Hopkins and his fellow officers decided that these Tea Partiers risked harming the organization and chose to "start weeding them out." "We're still in the process of recovering from it," explained Cindy Kemp, another officer.

Similarly, in a county in northern Ohio, the Tea Party generated huge interest locally; one Tea Partier challenged the county chair of the GOP and won the position. The new chair resigned a year later after the Republicans refused to adopt a prolife platform at the county level. Current GOP chair Connor Williams explained, "We're all prolife, but to adopt a prolife platform would inject a national touch into local politics. To me, our job is to fund and elect candidates. We're not here to tell them how to do their job." Later, an "America First" group emerged that "is more ideological [and] has pushed us a bit." Williams, like the other chairs confronted with such divisions, has sought to foster unity and keep the groups working together effectively. Like Novak, he also faced a far-right challenge to his chairmanship one year, and successfully fended it off. Nonetheless, these internal divisions—though taxing for leaders—do not appear to have harmed the local organizations. While these leaders deserve credit for skillfully navigating these obstacles, it is worth underscoring that as Republicans in a rural context today, they have been effectively paddling downstream, aided by the strong currents of interest in their party.

Returning to Michigan's Lower Peninsula, some counties show no evident party divisions; rather, the Republican organization has become fueled by Trump supporters, reinvigorated party old-timers, and newly active members working in tandem. In one such county, GOP Chair Kent Wilson explains that prior to 2020, only one or two dozen people had participated, but since then the organization has flourished. Previously, meetings were held in the middle of weekdays, preventing working-class people from attending, but he and others advocated to change them to weeknights. The gathering always starts with dinner at a restaurant to support local businesses. Wilson and others recruited younger people into leadership roles. Now, he reports, hundreds of people locally are active in the organization. They have become energized particularly around issues related to gun rights, and like most other rural counties in Michigan, have urged county commissioners to declare their county a "sanctuary" that will refuse to enforce federal or state gun control laws that they perceive as a violation of the Second Amendment.

Not far away in another county, Rick Swenson leads a GOP organization that became fired up in recent years. As he and fellow officer

Mary Bowers explained, the party resurgence happened in part in the wake of challenges to the 2020 election, when lawyer and conservative activist Matt DePerno filed a lawsuit challenging the vote count in nearby Antrim County. U.S. Attorney General William Barr disregarded the claim as "idiotic," and Republicans in the state senate rejected it as "demonstrably false."[3] Yet Swenson and Bowers found the claims convincing, and they feel certain that urban areas in the state rig election outcomes. During the COVID pandemic, Michigander Garrett Soldano started a group called Stand Up Michigan to protest the lockdowns as excessive—an issue that resonated with local residents. In addition, Swenson and Bowers explain, the Democrats dominating state government were creating policies with which they disagreed. Fueled by all these concerns, the local Republican Party is "stronger than it's been." The group hosts barbecues in the summer, and "everybody's welcome." Organizers invite candidates to speak or show movies such as *2000 Mules*—a 2022 film that falsely claims Democrats paid thousands of people to illegally collect and drop off ballots in swing states, thereby stealing the 2020 presidential election. They have also screened *Hillary's America*, a 2016 movie that portrays then–presidential candidate Hillary Clinton as dangerous and corrupt.[4] Says Swenson, "We're 'constitutional conservatives,' not true Republicans." They see themselves, along with many others in rural parts of the state, as part of a "Grassroots Army," a phrase coined by Soldano.[5]

Certainly some rural Republican groups, like this one, have become radicalized and enjoy broad support among members who agree with the direction it has taken. Other Republican county chairs find it hard to recruit people to run for local positions. Still, generally speaking, they benefit from a high level of support among local voters. Political developments since the 1990s have transformed rural places into fertile ground for GOP mobilization, and these local party groups are the beneficiaries.

Democrats Facing Headwinds

The Democratic county chairs in the same vicinity of Michigan face much greater challenges. For them, making progress is like paddling upstream. Current chair Sam Winant and his partner, Janet, herself a

former chair, requested that our interview take place at an outdoor location because the political climate in the town has become so divisive
that they feared repercussions if our conversation was overheard. A previous mayor displayed a Confederate flag on his truck, and after local
residents pushed back, his supporters convened in town, including
several men brandishing automatic rifles from the rooftops, "trying to
intimidate people." Flags and signs that say "F!#@ Biden" and other
obscene and insulting messages about Democrats were commonplace.

Conversing with us in a windy park, the pair explained that they became active in local politics decades ago. Janet said that when they were
dating, "I needed to get right to the meat of the matter, to know his out-
look and his philosophy. So I asked him who was the greatest living president. He said, 'Why Jimmy Carter, of course.' That cinched the deal."
Echoing a refrain we heard from many, Sam says that he is the chair
because "no one else wanted the job." "There's less people now in the party
than in the past," he says. "They've moved away or passed away." "It's a
party of old white people," Janet adds drily. Eight people had attended a
meeting earlier that week, and once a year, when the group throws a larger
social event (for which they have become known as "the party that has
parties"), usually twenty-five people show up. Sam says, "I decided to be
the chair because I thought, 'If I don't do this, there is no party.'" They
note that a larger group of progressive-minded local residents, particularly
younger people, have organized in recent years to address town issues, but
"they have no desire to get involved with the Democratic Party."

In a county in the fingertips area of Michigan's mitten, Democratic
county chair Debbie Ardent also describes a hostile atmosphere. "We do
try to recruit candidates to run, but right now it's dangerous." She explains how energized Republicans have become and notes that the local
sheriff has indicated he would not enforce certain laws, namely specific
restrictions on guns. She also remarked that white people—including
some of her own acquaintances—seemed more willing to make overtly
racist comments than in the past. "It's kind of scary," she added. "I've told
my friends, my single lady friends, 'Do not put political signs in your
front yard.' I do put out signs myself, but everybody knows who I am."

A bit further south in the state, however, Democrats in another
county—part of a different congressional district—have become newly

energized in recent years, and are making a point of being seen in public. In 2017, several individuals came together to form an "Indivisible" group. The existing Democratic party organization was "moribund," as current chair Stacy Conway described it. Members of the newly formed group started attending party meetings, and soon one of them was elected county chair. Since then, they have become well organized, sharing responsibilities among several people. They maintain a website, publish a newsletter, work with Democrats in surrounding counties, and join forces with local organizations like the League of Women Voters and the League of Conservation Voters.

As Conway explains, the group members "do a lot of door knocking and texting," and they recruit candidates for local office. "We are just trying to be more in the public eye," she says. "We are trying to be out there and to be part of things," through activities that include hosting a booth at the fair, raising money for food banks, writing letters to the editor, and working at vaccination clinics during the pandemic. They march as a group in all local parades; when they first began doing so some years back, they heard heckling, but now, Conway says, "People clap when we go by and give us a thumbs up." The Democratic vote share in recent elections is similar in their county to that in others we've discussed, but these organizers—perhaps due to their strong teamwork approach—have a sense of momentum and confidence that they are making progress.

While organizing at the local level in the current political climate isn't easy for either party, Democratic county chairs in rural areas face more obstacles. Next, we focus primarily on them, examining their approaches to the job and their experiences in several other states.

"Being the Face" and "Losing by Less": Rural Democrats' Approaches to Chairing

We found that most rural counties in our case study states do have Democratic Party chairs, and these individuals try valiantly to organize their districts, but they face steep odds. Since the 1990s, the party has lost supporters in rural counties nationwide, for the reasons discussed in earlier chapters. This means that fewer and fewer people show up at meetings, and those who do are typically older, with few under age seventy. As one county chair in Georgia put it, "I'm nearly seventy-four, and I'm one of the younger ones among the Democrats. We know there are younger Democrats here because they will vote. But the next generation are not joiners. They don't even go to church, much less join things." Some rural county parties *do* manage to organize all their precincts, hold annual dinners and fundraisers, and field a full slate of candidates, yet many others have had to scale back those activities due to dwindling numbers.

"Vicious circle" dynamics can easily set in: The less support the party receives in elections, the more difficult it is to find candidates who are willing to run for local positions; in turn, if the party cannot field a full slate, long-term Democrats wonder if it is even worth showing up to vote. Perhaps most dispiriting for the party, in many rural counties that we visited, in both the Southern and Midwestern states, some elected Democrats have changed their affiliation and become Republicans.

In these particularly challenging places, the mission of organized Democrats is very basic. County Chair Margaret Simpson, in Marjorie Taylor Greene's district in northwestern Georgia, has been a Democrat throughout her adult life. "In the 1990s, things began to get ugly. I watched our Democratic Party go from 90 percent of the people to 2 percent. We have a meeting this week, and five people might show up, and it's always the same five. But people will stop me in the grocery store and whisper to me, 'What are the Democrats doing?' They don't want to be seen. But somebody's got to be the face."[6]

For some rural dwellers, joining the Democratic Party is like "coming out," explains Barbara Jones, in Missouri—"coming out of the closet as Democrats." She describes the organization in her county as bringing together otherwise isolated residents who "hold progressive values, believe that all rights under the Constitution should be afforded to all. Some are gay; some are of a progressive faith like the UCC [United Church of Christ], and feel that the evangelical right are out of line."

In other rural counties, the local Democratic organization enjoys a greater sense of momentum. Usually this is due to leaders who have become involved in recent years, like those from the Indivisible group in Michigan. Several of the particularly active county parties include participants who are a bit younger, often recent retirees who are in their fifties or sixties and who joined the party more recently, unlike the long-term members, who tend to be in their seventies and eighties. Among the most vibrant parties are those in which several such individuals worked together as a team, each bringing different talents and ample energy. These factors seem more important in generating activity than the particular vote margin Democrats had gained locally.

For example, consider Frank Phillips, another chair elsewhere in Marjorie Taylor Greene's district in northwest Georgia. He and his wife moved to the area about fifteen years ago, and after the 2016 election, they became involved in the Democratic Party. They found that in their congressional district, out of 140 open seats for federal and county election that year, Democrats were on the ballot for only 8 of them; in each of the others, Republicans ran unopposed. They and others in the party determined that they needed to come up with a Democratic candidate for every race, and in 2018 and 2020 they very nearly did. "By getting people on the ballot, we got Democrats out to vote." Then in the runoff election for the U.S. Senate seat in January 2021, "We pushed really hard." They believed that "if we could get that extra 5 to 7 percent [of voter turnout compared to the November election], by making phone calls, text banking, and advertising, we could get [Jon] Ossoff and [Raphael] Warnock over the finish line" in the election. They succeeded: They ended up getting more of the Democratic candidates' supporters to show up in January than had turned out in November, the reverse of how the Republicans fared. Granted, both candidates won just 18 percent of the vote in the region, but the extra margin Phillips and his team struggled to attain helped them secure victory statewide. "In the past, they [local Democrats] said, 'Why bother [to run candidates]? They're not going to win.' But I said, We're not going to win *here*, but we're going to win on statewide federal elections. That's the message we want to hone."

The strategy of "losing by less" locally so that Democrats can win statewide is one several other rural chairs pursue. In a southwestern Georgia county in which Black Americans make up the majority of the population, county chair Ezekiel Willard explained that in the same

January 2021 Senate runoff election that Phillips described, "We raised about $30,000 and paid canvassers to go door to door. That was a biggie for us. Our turnout was about 88 or 89 percent of voters who had voted in the general!"[7] The strong turnout, like that in the northwestern part of the state, helped Warnock and Ossoff win their races. In southeastern Ohio, Bill Whittaker focuses relentlessly on losing by less. He figures that if a Democrat can claim at least 35 percent of the vote in his rural county and fare similarly in others, that candidate can win statewide, assuming good turnout in cities. Achieving 35 percent these days, however, presents an uphill climb for the Democratic Party in his area.

Rural county chairs use innovative approaches to organizing. One group in Michigan holds a luau party every winter. Another commits to running candidates for every local seat, because that "prevents Republicans from sending money they collect here elsewhere in the state to support other candidates," forcing them to spend it locally instead. North Carolinians in one county visit churches to tell congregants about their work. They also organize street cleanups, wearing their Democratic Party shirts while picking up litter. In a southeastern North Carolina county that has been attracting an influx of retirees, a few new leaders joined the party a decade ago and have since been transforming it. Chair Bruce Amato says, "We showed up at the same time as . . . a whole slew of retirees, with talent. We just happened to have niche capabilities: public relations, communications, digital, newspaper, etc. We all just gelled. We started attending festivals . . . with our signage, and being visible has helped us. We're out in public more, so that's generating more interest. We've tripled our newsletter readership in the last couple of years, and we have many more volunteers. We've gotten a lot of letters to the editor [published], and we're regularly in the newspapers."

Employing tactics that range from being the "face of the party" to simply "losing by less," Democratic county chairs maintain an organizational presence in a climate where it is under threat, offering voters an alternative. They do so, however, while facing strong political headwinds, and typically with little to no support in amplifying their message from either the state or national party.

Support for and Obstacles to Democratic Party Organizing and Voting

When we asked Democratic county chairs if they felt supported by the state-level party, they responded—in each county and each state—with a resounding "no." Some complained that the state organization tended to focus on urban areas to the exclusion of rural ones. Others said that it was typically run by people with little understanding of the important year-round, on-the-ground work that is necessary to organize in rural places. Richard Smith, in southeastern North Carolina, echoed several others when he said, "We have a whole bunch of technology, but not the experience—lots of young people who are technically wise but forget about grassroots politics." He felt that voters in the corridor from Charlotte to Wilmington were ignored by the state party, to its detriment. Shelly Martin, in the same part of the state, adds, "One-third of folks around here don't have broadband," so Zoom meetings don't work, and neither does email communication. Instead, phone calls are needed. Tina Wolford, a Texas Democratic Party chair explained, "We're not supported by state-level party leaders—we're ignored. We're supposed to do everything ourselves, but we are strapped. There's no infrastructure, it's a nonpaying position, and we're not getting financial help. It's all out of our own houses, on a shoestring budget. We feel like we're on our own."

Republican county chairs often felt the same way about their state organization. GOP Chair Bob Hopkins in Ohio explained, "This is the disconnect thing: Every office holder in this state knows that without the rural vote, they're not going to win anything, yet they still want the big cities to run the party." At the same time, Hopkins described weekly conversations with state-level organizers and elected officials, and he said, "I do believe the state [party] does care." Democratic county chairs did not report such communication, generally feeling that they had little contact with state leaders. And in some states, the party imposed particularly time-consuming paperwork requirements on the volunteer leaders, such as updating bylaws and filing numerous forms annually—with little support in return. Samantha Davis, a county chair in eastern

Georgia, described such responsibilities and sighed, saying, "No one's going to do this when I'm gone."

Rural Democratic chairs often feel that statewide candidates don't realize the difference their counties can make on Election Day, so they don't bother to campaign in rural locations. Then, in turn, potential Democratic rural voters feel ignored and don't show up to support the candidates. County chairs wince as they describe statewide races that Democratic candidates lost by only hundreds of votes, when in their view attention to rural places could have made the difference.

The consequences are grave. When we interviewed Bruce Amato in southeastern North Carolina in early 2023, he called the state Democratic Party at that time "highly dysfunctional." "We are not going to win North Carolina if we don't start making a dent across the rural landscape. I'm looking at 2030. We can continue to get crushed. We are hanging on by a thread . . . one vote away from enough to override the governor's veto." In fact, Republicans in the statehouse gained the supermajority needed to override a veto in April 2023, soon after this interview, when one Democratic representative changed her party affiliation to Republican. They held it until January 2025, and in the meanwhile overrode more than twenty bills that Democratic Governor Roy Cooper had vetoed.[8]

When it comes to national party leaders, local chairs felt that rural areas were not even "on their radar." Some complained that Democratic National Committee (DNC) leaders have chosen approaches that hasten the party's demise in rural places. They criticized a strategy known as "targeting": concentrating resources on a handful of swing states in presidential elections—and a few swing districts in congressional elections—and flooding them with television advertisements. This increasingly has led the party to pull resources away from the more rural states that have been trending Republican.[9] Debbie Ardent disparaged the Democratic Congressional Campaign Committee (DCCC), saying that it "doesn't jive with how rural Michigan works. They don't think that signs matter. They say, 'Signs don't vote, people do.' I wouldn't give them a dime." And rather than investing in the party infrastructure itself, the national leadership outsourced get-out-the-vote activities to advocacy groups, private companies, and others.[10]

As a result, those trying to organize for the party in rural places often feel neglected. Brent Jackson, an organizer in Missouri, explained that the state used to be considered a swing state in presidential elections, such that the national party routinely devoted resources to it. That's no longer the case, and the lack of party investment has hurt Democratic candidates at all levels. He said, "Now in Missouri, every two years, the whole party staff is displaced. . . . We go six months before people get added back in, and then those people are new. Most times, [the new organizers] are from out of state. So much of organizing is having authentic relations with people, so if you're trying to reach out to Democratic county chairs . . . it's hard to get people to answer. We must re-create all of those relationships," he sighed. "Whoever is at the top of ticket knows they need [rural] marginal votes [to win], but most of the resources go into already-blue parts of the state or purple, and all of these other areas are neglected."

Many national leaders in the Democratic Party are convinced that it makes more sense to devote time and resources to gaining votes in cities and suburbs, rather than in rural areas. As Senator Chuck Schumer put it in July 2016, "For every blue-collar Democrat we will lose in western PA, we will pick up two [or] three moderate Republicans in the suburbs of Philadelphia. And you can repeat that in Ohio and Illinois and Wisconsin. The voters who are most out there . . . are the college-educated Republicans who lean Republican or independent, and [live] in the suburbs."[11] Of course, come November of that year, white rural voters supported Trump at margins high enough to swing some of the states in the so-called Blue Wall. Nevertheless, the party has continued this approach.

Democrats Leave Rural Congressional Seats on the Table

One way of examining the strength of a party is to consider its ability to field candidates and run them for office. Competing in seats for federal office is especially important because such elections are high profile;

they signal that a party is present in a given area, which can encourage other people to participate in politics and even seek office down-ticket. As Deborah Evans in northwestern Georgia explains, "There's a small core of people in the county who still vote Democrat, religiously. The last election, I got a call from [one of them], an elderly lady who wanted to know why there's no Democrats on the ballot. And I had to explain to her that it was really expensive to run and that they knew they would lose." Evans realizes the trade-offs, though: With no Democrats on the ballot, it gets harder to turn supporters out to vote, and that hurts the party's candidates at the top of the ticket as well. "And that is unfortunately the reality of the situation right now."

We conducted an inventory of U.S. House races nationwide from 1984 to 2020 and found 788 in which one of the two major parties secured a seat without facing a challenger from the opposing party (see appendixes for details). As partisan competition has increased in recent decades, these uncontested seats have dwindled in numbers. By 2020, for example, only 15 seats were left uncontested nationwide. Yet even as late as the early 2000s, several dozen seats went uncontested.

Looking at the past four decades, who was the beneficiary of uncontested seats, and how did that vary by place? Overall, Democrats have in fact won more uncontested seats than Republicans, roughly 60 percent. This advantage owes largely to their ability to collect unchallenged seats in highly urban districts, where they typically won between 12 and 20 or more uncontested seats. Given their historical success in urban areas, this is perhaps not surprising.[12]

Yet starting in 1994, likely reflecting rural frustration with Democrats and the Democratic Party's poor party-building efforts, Republicans began to capture at least a dozen or so seats without competition in rural districts. Over the time period we examined, 317 of all uncontested seats were in the most rural districts in the country, and in the majority, 203, it was Democrats who left them uncontested. By 2010, Republicans could count on winning at least 10 uncontested seats in rural districts in most elections, and in 2016, the number had grown to 20.

Just a handful of such seats can be pivotal in lawmaking, especially as partisan competition has intensified. But they also matter for the health of democracy within the district. At least some semblance of competition between the two parties ensures not only that citizens have a choice, but also that those whose party is in the minority still feel they can express their views. To be clear, this applies to urban and rural areas alike; citizens in many cities could hold their elected officials more accountable if there were greater competition.

The rural-urban divide is fueling "us" versus "them"-style politics, but it doesn't have to be that way. Reinvigorating two-party government at the local level would be crucial step toward fostering healthier politics.

Democratic Resurgence in Rural Areas, 2004–2008

Could the Democratic Party still have rallied in rural states and districts despite all the obstacles it faced, or was its decline inevitable? By the late 1990s, some party officials had concluded that the targeting approach was inadequate and was hastening the party's demise in many locations. From 1999 through 2004, the DNC began working more collaboratively with state parties and started to build a national voter file.[13] These steps were modest, and by 2004 they had not begun to stem the tide.

The next year, former Vermont governor and presidential candidate Howard Dean became DNC chairman and promised a sea change in organizational strategy: a vast and widespread effort to rebuild the party from the ground up nationwide. At the 2004 Democratic convention, Dean had met with delegates from eighteen states that had not been targeted by the party and hence had been ignored. Speaking with *New York Times* reporter Matt Bai, an appalled Dean said, "The best window we have to talk to Democrats, the time when they pay the most attention, is in the presidential campaign, and we're just saying to the people of those 18 states, 'We're not interested in you.' You cannot be a national party if you say that to anybody. Anybody." Dean also learned from pollster Cornell Belcher that rural and small-town voters cared more about "their faith and the character of their communities than they do about individual issues." What Dean took away from this was that "any voter in any state can be a Democrat, but only if you bother to talk to him and if only you make the right kind of argument."[14]

In the absence of a Democratic president, who normally selects the head of the DNC, Dean had been elected by 365 grassroots DNC members, who are themselves elected by state parties. They greeted his approach with enthusiasm.[15] Congressional leaders Harry Reid and Nancy Pelosi tried repeatedly to find another candidate who could win the position, but they failed to do so, given Dean's popularity with state-level party leaders.[16] Referring to his support among Democrats from states across the country, Dean told us, "They understood what I was about right away, which is that you cannot do this from the top down." Dean's perspective was influenced by his previous experience: He himself had started his work in politics as a county party chair. He understood the role: to raise a little money, go out and find candidates, and "support them with know-how and volunteers."

Dean began in his role at the DNC by conducting an assessment of the party in every state. As he described it to us, he found that "they were in terrible shape. They had no money. They did have good people, but no facilities and no interest from the Washington crowd in helping them." Drawing on these insights and assessments, Dean promoted what became known as the "fifty state" strategy. This entailed placing at least three or four organizers in *every* state, who would in turn promote party organization in counties and precincts. It also involved providing extensive training for state and local party operatives and volunteers, and giving them access to a national voter file called Vote Builder, and to an organizing tool called Party Builder.[17] Rather than focusing only on the presidential election in swing states, in red states these organizers would try to help Democrats improve their performance in contests for state legislative seats or gubernatorial races, and in blue states they would try to flip statewide offices that Republicans held or to improve Democratic turnout in rural districts.[18]

Janet Winant, the former Democratic county chair in Michigan who has been deeply involved for decades, remembered, "Howard Dean revitalized the Democratic parties in this region." She ticked off the names of numerous counties in northern Michigan. "We've got decades-long relationships with people in outlying counties because of him." Specifically, she recalled that Dean had used the internet's emerging capabilities to bring people together. "We could connect and feel like we had support, moral support, even if it was far-flung."

Yet Dean's approach incurred the wrath of the Washington-based party leaders. In advance of the midterms, Representative Rahm Emanuel, who served as chair of the DCCC, and Senator Chuck Schumer, who chaired the Senate counterpart, recruited some strong candidates, and owing to Dean's approach, those individuals benefited from better-organized states and districts than had been the case for many years. As the election drew close, Emanuel requested that Dean contribute $10 million from DNC coffers to help with races in swing districts. Dean refused, adamant that to do so would harm the longer-term goal of party building to which he was dedicated. This infuriated Emanuel and other leaders, for whom the immediate goal of winning the election was paramount—and seemed essential to party building.[19]

On Election Day 2006, Democrats triumphed. The party took back both chambers of Congress, gained control of more state legislatures than it had since 1994, and picked up six governorships. As political scientist Elaine Karmarck wrote, "It looked like everyone had won."[20] Yet even then, two Democratic consultants—James Carville and Stan Greenberg—complained to reporters than the victory would have been even greater if Dean had not been so insistent on the fifty-state strategy. Carville even suggested that Dean should be replaced as DNC chair. But state party chairs rallied to Dean's defense, the controversy quieted down, and Dean stayed on.

As Kamarck noted, the conflict stemmed from a classic question that political scientists often ask as they look back at campaigns: "How much of the outcome is due to the actions and tactics of the campaigns and how much is due to forces beyond [their] control?"[21] She observes that this question is impossible to answer in the case of the statewide races, since Dean had sent organizers to every state, and Americans everywhere were subject to larger political trends such as weariness with both the war in Iraq and the Bush presidency. But congressional races are another story, because Dean had sent organizers to some districts and not others, and to many districts before it was evident that a viable candidate would run. She identified thirty-nine districts in which Dean had made an organizing commitment. Then she assessed the average change in Democratic vote share in those districts in 2006 versus 2002, compared to the changes in all other contested districts. Notably, the places that had organizers on the ground for over a year before the election "doubled the Democratic vote over what would have happened due to forces outside the control of the Party," increasing the vote share by 9.8 percent compared to 4.7 percent.[22] To be sure, we should interpret these findings with some caution; they are based on a relatively small sample of congressional districts, are descriptive in nature, and do not account for other important factors—such as district demographics or economic conditions. But they are nevertheless suggestive, and as Kamarck notes, they are "a powerful testament to the value of a long-term party building approach."[23]

Two years later, when Obama won the Democratic presidential nomination, he inherited, as Galvin observed, "a party that was active in more states and that reached more deeply into local communities than at any time in recent memory." Obama's campaign worked in concert with the DNC to conduct a voter registration drive in all fifty states. Obama's personal charisma helped facilitate the outpouring of volunteer energy that emerged. The campaign aimed to organize and channel resources not only into swing states for the presidential race, but also, as Galvin notes, to "help down-ticket Democratic candidates and lay the groundwork for redistricting in 2011."[24] The number of rural congressional seats Democrats left uncontested had already dropped from more than a dozen in 2004 to just five in 2006 and eight in 2008, as our analysis finds (see appendixes). Come the November election, the years of nationwide organizing paid off as Obama triumphed and the party picked up eight Senate seats, twenty-one House seats, and helped sixty of ninety-nine state legislative chambers.[25] Many of those, as we saw in chapter 6, were in rural areas. The question is, once Obama became president and head of the Democratic Party, what would become of the fifty-state strategy and the vast volunteer network that had been mobilized?

The Grassroots Perish

When Obama named a new DNC chairman, Tim Kaine, he took the opportunity to stress the need to build on the widespread political mobilization that had powered his victory. The president-elect implored,

"We must build a movement for change that can endure beyond a single election, and that will require redoubling our efforts to reach out to Americans throughout our 50 states, north and south, east and west. It will require finding candidates for elective office whose policies and plans are rooted not in ideology, but in what works."[26] Obama praised Dean and his fifty-state strategy, which "made Democrats competitive in places they had not been in years."[27]

Indeed, even before Obama won the nomination, some of his advisors were already strategizing about how the grassroots energy his campaign had ignited could be channeled into an enduring progressive organization. They hoped it could wield the power to build support for his policy agenda and more, fueling progressive politics far and wide. By the time he was elected, Obama's campaign had thirteen million email addresses, three million donors, and two million individuals active on its social networking platform.[28] Volunteers had devoted themselves passionately to his campaign and were poised to carry on. As one in Pennsylvania wrote shortly after the election, "We're all fired up now and twiddling our thumbs! ALL the volunteers are getting bombarded by calls from volunteers essentially asking: Nowwhatnowwhatnowwhat?"[29]

But just as Howard Dean had clashed with Washington insiders, the proponents of continued grassroots organizing met with resistance as well. The two hundred DNC staffers who had implemented the fifty-state strategy were laid off.[30] On the question of how to sustain the energy from the Obama campaign, the debate focused on organizational structure: whether it would operate independently, outside of party politics, as its chief proponents desired, or be included within the DNC, as Obama's high-ranking campaign advisors favored. The latter group prevailed, and the army of volunteers was folded into the DNC as Organizing for America. Within the confines of the DNC—which was not oriented toward ongoing grassroots organizing—the bold vision of those energized by Obama's campaign came to naught. Rather than enduring as a group, OFA withered into a mailing list for the DNC, and not a particularly effective one. The campaign's chief technology officer, Michael Slaby, lamented years later, "Our party became a national movement focused on general elections, and we lost touch with nonurban, noncoastal communities."[31]

The Democratic Party today operates largely out of Washington, DC, led by operatives and consultants who are mostly based there. It is subject to the whims of big donors in the Democracy Alliance, interest groups and individuals alike. The donors channel dollars to DC-based groups rather than local parties, feeding what political scientist Daniel Schlozman calls a "Washington-centric Blob." Meanwhile, the party's nationwide organizational apparatus, which was once more in touch with voters and had the capacity to mobilize them, has been starved for resources and has atrophied as a result. The volunteers activated by Obama have long since disappeared, and "the threadbare state parties [are] now barely able to keep the lights on."[32]

Building Relationships

A shared conviction among the most active Democratic party chairs we interviewed is that politics can be improved by talking to people, building relationships, and rebuilding the party, bit by bit. Richard Smith of southeastern North Carolina said, "We have to go back to the practices of . . . going door to door, building relationships in communities . . . so [voters] can make a conscientious decision. Robocalls don't tell me that you have my interests in mind. Politics is a social issue; . . . you need to reach out and touch people. Without it, you won't get people elected to office in this highly competitive environment that we are in."

And in northeastern North Carolina, Belinda Mason said, "I do feel like relationship building is crucial, because if you can and you are credible, that can help influence people to be able to think independently and critically." In her small town, Democrats serve as the town manager and as mayor, and Mason described them as doing a "phenomenal job," having a "vision," and getting everyone "working together for the greater good." She explained, "That helps dispel those myths—'You are a Democrat, a socialist, and a baby killer.' You can say that to someone you don't know, but not once you know them. That's how you make a difference. It's slow and it takes time."

10

Conclusion

BILL WHITTAKER was raised in rural southeastern Ohio, in a household that he describes as "public-servant minded." Now, while raising his own children in the area, he is continuing the tradition by serving as the chair of his county's Democratic Party. The county is part of the sixth congressional district, which was long competitive between Democrats and Republicans but swung hard to the Republicans from the Tea Party wave in 2010 through the rise of Donald Trump. Whittaker often finds himself in a conversation with a local person who will tell him, "For a large majority of my life I voted Democrat. But the Democrats, they left me."

"I always respond and ask, 'Where did we go? We're still right here!'" says Whittaker. "They'll look at me funny, and I'll laugh, but I'll say, 'I'm serious. Let's break it down.'"

First, he explains that local government at the township level in Ohio—the three township trustees and a fiscal officer—is nonpartisan on the ballot. "So we can take those out," he says. "Now we go up to the county level. Our sheriff, the county recorders, the county treasurer, the county auditor and the county prosecuting attorney—they are all Democrats. Everybody's a Democrat except the three county commissioners, and that only changed in the past three years. So are you telling me that the Democratic Party left you at the county level? Where did they go? Well, they didn't go anywhere, did they? They're the same people today as they were ten years ago or twenty years ago, and you even knew some of them thirty years ago, and they're still the same people."

The individual responds, "Yeah—I'd agree with that. They're still the same people."

Whittaker presses on, "Okay, so now we're up to state representatives and state senators." He mentions the name of the state senator, who is a Democrat. "Do you personally know him?" he asks.

"No."

Whittaker replies, "He was one of the best state representatives, now a state senator. While he served in the assembly, he was elected [by his colleagues as] one of the most bipartisan members almost every year he was in office!" He continues, "Well, then who left you? We haven't found anybody yet who left you."

The person typically says, "I don't like AOC [Alexandra Ocasio-Cortez]. I don't like Ilhan Omar. I don't like this one. And I don't like that one."

"Oh, so you're talking about *national* politics. There—yep, that's what we're talking about. Excuse me, was Ilhan Omar on your ballot for U.S. congressperson?"

"No, she's not from here."

"So you elected someone to represent you, and the folks in Minnesota elected someone to represent them, right?"

"Yeah, but I still don't like her."

"But everyone has the opportunity to send a representative to Congress based on geographic location. Is that true?"

"Yeah, that's true."

"Well, then why are you so mad that the folks in her area voted for her? They must have thought that she was the best choice. You thought that [our Republican Congressman] Bill Johnson was the best choice, but maybe people in Minnesota don't like Bill Johnson! Did you ever think of that?"

"No, I never thought of that."

"That's like saying that you or I have all the right answers. And we don't, we don't have all the right answers. And guess what? They don't have all the right answers either. And if you ask them, they'll probably tell you. Alexandria Ocasio-Cortez will probably tell you, 'No, I don't have all the right answers.' No one has all the right answers. We try to work together to find an answer that is common ground that most people can live with."

Through conversations such as these, Bill Whittaker and his fellow Democrats try to stem the tide they have faced for years as their rural counties—like several hundred nationwide—have seen their politics move dramatically to the right. The Democratic Party—once embraced by many rural voters, considered an occasional alternative by many others, and viewed as a legitimate opponent by most of the rest—is now regarded with disdain. Since the 1990s, many white rural Americans have shifted their political loyalties to the Republican Party, even as it became more extremist. Beyond the local level, this new national divide between rural and urban is transforming American politics and, more fundamentally, endangering democracy.

Understanding the Rural-Urban Divide

The first step toward mitigating the rural-urban divide is to understand it. Many highly educated urbanites have been quick to assume they already do, and they readily assert that rural people, particularly those who are white, are irredeemably racist, bigoted, or backward. The empathy that liberals typically extend to marginalized groups tends to be in short supply when it comes to rural people. It should go without saying that sheer intolerance, aside from being an inappropriate way to regard a group of fellow citizens, is no way to build a winning political coalition. It is downright bad politics.

The rural-urban divide began when rural communities were ravaged by economic changes that matched the Industrial Revolution in their scope and power. Key shifts were exacerbated by policy choices: The United States' embrace of deregulation and free trade removed the regulatory supports that had long been built into the political economy to sustain rural places. In the agricultural sector, small family farms were replaced by agribusinesses. In mining and other extractive industries, technological change and trade reduced the size of the workforce. Counties that relied heavily on manufacturing witnessed the shuttering of factories or severe downsizing of the workforce. Meanwhile, urban places were subject to some of these same forces, but many more easily rebounded. Public officials aided them in doing so by promoting the knowledge economy, with its bevy of good-paying jobs for highly educated people.

In combination, these changes led to *place-based economic inequality*. During the 1990s and early 2000s, counties that suffered most from these developments shifted away from supporting Democratic candidates and toward favoring Republicans.

In the next phase, from 2008 onward, the rural-urban divide deepened, driven by a trend activated by the first phase. Rural Americans grew to resent what they perceived as overbearing Democratic elites— from urban places—advancing policies in which they felt they had little voice. This is especially striking because on most policy issues, rural and urban residents differ very little—if at all—in their views. What links numerous issues together, though, is that rural dwellers felt imposed on by outsiders, who happened to be benefiting far more from the contemporary economy. This sense of *elite overreach* pushed them more firmly toward the Republican Party.

A third trend compounded the other two: *conservative mobilization*. Political parties and organizations can play a crucial role in connecting the dots for citizens, interpreting events such as those reflected in the trends noted above and assigning blame for them. As political parties have grown weaker over time, Republicans have been aided electorally by vibrant civic organizations, particularly those concentrated in rural places. Evangelical churches, Right to Life organizations, and gun clubs affiliated with the National Rifle Association politicize their members in ways that help GOP turnout. The Democratic Party, meanwhile, lost out as the labor unions that for decades had bolstered it saw their ranks decimated by deindustrialization and Republican attacks on both public- and private-sector unions. This has harmed rural support for the party. Together, in a process we call sequential polarization, these forces have profoundly polarized America by place.

We have not been able to assess the role of conservative media given a lack of appropriate data, but we suspect that like civic organizations, it may help point citizens to GOP voting. This impact is likely amplified given the demise of local newspapers in so many places, and the absence of less partisan civic organizations that might have served as a countervailing force.[1] Bill Whittaker talked about the rise of Fox News and how it might matter. "Absolutely—it's a problem. It's probably a bigger problem in the rural areas because you don't have a lot of other alternatives, you don't have a lot of loud kickback. You don't have a lot of loud voices saying, 'Hey, they're really lying to you.' I mean, [Fox] went to court and said, 'No, we're not a news outlet—we're an entertainment outlet.' You don't have people here shouting that from the rooftops."

The resulting place-based cleavage has fueled partisan polarization at the highest levels of government. It has put out of reach numerous policy changes that enjoy broad public support, from labor and employment law reform to gun control measures and immigration reform. It has stood in the way of updating and improving existing policies, whether on voting rights or environmental protection. Once again, the cause is not that rural people hold strikingly different views on public policies than urbanites. To the contrary, it is because the nation has been severed into two factions, and those in rural places now routinely elect members of a party that is governing from a posture out of step with its own history and to the right of most Americans—including rural ones—on numerous issues.

Why the Rural-Urban Divide Is a Threat to Democracy

The United States' relatively new, searing place-based divide is harming democracy in several ways. In rural communities, it subjects residents to one-party governance, which can undermine accountability and make corruption more likely. It can discourage the presence of political opposition; as a party loses vote share in each national election, it becomes more difficult to field candidates and maintain an organized presence. In many places, openly supporting the Democratic Party makes residents fearful of losing customers, their jobs, or even their friends. The lack of meaningful competition in general elections can in turn spur extremism among the dominant party, as candidates face challengers only from fellow partisans in primaries, and voters in such contexts tend to be relatively unengaged.[2] These developments threaten the democratic ideal of pluralism, where citizens with diverse views and identities can live together peacefully and participate freely in the political process. For the nation as a whole, this growing divide exacerbates partisan polarization and reinforces a nasty and dangerous "us" versus "them" politics.

Of course, Americans have grown increasingly divided along several dimensions in recent decades. So what, if anything, sets this latest place-based division apart? At first glance it may seem like just another fracture layered on top of existing ones: race, religion, views on gender, educational level, attitudes about immigration, and now, geography. A skeptic might also point out that rural dwellers make up, at most, only about one in five Americans, so how important can this division be?

Our deepest concern is that the contemporary rural-urban divide matters in a distinctive way, one not shared by any of the other sources of division. It grants to one party all the institutional advantages of place embedded in the U.S. Constitution. Indeed, the combination of changes in rural Americans' political behavior, on one hand, and these institutional arrangements, on the other, makes the divide especially powerful and consequential. To be clear, it does not allow rural Americans themselves, at the mass level, to dominate politics. Rather, it empowers the recipients of their votes—the Republican Party—giving it extra leverage over its competitor. There is one clear winner from the developments we've described, and that is the Republican Party.

The Republican Party, with rural voters consolidated within it nationally, now enjoys a greater chance than the Democrats of dominating all three branches of federal government. The Electoral College system gives it an edge in presidential elections. The use of single-member, winner-take-all districts for House elections and the inefficient distribution of Democratic voters benefits the Republicans in gaining seats in the lower chamber. But it is in the Senate that the rural-urban divide is most firmly rooted, given the considerable power it grants to lower-population states. Since Democrats John Tester of Montana and Sherrod Brown of Ohio were defeated in the 2024 election, and Kentucky voters also flipped a seat in replacing Joe Manchin, who retired, it will be extremely difficult for Democrats to gain a majority in the chamber for the foreseeable future. In other words, unless Democrats can overcome the rural-urban divide, they are likely locked out of power in one of the most powerful chambers of governance in the world.

The consequences of long-term Republican dominance of the Senate are immense. It means that Republicans will have the ability to advance many of their legislative goals and, just as important, block those favored by Democrats. It also means Republicans will control nominations to cabinet positions and administrative agencies, influencing the shape of the executive branch. When a Democratic president is elected again, that president may face significant challenges in getting appointments confirmed, let alone legislation passed to address the needs of urban and rural dwellers alike. Perhaps most significantly, it allows Republicans to shape an entire branch of government—the judiciary—for years, and likely decades, to come.

Finally, as it currently stands, the rural-urban divide facilitates the radicalization of the party that controls the institutional advantages. A key implication of the patterns we have identified is that the party benefiting from them can, through various pathways, secure political power even with just a minority of the population supporting it electorally. This makes its elected officials less responsive to the broader public, enabling them to maintain power even as they double down on unpopular policies and extremist positions.

Now that party is dominating the political system, and it is running roughshod over the basic procedures that undergird democracy. These include free and fair elections and abiding by their outcomes, the rule of law, the legitimacy of the political opposition, and the integrity of rights.[3] This occurred in 2020, when Republican leaders denied the outcome of the presidential election and condoned the actions of those who tried to overturn it. It happened once Trump took office again in 2025 and quickly issued numerous decisions—from firing civil servants to shuttering agencies—that seized powers rightly belonging to Congress. Though Republicans control both chambers, they failed to respond vigorously to defend their authority. Again, it is not that rural Americans themselves hold more authoritarian views than urban Americans. Rather, it is that many of the officials they have elected have prioritized keeping their party in power over protecting democracy, and they have not faced retribution at the ballot box for their behavior.[4]

In sum, the rural-urban divide is wreaking havoc on American politics. It consolidates the long-standing institutional advantages of rural and less-populated areas within one party, granting it disproportionate power and enabling it to further tilt the system in its favor. In congressional elections, this divide has ended meaningful two-party competition in many rural places, ushered in extreme candidates, and eliminated the moderate rural politicians of the past who often helped Congress overcome legislative gridlock. Ironically, although rural areas increasingly elect conservatives who reject government intervention, these places disproportionately depend on government for both employment opportunities and social programs. In short, the rural-urban divide is fueling polarization, deepening political dysfunction, and threatening democracy itself.

Mending the Divide

What can be done? Some reformers highlight the need for institutional changes, such as abolishing the Electoral College or changing the structure of the Senate. While these changes seem logical, the obstacles to enacting them are formidable. Either would require a constitutional amendment—a daunting prospect considering that over eleven thousand amendments have been proposed but only seventeen have succeeded since the original ten in the Bill of Rights. Given the nation's present political climate—in which Congress and the states are deeply polarized—the likelihood of overcoming the arduous ratification process in both venues is next to nil. Other reforms that could strengthen democracy—such as ending winner-take-all House elections and moving to an electoral system based on proportional representation—do not face such high hurdles, but even then, our divided polity would likely stymie them. We are sympathetic to those who favor moving to multimember districts in the House of Representatives; such a reform would not only make Congress more representative of the nation as a whole, but also likely reduce polarization, as several political scientists have shown.[5] Yet we are doubtful that lawmakers would take the bold steps of putting their own seats at risk by passing the legislation necessary for such a change.[6]

Other reformers focus on public policies aimed at improving the economies of rural places. While such policies are certainly necessary, they offer no guarantee of reducing political polarization in the near term, given how deeply entrenched the divisions have become. Nor can mere changes in political messaging alter patterns built over years of growing distrust.

Rather, our research suggests that the most promising path forward involves listening, organizing, and political engagement. For democracy to thrive, the United States needs vibrant party competition that flourishes in both rural and urban areas. This is crucial for localities, to prevent the downward spiral associated with one-party government, and it is vital for the nation as a whole, to combat polarization and extremism. But reinvigorating Democratic politics in rural places cannot be achieved simply by sending volunteers from cities to rural districts for a few months before each election.

To former Democratic Congresswoman Cheri Bustos, who in 2012 flipped a Republican seat in Illinois's heavily rural seventeenth congressional district and won it four more times, success required maintaining a consistent presence. She told us, "Every two years I had a barn burner of a campaign. They were never easy." What Bustos learned is that showing up just prior to elections wasn't enough; she emphasized that "being there" year-round with her constituents was crucial. She added, "It's expensive, its time-consuming, and it takes organization." Seeking to meet her constituents in settings conducive to civil conversation, she held town hall meetings "at virtually every small library" in the district. On "Supermarket Saturdays," she walked the aisles of grocery stores and Dollar General stores, asking people, "I'm flying back to Washington on Monday. What's on your mind? What do you want me to know?" When election time came, she said, "I didn't have to poll. I knew what people were thinking."

She started an initiative called "Cheri on Shift," in which she job-shadowed 120 constituents over time. "They were a huge help to me," she said. "If there was one takeaway, it was how hard people work, in some really, really hard jobs, but they take pride in them. And it is how they support their families and themselves and their communities." She mentioned, for example, "the fisherman who catches carp in the Illinois River and takes it into the processing plant, who's been doing it since he was sixteen years old. You know, as he's standing knee deep in fish guts. . . . He loved that. And he didn't want to do anything else." Even with these constant efforts to understand her constituents and their needs, defying the typical image that many rural people have of Democrats, Bustos faced an uphill battle politically. Yet she managed to defy the odds, continuing to win while other rural Democrats in Congress vanished.

The first principle, Bustos will insist, is listening. She recalls assisting with Barack Obama's 2008 campaign in rural Iowa. They held meetings where attendees were asked their views on what a good health care policy would look like, helping to shape the party platform. Since then, Democrats have largely abandoned such efforts. Some ignore the well-being of rural people entirely, focusing primarily on urbanites who are in need. For a party that claims to prioritize economic inequality and the needs of lower- and middle-income Americans, this myopia excludes a large share of those in need and weakens the party. Other Democrats believe the party should engage with rural areas, but often the policies they advance do little to involve rural people in the process. If the Democratic Party is to build a strong political coalition that spans all areas, it must begin by listening to rural people, even when what they say is difficult to hear.

Rural Democrats in Republican-dominated states—and rural Republicans in Democratic-dominated states—need to make their voices heard in the policymaking and implementation processes. Sometimes rural dwellers feel that even their fellow partisans in state government give little heed to their concerns, even when policies will directly affect them. For example, with environmental policies, rural people are often more attuned than urbanites to how implementation will actually be carried out. Bustos recommends that candidates and elected officials meet regularly with rural people, listen to their ideas and concerns, and fashion policies that respond to them, both in design and in plans for implementation.[7]

Mitigating the rural-urban divide will require serious, year-round organizational efforts focused on party building. For decades, leaders in the Democratic Party have prioritized short-term victories at the expense of building and maintaining the party at the grassroots level across broad swaths of the United States. Particularly now, in an age of disinformation, there is no substitute for fostering these face-to-face, long-term relationships within communities. Local party leaders know the potential is there, but they need help from both the state- and national-level organization. As Tina Wolford said of Texas, "We're not a Republican state; we're a nonvoting state." She explained that part of the problem owed to Republican leaders making voting more difficult, but she also criticized the state Democratic Party for failing to adequately support the county chairs—particularly those in rural counties. The Democratic Party should hire full-time, year-round organizers—ideally people from the same region—to shore up and expand the efforts of county chairs. The party should aim to build and fortify itself everywhere—not just in swing states, but across the nation.

In many rural counties, Democratic candidates—who used to win majorities—now secure only about 20 percent of the vote. Yet as several county leaders in various states noted, statewide candidates often win by tiny margins, and better mobilization of rural voters could be enough to swing the results. In recent general and run-off elections, organizers in rural Georgia worked hard to get out the vote for Senate candidate Raphael Warnock. They took pride in the high voter turnout among Democratic supporters and believed it contributed to his improbable victories. Simply by "losing by less," rural voters can make a difference far beyond their localities.

Democratic candidates for statewide office should include rural areas in their campaign visits. Doing so would not only improve Democrats' prospects in statewide elections by increasing their share of the rural vote, but more importantly, it would signal that two-party governance is alive. The Democratic Party must also make a concerted effort to re-cruit candidates for state legislatures and the U.S. Congress in all rural districts. This strategy matters both for giving voters a choice and because circumstances can change, even in districts that once seemed unwinnable. Republicans would do well to adopt the same approach in urban districts; even when the odds appear tough, citizens deserve a meaningful choice on the ballot, and providing that choice promotes a more vibrant political community.

We also acknowledge that in some rural places, the barriers to running candidates on the Democratic ticket may seem insurmountable until the party manages to restore trust and build ties in the local community. Candidates who wish to present an alternative choice to the Republican Party in the meanwhile may view running as an independent as a more viable option. Independents like Bernie Sanders of Vermont and Angus King of Maine—both rural states—currently hold seats in the Senate and caucus with the Democratic Party. In 2024, Dan Osborn, a mechanic and labor leader, ran as in independent in Nebraska against incumbent Republican Deb Fischer. Though he lost, he netted an impressive 47 percent of the vote, far surpassing Democratic presidential candidate Kamala Harris, who won 39 percent statewide. This strategy offers another path to restoring competitive elections in rural places.

Abraham Barton is a Black Democrat and long-term party chair in rural North Carolina whose county organization has enjoyed considerable success. He explains, "The secret is building relationships in your community." Barton manages to organize all the precincts in the county, despite disinvestment from the state and national party. He and a party leadership group routinely share announcements in the local newspaper, make phone calls, talk to people in person, and teach new precinct chairs how to run meetings. They place information about voter registration in churches and stores, and work with the NAACP and Lions Club. They reach out to welcome newcomers. "We are steadily getting younger people involved. We are trying to teach them how politics works, to teach them it controls everything." Reflecting on decades of organizing, he says, "It doesn't just happen. It's about building relationships over the years."

Despite the challenges faced in rural places, those who have chosen to live in them are glad they did. Said one party chair after another, "I love it here," and, "The best decision I ever made was to move here." They have invested precious time and energy in the civic renewal of their communities, and their efforts—if bolstered and supported—may revitalize the nation as a whole.

ACKNOWLEDGMENTS

DURING THE COURSE of this project, we received help from numerous individuals and organizations, without which this book would not have been possible.

We began researching the rural-urban political divide in the early months of the COVID-19 pandemic and talented Cornell undergraduates assisted us from the start. Samantha Puzzi helped us conduct initial research, including mapping political trends, that was eventually published in *The Forum*. La'Treill Allen and Abraham Reiss joined Samantha in investigating our case study states. Michaela Ferrario researched numerous topics and examined Right to Life organizations in Michigan. Lauren Weintraub carried out the analysis that led to Figure 5.3, detailing the prevalence of NRA-affiliated gun groups in the case study states. Later on, Varsha Gande studied counties we traveled to for interviews, helping us to prepare in advance. Eddie Elliott and Saad Razzak aided with numerous tasks involving data coding and fact-checking. Eddie's assistance was crucial as the book reached completion. Additional help came from Richard Li, Andreas Psahos, Daniel Chayet, and PhD student Thomas Gareau-Pacquette. Two other Cornell PhD students, Gisela Pedroza Jauregui and Marissa Rivera, joined us to study how political behavior among rural dwellers who identified as Black or Latino compared to that of white residents; our findings, some of which are discussed in Chapter 1, were published in *Politics, Groups, and Identities*.

Once the pandemic subsided, we began our field research in earnest, traveling to rural counties in our four main case study states to interview political party chairs, both Democrats and Republicans. We are enormously grateful to these individuals, each of whom was willing to accept a request from a stranger, take the time to meet with us, and welcome us warmly. Their thoughtful and candid responses to our questions tremendously deepened our understanding of how rural areas have changed over time and how politics has developed there.

Meanwhile, the Kluge Center at the Library of Congress generously hosted Suzanne Mettler as a scholar-in-residence for several months. That provided the opportunity to interview twenty policymakers, including former U.S. senators and representatives who had been elected from more rural states and districts. Their stories and reflections proved to be deeply illuminating, and we are appreciative of their willingness to share them with us. Also during this time period, Jon Cardinal magnanimously convened a gathering of Capitol Hill staffers and agency personnel who focus on rural issues. They listened to us describe our evolving research and provided insightful feedback. Conversations with numerous people proved crucial to our research, and we thank them all, including Janna Deitz, Tom Hamburger, Michael Levy, and Bob Reklaitis.

We were fortunate to team up with Danielle Thomsen to study how the emergence of the rural-urban divide has shaped the U.S. House of Representatives. We've learned so much from Danielle, and the conference papers we wrote with her provided some of the key analyses included in chapter 6.

We've benefited from the probing questions, helpful suggestions, and tough-minded criticism offered by a marvelous community of scholars. An early presentation at the University of Wisconsin at Madison permitted us to learn from Barry Burden, Katherine Cramer, Virginia Sapiro, Rochelle Snyder, and their colleagues. Daniel Carpenter, Dan Lichter, Ken Roberts, Eric Schickler, and Jeff Stonecash took the time to read our papers and offer valuable feedback. Our colleagues in American politics at Cornell read an early paper and helped us improve it; we thank David Bateman, Richard Bensel, Doug Kriner, Peter Enns, Jamila Michener, and Isabel Perera. We learned so much from conversations with the late Elizabeth Sanders and from her indispensable scholarship on the nineteenth-century agrarian movement; we only wish she were with us still. Fascinating discussions with Kristi Andersen, Charles Bullock III,

Chris Cooper, and Barry Rabe aided our research. A presentation at the University of Toronto for the Malim-Harding lectureship and at the University of Pennsylvania's American Politics workshop offered wonderful opportunities for feedback. We have presented our work at numerous conferences, including those of the American Democracy Collaborative, the Consortium on the American Political Economy (CAPE), the Princeton University conference on Identity and Inequality, the Princeton University conference on Democratic Frontsliding, the University of Virginia's Democracy and Capitalism conference, and annual meetings of the American Political Science Association, Midwest Political Science Association, and Southern Political Science Association. Among those who've provided valuable insights along the way are Larry Bartels, James Conran, Rachel Funk Fordham, Daniel Hopkins, Larry Jacobs, Matt Lacombe, Frances Lee, Matt Levendusky, Tali Mendelberg, Jim Morone, Robert Lieberman, Sid Milkis, Alexander Sahn, Theda Skocpol, Rogers Smith, Laura Stoker, Mary Summers, Daniel Ziblatt, and numerous others. Anonymous reviewers for *Perspectives on Politics* and Princeton University Press provided excellent guidance as well.

Funding for this project was generously provided by Cornell University, particularly through a New Frontier grant from the College of Arts and Sciences. In addition to the Kluge Center at the Library of Congress, the Guggenheim Foundation also supported Suzanne Mettler's time in working on the research and writing. Jerrica Brown, Laurie Dorsey, and Dinnie Sloman provided indispensable administrative help throughout the duration of the project.

An early version of some of the arguments in chapter 2 is published in a volume edited by Sidney Milkis and Scott Miller, *Can Democracy and Capitalism Be Reconciled?*, from Oxford University Press. An early version of some of the arguments in chapters 3 and 4 is published in *Perspectives on Politics*.

We greatly appreciate Princeton University Press for publishing this book. Our agent, Lisa Adams, aided us in myriad ways, not least in helping us gain a better understanding of how to frame and write the book. We are so thankful, as always, for her sage counsel. Editors Bridgette Flannery-McCoy and Alena Chekanov offered superb advice on how to improve the readability of the manuscript. We are also grateful to everyone who brought the book to press with such professionalism and care: Eric Crahan, David McBride, and Steve Stillman at Princeton University Press; Angela Piliouras of Westchester Publishing Services; and freelance editor Kelley Blewster.

Several institutions provided access to data that made analysis for this project possible. These include the Bureau of Economic Analysis; Cornell Center for the Social Sciences; the Cooperative Election Study (CES) at Harvard University; the Inter-university Consortium for Political and Social Research (ICPSR) at the University of Michigan; the American National Election Studies (ANES); the MIT Election Lab; and the National Center for Education Statistics. Staff associated with each of these initiatives offered swift help and guidance. Briane Thiede and Michael Zoorob also shared helpful data.

———

Suzanne adds: Over these years, I have been nurtured by the warm support of dear friends and family. Most of all, my husband has—as always—listened to my ideas as they evolved, day after day, offering wise suggestions and encouragement, and he has provided the best company along the journey that became this book.

I grew up in a rural county. My father was raised on a farm there; my mother was a city girl whose parents owned a home in the area. Theirs was a beautiful marriage of rural and urban, and they each devoted themselves to the local community. Two of my siblings live in the same county today and continue that tradition of civic engagement. I dedicate this book to each of my five siblings, with whom I share a love of the place that so profoundly shaped all of us.

———

Trevor adds: As we researched and wrote this book, I have benefited from the love and help of many friends, at Cornell and elsewhere. They include Ariana Shapiro, Rachel Funk Fordham, Danny Daneri, Nat

Schwartz, Mackenzie Speer, Matt Lacombe, and Jeanne Kuang. Above all, my family, particularly my parents and Aunt Tammy, have offered endless support.

I spent most of my childhood in a rural Rust Belt area just outside Springfield, Ohio. In addition to my immediate and extended family, I was shaped by the care of an army of dedicated public school teachers, sports coaches, and family friends. I dedicate this book to them and to Donnelsville, Ohio, a town of around two hundred people where I played most of my little league baseball. The people and community there taught me, among many other valuable lessons, that we should view each other as neighbors, not enemies.

Appendixes

Measuring Rural

Throughout the book, we primarily use two different measures of "rural." In county-level analyses, we rely on the Office of Management and Budget's (OMB's) metro (urban) versus nonmetro (rural) distinction. We use this measure because it captures counties' (1) population size, and (2) social and economic integration into major cities.[1] The OMB updates the measure each decade. However, the OMB has changed the classification criteria a number of times, rendering many decades incomparable to others.[2] Therefore, following other scholars, throughout the book we primarily rely on the 1993 rural-urban distinctions, a year that sits roughly in the middle of the time frame for most of our analysis (i.e., 1976–2020).[3] However, we note that virtually all our findings are substantively the same when allowing the rural measure to vary across decades by different OMB delineations.[4] Where we use an OMB classification different from the 1993 version, we note it in these appendixes.

In analyses of states and congressional districts, we primarily use the U.S. Census Bureau's measure of rural-urban. Rurality is demarcated by the Census at the block level based on land use (i.e., housing density) and population density. For example, under the 2010 definition, rural areas consist of open countryside with fewer than five hundred people per square mile and places with fewer than twenty-five hundred people. To generate estimates at the district level, the Census Bureau "crosswalks" or aggregates smaller measurements up to congressional districts and states.[5]

Chapter 1

County-Level Descriptives

Figures 1.1, 1.2, and 1.3 are produced by aggregating county-level vote returns by year and place. Figure 1.1 does so for the nation as a whole; Figure 1.2 does so for each region; Figure 1.3 does so for each state. Following David Bateman and his colleagues, we define the South as the seventeen-state bloc in which racial segregation in schools was mandated by law, prior to the *Brown v. Board of Education* decision in 1954. This included Alabama, Arkansas, Delaware, Florida, Georgia, Kentucky, Louisiana, Maryland, Mississippi, Missouri, North Carolina, Oklahoma, South Carolina, Tennessee, Texas, Virginia, and West Virginia.[6] Election returns come from Dave Leip's Atlas of U.S. Presidential Elections. Rural-urban is designated by the 1993 OMB measure.[7]

Our county-level voting trends are fairly consistent with individual-level analysis of non-Hispanic white voters from the American National Election Studies (ANES) and the Cooperative Election Study (CES, formerly the Cooperative Congressional Election Study). Those estimates are illustrated below, using the appropriate survey weights, as well as the 1993 OMB definition of rural-urban for each respondent's reported county of residence (figures A1.1 and A1.2).[8]

Policy Preferences

Figures 1.4 and 1.5 display averaged answers to several policy preference questions. These calculations were made using the CES Policy Preferences dataset.[9] The CES offers the county of residence of each respondent, allowing us to merge them with the OMB's measure of rural-urban. Because the questions were asked in the 2010s, we used OMB's 2013 metro (urban) and nonmetro (rural) measures here; we note that our findings are consistent with using the 1993 measure. Survey weights provided by CES were used to calculate estimates.

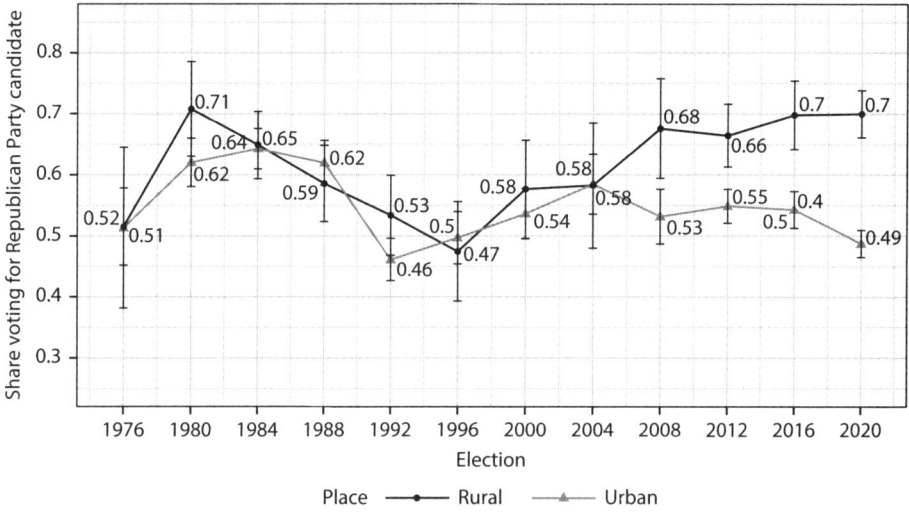

FIGURE A1.1. The emergence of the rural-urban divide among non-Hispanic white individuals, 1976–2020
Source: ANES; measure of respondents' rural-urban status from OMB

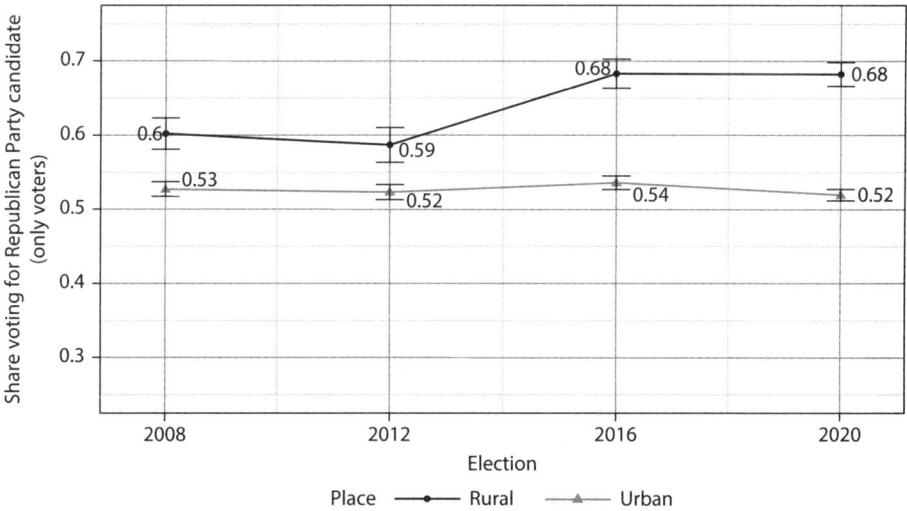

FIGURE A1.2. The rural-urban divide among non-Hispanic white individuals, 2008–2020
Source: ANES; measure of respondents' rural-urban status from OMB

As for questions related to public spending, in years 2014, 2016, 2018, and 2020, respondents were asked the following: "State legislatures must make choices when making spending decisions on important state programs. Would you like your legislature to increase or decrease spending on the five areas below?"

For education, infrastructure, health care, welfare, and policing, respondents were offered the following responses: "greatly increase; slightly increase; maintain; slightly decrease; greatly decrease."

We assigned each response a score from 0 ("greatly decrease") to 4 ("greatly increase"), placed those answers on a scale of 0 to 1 for interpretability, and averaged them together by respondents' place of residence. We pooled all years together for simplicity and to generate a more reliable sample size; we note that, if we conduct the analysis for each individual year, the differences between rural and urban respondents are fairly stable over time.

As for questions related to social issues or "culture war" issues, the CES asked respondents a battery of questions we used to create scales for support or opposition, available from 2012 to 2021. These included questions on immigration, abortion, gun control, gay marriage, and environmental regulation. We tested the items for internal consistency by calculating Cronbach's alpha, which confirmed that they formed a reliable scale. Those interested in the alpha estimates and/or the wording of the questions should consult the supplementary material from Brown et al. 2024.[10]

Feeling Thermometer Questions

The feeling thermometer estimates in chapter 1 were generated using ANES's single-year and cumulative files.[11] In particular, each respondent was asked how warmly they feel toward the groups discussed in chapter 1, on a scale of 0 to 100. We gained access to respondents' county of residence at the time of the survey, which is restricted data, through an agreement with the University of Michigan and Inter-university Consortium for Political and Social Research (ICPSR). We then merged respondents' answers with the OMB measure of rural-urban. Appropriate survey weights were used to calculate estimates.

Chapter 3

Figures 3.1 and 3.2 were produced by aggregating county-level population and employment statistics by place and year up to the national level. Figure 3.1 uses employment data from the Bureau of Economic Analysis (BEA), housed within the U.S. Department of Commerce.[12] To produce estimates for Figure 3.1, we subtracted all public-sector jobs in each county from "Total Employment," using data from tables "CAEMP25N" and "CAEMP25S." We pegged raw employment growth for all rural and urban counties to the year 1970, showing the increase (in full percentage points) in jobs, by place, over time. Figure 3.2 relies on the aggregation of county-level population estimates from various iterations of Decennial Census of Population and Housing, conducted by the U.S. Census Bureau.[13]

Figure 3.3 was produced by aggregating the number of workers who received assistance from the Trade Adjustment Assistance (TAA) Program, which allows workers to apply for training and temporary income assistance if they have been laid off due to rising imports or offshoring. Data on local, industry-specific employment that might be more affected by trade are surprisingly hard to come by. For reasons related to privacy, the BEA avoids disclosing industry-related employment information for many counties, particularly those that are sparsely populated.[14] This makes it tough to draw inferences about industry-specific employment effects in rural counties especially.

One way to proceed is to analyze programs such as TAA. Of course, these estimates likely do not reflect the entire population of trade-related job displacements. Many workers do not file claims for various reasons, including a lack of knowledge about the program or the hassle of applying, otherwise known as "administrative burden."[15] Still, we think this is a fair measure. To the extent that either lack of knowledge about the program or the reduced presence of nonprofits and worker-friendly civic infrastructure discourages workers from applying, we would expect those factors to be more acute in rural areas, implying relatively more rural job losses are missed by this measure.

Petitions were retrieved from the Department of Labor and cleaned with the help of research assistants.[16] Note that only successful petitions were included, further making this a relatively conservative measure of trade's impact on workers and their surrounding communities. To adjust the estimates for the significant population differences between rural and urban areas, we created a per capita measure by aggregating county populations by year. Single-year population data here come from the BEA, which generates estimates using the Census Bureau's annual midyear (July 1) population estimates.[17]

Chapter 3 also includes discussion of poverty rates and per capita income. To generate the poverty estimates for 2019, we used data from the Small Area Income and Poverty Estimates (SAIPE) Program.[18] We used the 2013 OMB metro (urban) and nonmetro (rural) category to aggregate the estimates by year and place. For per capita income, we used data from the BEA; in particular, we used the measure "personal income," defined as:

> the income that persons receive in return for their provision of labor, land, and capital used in current production as well as other income, such as personal current transfer receipts. In the state and local personal income accounts the personal income of an area represents the income received by or on behalf of the persons residing in that area. It is calculated as the sum of wages and salaries, supplements to wages and salaries, proprietors' income with inventory valuation (IVA) and capital consumption adjustments (CCAdj), rental income of persons with capital consumption adjustment (CCAdj), personal dividend income, personal interest income, and personal current transfer receipts, less contributions for government social insurance plus the adjustment for residence.[19]

It was retrieved from table "CAINC1."[20] Here we also used the 2013 OMB rural-urban delineation.

Regression Analyses and Modeling Choices

Figures 3.4 and 3.5 are based on ordinary least squares (OLS) multivariate regressions. Our models use county-level Republican vote share in presidential elections as the dependent variable to proxy the extent to which rural and urban counties have diverged politically. In most regression models throughout the book, we use the vote share going to the Republican party among all candidates. In models that use the Republican share of just the major two-party vote, our results are almost entirely the same.[21]

In models underlying analysis in chapter 3, our key independent variables are: rural versus urban, county-level job growth, and county-level population growth. Rural is again retrieved from the OMB; job growth comes from the BEA; and population totals from the U.S. Census Bureau. To generate employment and population growth, we calculated the percentage increase or decrease from the previous election year; we then transformed and logged each value, a typical practice in econometric analysis to ensure the data meet the assumptions of OLS estimators.

To investigate change over time, we pooled the data into three time periods: elections from 1976 to 1988, 1992 to 2004, and 2008 to 2020. Theoretically, these periods have substantive importance. As displayed in figure 1.1, the first period acts as a baseline, or a period before the rural-urban political divide emerged; the second period covers the time period when the divide began to emerge; and the third period marks its intensification. These periods also track well with social and economic descriptive changes illustrated and discussed throughout the book. Methodologically, these three pools offer a relatively well balanced set of models, each encompassing the same number of elections and roughly the same number of observations, with one exception.[22] To detect change over time, tests for equality of coefficients were conducted in Stata by combining the results from the two periods with the "seemingly unrelated estimates" command, *suest*. Wald tests for equality of coefficients were then estimated using Stata's *test* command.[23] While our data might seem like good candidates for dynamic time series models, we are concerned that the number of time periods is too few. Our total time frame includes thirteen elections, and the time period that marks the ascendance of the rural-urban political divide includes only seven elections. As Nathaniel Beck argues, dynamic cross-sectional time series models tend to require at least ten time periods, and preferably more.[24]

In addition, we control for the share of the county-level population that identifies as white; the share of the county-level population aged sixty-five or older; and the share of the county-level population aged

TABLE A3.1. Place and Presidential Voting

	Dependent Variable		
	County-Level Republican Vote Share		
	(1976–1988)	(1992–2004)	(2008–2020)
Rurality	0.002	0.007	0.024***
	(0.004)	(0.004)	(0.005)
Share College	0.175***	−0.048	−0.538***
	(0.037)	(0.030)	(0.026)
Share White	0.233***	0.229***	0.456***
	(0.010)	(0.011)	(0.013)
Share Senior (65+)	−0.144***	−0.089*	−0.168***
	(0.048)	(0.048)	(0.050)
Constant	0.244***	0.135***	0.206***
	(0.012)	(0.014)	(0.015)
Year Fixed Effects?	Yes	Yes	Yes
Region Fixed Effects?	Yes	Yes	Yes
Observations	12,430	12,443	12,434
R^2	0.366	0.467	0.511
Adjusted R^2	0.366	0.467	0.510

Note: Estimates generated using OLS multivariate regressions; robust standard errors clustered at county level.
$*p < 0.1$; $**p < 0.05$; $***p < 0.01$

twenty-five and over with a four-year college degree. These data come from the U.S. Census Bureau. Because rural counties on average tend to have older populations, contain a higher share of white residents, and have relatively fewer residents with college degrees, including these variables in our model is key to ensuring that race and ethnicity, age, and/or education do not confound our results. When necessary, we used linear interpolation to calculate off-decade, election-year estimates; such interpolation has been shown to perform quite well in producing reliable demographic estimates.[25] In all our models, we include year fixed effects to ensure that no single election is driving our results. We also include region fixed effects to ensure no unobserved variation across region (such as between South versus non-South) might be

TABLE A3.2. Employment Growth and Presidential Voting,
Rural and Urban Counties

	Dependent Variable		
	County-Level Republican Vote Share		
	(1976–1988)	(1992–2004)	(2008–2020)
Rurality	−0.026***	−0.064***	−0.004
	(0.007)	(0.008)	(0.011)
Log Job Growth	0.126***	0.148***	0.207***
	(0.016)	(0.018)	(0.022)
Log Pop Growth	0.065***	0.028	0.060
	(0.012)	(0.020)	(0.048)
Share College	0.116***	−0.049	−0.572***
	(0.038)	(0.031)	(0.027)
Share White	0.214***	0.218***	0.448***
	(0.011)	(0.012)	(0.013)
Share Senior (65+)	−0.093**	−0.063	−0.119**
	(0.046)	(0.051)	(0.051)
Rurality x Log Job Growth	−0.104***	−0.205***	−0.078***
	(0.017)	(0.019)	(0.023)
Constant	0.332***	0.209***	0.326***
	(0.015)	(0.018)	(0.029)
Year Fixed Effects?	Yes	Yes	Yes
Region Fixed Effects?	Yes	Yes	Yes
Observations	12,205	12,222	12,224
R^2	0.379	0.477	0.521
Adjusted R^2	0.378	0.476	0.521

Note: Estimates generated using OLS multivariate regressions; robust standard errors clustered at county level.
*p < 0.1; **p < 0.05; ***p < 0.01

confounding our results. We cluster robust standard errors at the county level to address heteroscedasticity.

Results from models in chapter 3 are shown here. Table A3.1 includes a simple model to illustrate that place matters above and beyond simple county-level demographic factors. Table A3.2 presents results in which

TABLE A3.3. Population Growth and Presidential Voting,
Rural and Urban Counties

	Dependent Variable		
	County-Level Republican Vote Share		
	(1976–1988)	(1992–2004)	(2008–2020)
Rurality	−0.060***	−0.164***	0.010
	(0.011)	(0.016)	(0.039)
Log Pop Growth	0.188***	0.339***	0.094
	(0.022)	(0.031)	(0.088)
Log Job Growth	0.040***	−0.025***	0.141***
	(0.007)	(0.008)	(0.014)
Share College	0.128***	−0.059*	−0.569***
	(0.038)	(0.031)	(0.027)
Share White	0.214***	0.219***	0.448***
	(0.011)	(0.012)	(0.012)
Share Senior (65+)	−0.104**	−0.088*	−0.124**
	(0.047)	(0.052)	(0.049)
Rurality x Log Pop Growth	−0.160***	−0.398***	−0.042
	(0.024)	(0.036)	(0.082)
Constant	0.358***	0.286***	0.314***
	(0.016)	(0.021)	(0.044)
Year Fixed Effects?	Yes	Yes	Yes
Region Fixed Effects?	Yes	Yes	Yes
Observations	12,205	12,222	12,224
R^2	0.380	0.483	0.521
Adjusted R^2	0.379	0.482	0.520

Note: Estimates generated using OLS multivariate regressions; robust standard errors clustered at county level.

*p < 0.1; **p < 0.05; ***p < 0.01

we interacted rural with employment growth, as presented in figure 3.4. Table A3.3 presents results in which we interacted rural with population growth, as displayed in figure 3.5.

Chapter 4

Figure 4.1 relies on county-level estimates from the U.S. Census Bureau's various years of Decennial Census of Population and Housing.[26] Using the 1993 OMB measure of rural-urban, we calculated the share of the population nationwide aged twenty-five and older with a four-year degree by all rural and urban counties and by decade.

Figure 4.2 was generated using OLS regressions similar to those discussed above. Instead of interacting our measure of rural with job or population growth, we interacted our measure of rural with the share of the population aged twenty-five and older with a four-year degree. Full results are presented in table A4.1. We note these results are robust to allow the OMB rural definition to vary by decade.

Figure 4.3 uses the ANES cumulative file to proxy anti-Black attitudes among non-Hispanic white respondents. In particular, ANES asks respondents, "Some people feel that the government in Washington should make every effort to improve the social and economic position of blacks. Others feel that the government should not make any special effort to help blacks because they should help themselves. Where would you place yourself on this scale, or haven't you thought much about it?"[27] Crucially, the question was asked for every election year from 1976 to 2020.

Respondents were given a seven-point scale ranging from "Government should help blacks" to "Blacks should help themselves." We note that this measure correlates strongly with racial resentment, the traditional measure used for anti-Black attitudes ($r = .65$, $p < .001$).[28] It is also the only measure that consistently proxies anti-Black attitudes across our time period of interest. We rescaled the responses so higher scores indicated greater support for government efforts to help Black Americans; we then transformed and placed the responses on a scale of 0 to 100 for interpretability. Those who answered "don't know" or "haven't thought about it" were dropped from analyses.

TABLE A4.1. Education and Presidential Voting, Rural and Urban Counties

	Dependent Variable		
	County-Level Republican Vote Share		
	(1976–1988)	(1992–2004)	(2008–2020)
Rurality	−0.026***	−0.037***	0.018
	(0.009)	(0.011)	(0.011)
Share College	0.008	−0.169***	−0.596***
	(0.045)	(0.039)	(0.034)
Log Job Growth	0.040***	−0.022***	0.140***
	(0.007)	(0.008)	(0.014)
Log Pop Growth	0.075***	0.045**	0.073
	(0.012)	(0.020)	(0.047)
Share White	0.213***	0.216***	0.446***
	(0.011)	(0.012)	(0.013)
Share Senior (65+)	−0.072	−0.060	−0.122**
	(0.046)	(0.052)	(0.051)
Rurality x Share College	0.266***	0.266***	0.053
	(0.071)	(0.063)	(0.050)
Constant	0.323***	0.180***	0.313***
	(0.015)	(0.018)	(0.026)
Year Fixed Effects?	Yes	Yes	Yes
Region Fixed Effects?	Yes	Yes	Yes
Observations	12,205	12,222	12,224
R^2	0.379	0.473	0.521
Adjusted R^2	0.378	0.473	0.520

Note: Estimates generated using OLS multivariate regressions; robust standard errors clustered at county level.

*$p < 0.1$; **$p < 0.05$; ***$p < 0.01$

To investigate the relationship between place and racial attitudes, we gained access to users' county of residence through an agreement with the University of Michigan and ICPSR. We then coded whether each resident lived in a rural or urban county, as defined by the OMB's 1993 categories. Figure 4.3 reflects the average scores for rural and urban respondents. It is worth noting that, if we allow the OMB

TABLE A4.2. Anti-Black Attitudes and Individual Vote Choice Among
Non-Hispanic Whites, Rural and Urban Counties

	Dependent Variable		
	Individual-Level Republican Vote Choice		
	(1976–1988)	(1992–2004)	(2008–2020)
Rurality	−0.442* (0.182)	0.0993 (0.166)	0.343* (0.141)
Support for Gov't Aid to Black People	−0.0253*** (0.00188)	−0.0208*** (0.00172)	−0.0418*** (0.00123)
Rurality x Support for Gov't Aid to Black People	0.0146*** (0.00335)	−0.00123 (0.00365)	0.000976 (0.00281)
Share Hispanic	−0.322 (0.329)	−0.491 (0.303)	−1.110*** (0.206)
Education	0.147** (0.0463)	0.205*** (0.0503)	−0.117** (0.0398)
Income	0.281*** (0.0403)	0.202*** (0.0410)	0.179*** (0.0307)
Gender	−0.171* (0.0774)	−0.259** (0.0806)	−0.0806 (0.0582)
Age	0.00321 (0.00244)	0.00795** (0.00251)	0.0114*** (0.00190)
Constant	−0.172 (0.292)	−1.210*** (0.247)	1.028*** (0.210)
Year Fixed Effects?	Yes	Yes	Yes
Observations	3,133	3,257	12,022

Note: Estimates generated using logistic multivariate regressions; robust standard errors in parentheses.
$^*p < 0.05$; $^{**}p < 0.01$; $^{***}p < 0.001$

TABLE A4.3. Racial Demographics and Individual Vote Choice,
Rural and Urban Counties

| | *Dependent Variable* | | |
| | Individual-Level Republican Vote Choice | | |
	(1976–1988)	(1992–2004)	(2008–2020)
Rurality	0.126	0.0897	0.553***
	(0.0959)	(0.0997)	(0.0787)
Share Hispanic	−1.265***	−0.915**	−1.461***
	(0.319)	(0.296)	(0.181)
Rurality x Share Hispanic	2.878**	2.048*	−0.00420
	(0.888)	(0.864)	(0.506)
Education	0.0824	0.0750	−0.186***
	(0.0423)	(0.0437)	(0.0309)
Income	0.319***	0.236***	0.229***
	(0.0363)	(0.0358)	(0.0234)
Gender	−0.163*	−0.260***	−0.153**
	(0.0711)	(0.0711)	(0.0469)
Age	0.00412	0.00759***	0.0142***
	(0.00221)	(0.00222)	(0.00144)
Constant	−1.242***	−1.705***	−0.487**
	(0.253)	(0.218)	(0.158)
Year Fixed Effects?	Yes	Yes	Yes
Observations	3,468	3,954	13,215

Note: Estimates generated using logistic multivariate regressions; robust standard errors in parentheses.
*p < 0.05; **p < 0.01; ***p < 0.001

delineation of rural to vary by decade, the results remain remarkably consistent.

Figure 4.4 relies on a set of individual-level logistic regressions using the ANES cumulative file. Similar to the county-level regressions, we pooled the data into three periods (1976–1988; 1992–2004; 2008–2020). Our dependent variable was whether a respondent voted for the Republican candidate in each presidential election. We restricted our analysis to non-Hispanic whites, using the appropriate survey weights. To test

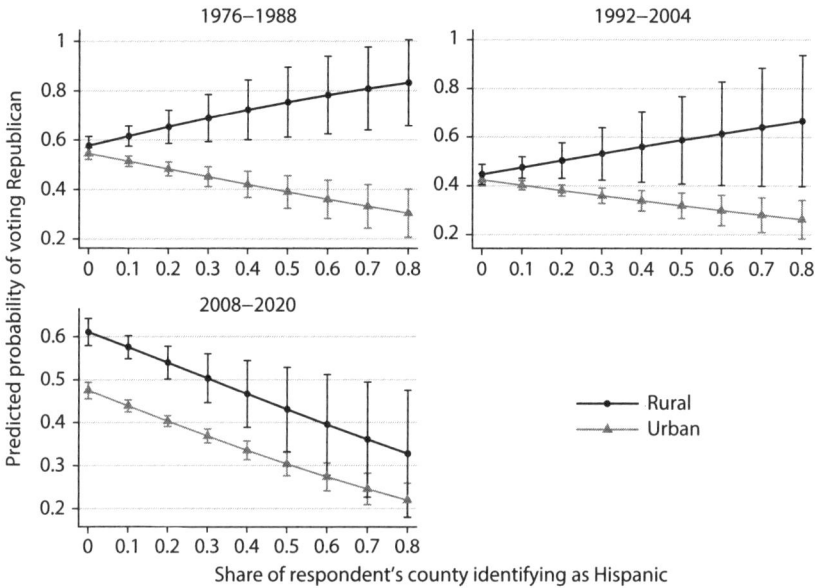

FIGURE A4.1. Racial demographics and presidential vote choice, rural and urban non-Hispanic white individuals
Source: ANES; measure of respondents' rural-urban status from OMB

whether anti-Black attitudes influenced Republican vote choice differently across place, we interacted our measure of rural with respondents' level of racial animus, as proxied by the measure above. We included controls for respondents' education, income, age, and gender, as provided in the ANES cumulative file. Full results are listed in table A4.2. We note that our results are consistent with allowing the OMB rural measure to vary by decade.

In addition to anti-Black attitudes, we also wondered if racial/ethnic status threat might be influencing vote choice across place.[29] To probe this possibility, we again used data from the ANES. Along with the respondents' rural-urban status based on the OMB measure, we also included the share of the Hispanic population residing in each respondents' county, retrieved from the U.S. Census Bureau. The models that follow are similar to the structure of the ones above, except here we interacted our measure of rural with the share of the county population that identifies as Hispanic. Results are listed in table A4.3 and displayed in figure A4.1. In short, we do not find evidence that racial threat is contributing to the rural-urban divide, at least as measured here. We note that these results are similar when allowing the rural measure to vary across decade; using county share of population that is nonwhite (instead of Hispanic); and using the change (rather than levels) of various racial/ethnic demographic groups over time.

Finally, chapter 4 includes discussion of the changing racial and economic demographics of rural and urban counties. To generate our estimates, we use data from various iterations of the Decennial Census of Population and Housing Data.[30]

Chapter 5

Chapter 5 includes discussion of union election activity and place. Figure 5.1 shows the number of union elections petitioned to the National Labor Relations Board (NLRB), per job by place, from 1969 to 2010. Estimates were generated by cleaning and aggregating union election activity from John-Paul Ferguson and the NLRB; single-year employment data came from the BEA.[31] No measure of union coverage is available at the county levels and, to be sure, this is a limited measure. It tells us little about the number of workers covered, represented, and engaged by a union, among other things. Nevertheless, below the state level, traditional union power measures are notoriously difficult to come by.

Beyond unions, chapter 5 includes discussion of church density by place, over time. To generate these estimates, we used data from the U.S. Religious Census and the Association of Statisticians of American Religious Bodies.[32] We aggregated the number of evangelical and Catholic churches, respectively, by rural and urban, for each year. We used the 1993 OMB rural measure. As of this writing, data on congregation density were not available at the county level for 2020.

Figure 5.2 rests on OLS regression results, similar to those discussed above, in which county-level Republican vote share in presidential

TABLE A5.1. Rurality, Evangelical Congregations, and Presidential Voting

	Dependent Variable		
	County-Level Republican Vote Share		
	(1976–1988)	(1992–2004)	(2008–2012)
Rurality	0.019***	0.029***	0.022**
	(0.006)	(0.008)	(0.010)
Evangelical Per 10k Residents	0.002**	0.006***	0.006***
	(0.001)	(0.001)	(0.001)
Catholic Per 10k Residents	0.003***	0.004***	0.005***
	(0.001)	(0.001)	(0.001)
Log Job Growth	0.039***	−0.019**	0.130***
	(0.007)	(0.008)	(0.020)
Log Pop Growth	0.081***	0.088***	0.153*
	(0.012)	(0.021)	(0.088)
Share College	0.152***	0.019	−0.415***
	(0.041)	(0.035)	(0.032)
Share White	0.220***	0.210***	0.423***
	(0.011)	(0.012)	(0.014)
Share Senior (65+)	−0.099**	−0.172***	−0.326***
	(0.047)	(0.053)	(0.064)
Rurality x Evangelical	−0.002***	−0.004***	−0.002**
	(0.001)	(0.001)	(0.001)
Constant	0.288***	0.157***	0.328***
	(0.014)	(0.018)	(0.041)
Year Fixed Effects?	Yes	Yes	Yes
Region Fixed Effects?	Yes	Yes	Yes
Observations	12,205	12,222	9,168
R^2	0.381	0.485	0.531
Adjusted R^2	0.380	0.485	0.530

Note: Estimates generated using OLS multivariate regressions; robust standard errors clustered at county level.

*p < 0.1; **p < 0.05; ***p < 0.01

elections is the dependent variable. We interacted our measure of rural with a per capita measure of evangelical congregations. In addition to controlling for county-level measures of educational level, racial and ethnic demographics, and age, we included a per capita measure for the presence of Catholic churches. Year and region fixed effects are included. Robust standard errors are clustered at the county level to address heteroscedasticity. Full results are listed in table A.5.1. We note that these results are consistent when allowing the rural measure to vary across decade.

Figure 5.3 generates place-based estimates of National Rifle Association–affiliated gun and rod clubs across our case study states. In the summer of 2022, using the "Locate Clubs and Ranges Near You" feature under the Clubs and Associations tab on the NRA website, we collected data on each active club as well as the county in which it was located.[33] We then merged chapters with the 2013 OMB rural-urban measure. Single-year population data used to produce per capita calculations come from the BEA, which generates estimates using the Census Bureau's annual midyear (July 1) population estimates.[34]

Finally, chapter 5 includes discussion of Right to Life groups in Michigan. In the fall of 2022, we used their affiliates page to find active chapters.[35] After finding all active chapters in the state, we matched their county with the 2013 OMB measure of rural. Single-year population data used to produce per capita calculations come from the BEA, which generates estimates using the Census Bureau's annual midyear (July 1) population estimates.[36]

Chapter 6

Rurality of Districts

Several figures in chapter 6 rely on a scale of how rural or urban a U.S. congressional district is, ranging from 1 (most urban) to 5 (most rural). These were generated using the share of the population in each district that is considered rural, as defined by the Census Bureau.[37] To create

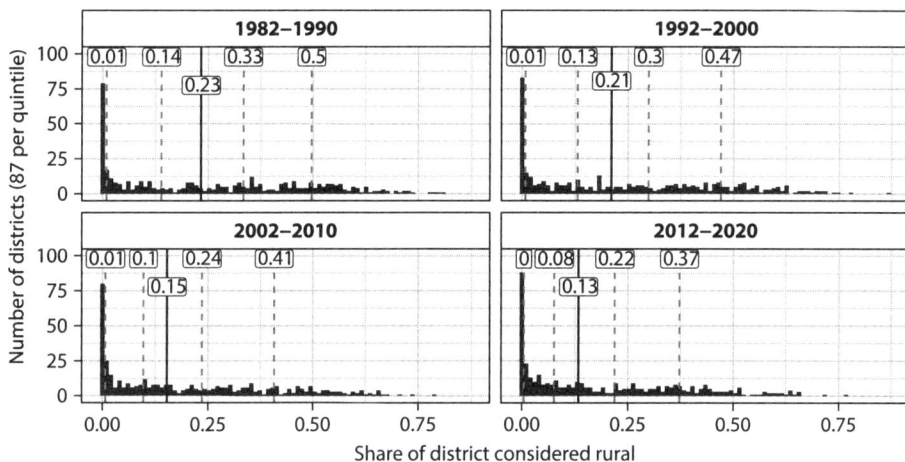

FIGURE A6.1. Distribution of congressional districts by rurality, by each redistricting cycle

Source: Measure of rural from U.S. Census Bureau

the scales for each redistricting cycle (1982–1990; 1992–2000; 2002–2010; and 2012–2020), we reranked districts into quintiles based on the share of their populations considered rural. Each quintile consists of roughly eighty-seven districts or seats. The distribution of districts in terms of share rural population is displayed in figure A6.1; each quintile is marked by a dashed vertical grey line, while the solid black line represents the median district.

Figure 6.1 displays the raw number of Republicans who replaced incumbent Democrats in the 1994 House election. Region codes reflect the U.S. Census's definition, with the caveat that we define the South using the same seventeen-state bloc described above in the appendix for Chapter 1. Data on the partisanship of each member of Congress come from Voteview.

Figure 6.2 shows the number of Republicans and Democrats elected, by how rural or urban their district was, in 1992, 1994, 2008, and 2010, using the same quintile scheme as described above. Data on rurality come from the U.S. Census Bureau; partisanship of each member of Congress from Voteview.[38] Figure A6.2 displays the full time series.

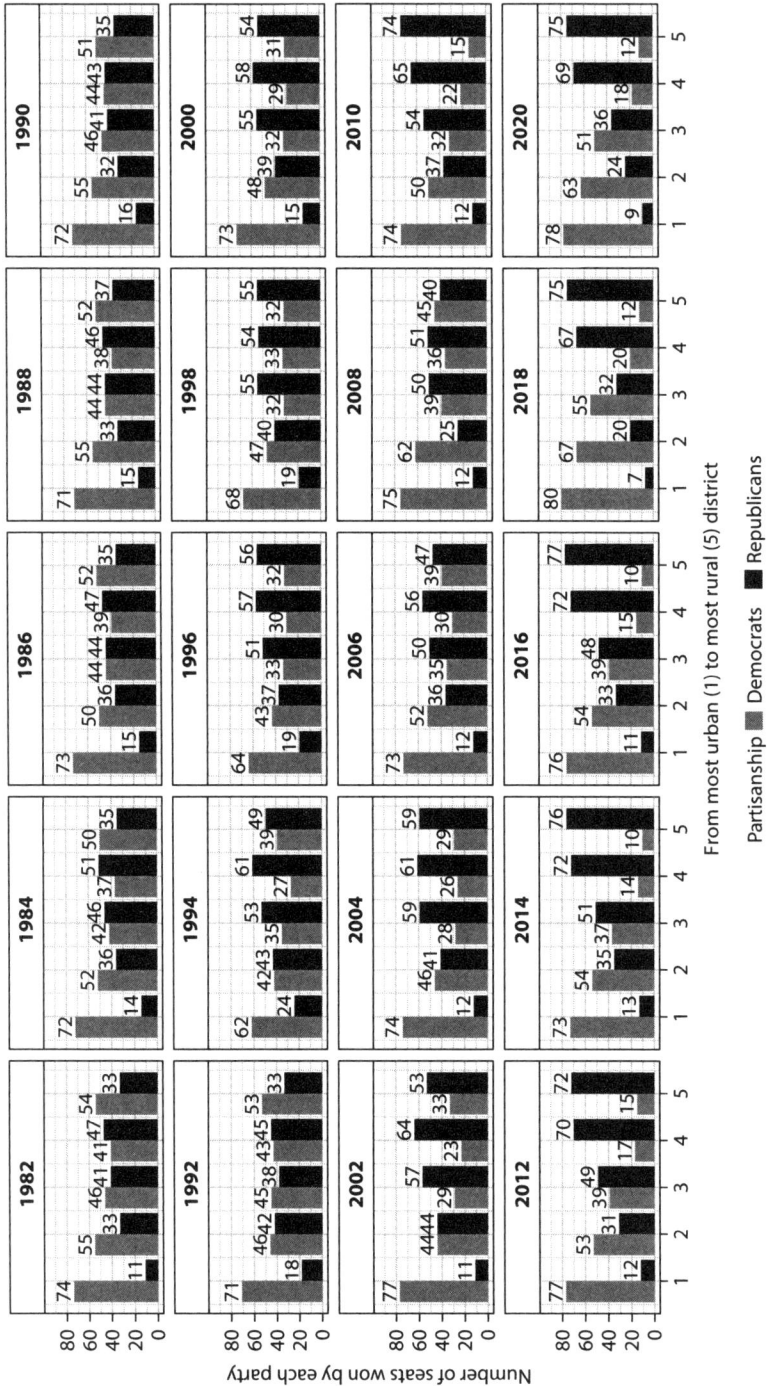

FIGURE A6.2. U.S. House members' partisanship by rural-urban composition of districts, 1982–2020

Source: Voteview; measure of rural from U.S. Census Bureau

Partisanship ■ Democrats ■ Republicans

From most urban (1) to most rural (5) district

Number of seats won by each party

Figure 6.3 displays the relationship between place and elected officials' ideology over time, using OLS multivariate regressions. In particular, we pooled all members across all Congresses from 1982 to 2020, and regressed each member's first-dimension DW-Nominate score—a widely used measure of how conservative or liberal a member is—on the share of the population in their district considered rural. Our measure of rural is interacted with year to demonstrate how the relationship is changing over time. We include controls for district-level demographics, such as age, race and ethnicity, education, and region.[39]

Figure 6.4 uses the quintile scale of how rural each district was for election cycle 2002–2010 to display how rural and urban Democrats and Republicans voted on passage of the Affordable Care Act. Data on the votes and partisanship come from Voteview.

Figure 6.5 uses the quintile scale of how rural each district was for election cycle 2012–2020 to display how members of Congress voted on the certification of the 2020 election. Data on the votes and partisanship come from Voteview.

Chapter 7

Figure 7.1 expresses the average number of people each senator from each party represents, by Congress. Calculations were made by determining the number of people in each state represented by each senator, for each year. Populations were then aggregated for each party and divided by the number of senators in each caucus. Data on partisanship of senators come from Voteview. Single-year state-level population data come from the BEA, which generates estimates using the Census Bureau's annual midyear (July 1) population estimates.[40]

Figure 7.2 shows the share of the U.S. population represented by the political party in control of the Senate, for each Congress back to 1980. Estimates were generated by summing the population of each state represented by each party, and dividing it by the entire U.S. population. Data on partisanship of senators come from Voteview. Single-year state-level population data come from the BEA, which generates estimates using the Census Bureau's annual midyear (July 1) population estimates.[41]

Figure 7.3 illustrates the share of the U.S. population represented by the "yes" votes for each successful Supreme Court nominee since 1981. Estimates were generated by summing the population of states represented by each "yes" vote, by party, and dividing them by the entire U.S. population. Data on partisanship of senators come from Voteview.[42] Single-year state-level population data come from the BEA, which generates estimates using the Census Bureau's annual midyear (July 1) population estimates.[43]

Figure 7.4 shows the efficiency gap for U.S. House elections for each case study state in the book, running back to 1982. For each state, following other scholars who use the measure, the efficiency gap was calculated as follows:

(Republican Seat Margin − 50%) − 2 × (Republican Vote Margin − 50%)[44]

The Republican vote margin for each state was generated by summing all Democratic votes in each election by year and subtracting them from all votes to Republicans in the state. In uncontested elections, following other scholars, we imputed votes for fictional opposition candidates (and subtracted them from votes for the uncontested candidate) by assuming the fictional opposition candidate would have received the minimum share received by their worst-performing copartisan running in the state that year. For example, if the worst-performing Republican in a given state-year received 20 percent of the vote, each election won uncontested by a Democrat would receive a fictional Republican candidate securing 20 percent of the vote, and the Democrat's total votes would be adjusted appropriately. After generating an efficiency gap for each year, we then smoothed them across redistricting cycles (1982–1990; 1992–2000; 2002–2010; and 2012–2020) for ease of interpretation. Data on election returns come from the MIT Election Data and Science Lab; seat margins for each state (or the number of Republicans and Democrats in each state's congregation) were pulled from Voteview.[45]

Figure 7.5 shows the average efficiency gap for all U.S. House races from 1982 to 2020. We calculated it in the same way as for figure 7.4. Data on election returns come from the MIT Election Data and Science Lab; seat margins for each state were pulled from Voteview.

Chapter 8

Figure 8.1 aggregates all social transfers from governments to individuals in rural and urban counties, by year, and adjusts them for population and inflation. Data on all social transfers come from the BEA, using the "Current transfer receipts of individuals from governments" measure. As defined by the BEA, current transfer receipts of individuals from governments consist of: "Retirement and disability insurance benefits, medical benefits, income maintenance benefits, unemployment insurance compensation, veterans' benefits, education and training assistance, and other transfer receipts of individuals from governments."[46] The measure comes from table "CAINC35."[47] Transfer value estimates were adjusted for inflation and pegged to 2019 dollars using the consumer price index (CPI), retrieved from the Federal Reserve.[48] Single-year population data used to create the per capita measure come from the BEA, which generates estimates using the Census Bureau's annual midyear (July1) population estimates.[49]

Figure 8.2 aggregates social transfers from various programs to individuals in rural and urban counties, by year, and adjusts them for population and inflation. They are calculated using the same method as for figure 8.1. Measures for Medicare, Social Security, Earned Income Tax Credit, and SNAP receipts also come from table "CAINC35."[50] Transfer value estimates were adjusted for inflation and pegged to 2019 dollars using the CPI, retrieved from the Federal Reserve.[51] Single-year population data used to create the per capita measure come from the BEA, which generates estimates using the Census Bureau's annual midyear (July 1) population estimates.[52]

Figure 8.3 aggregates public employment, net military service, by place and year, and adjusts it for population size. Public employment includes all state and local employees, as well as federal civilian workers.

Those measures are in tables "CAEMP25S" and "CAEMP25N."[53] Single-year population data used to create the per capita measure come from the BEA, which generates estimates using the Census Bureau's annual midyear (July1) population estimates.[54] Our estimates differ slightly from Rodden 2024 because we include federal civilian employment; Rodden only includes state and local employees.[55]

Figure 8.4 shows the number of residents of rural and urban counties who died while serving in the military from 2001 to 2019, and adjusts those estimates for population. Data were retrieved from the Department of Defense's (DoD's) Defense Casualty Analysis System.[56] Within each military operation, the DoD lists all names of those who have died while in military service (under "Names of the Fallen"), along with their home county. We aggregated each death from each type of county (that is, rural versus urban) by year. Our analysis is largely restricted to interventions in Afghanistan and Iraq. Single-year population data used to create the per capita measure come from the BEA, which generates estimates using the Census Bureau's annual midyear (July 1) population estimates.[57]

Chapter 8 also includes discussion of the prevalence of community colleges. To probe the presence of community colleges across place, we acquired data on institutions of higher education from the Department of Education's Integrated Postsecondary Education Data System (IPEDS), which includes and surveys all accredited institutions of higher education in the country.[58] We limited our definition of community colleges to postsecondary schools that meet both of the following criteria: (1) grant at least one-year degrees but less than four-year degrees, and (2) are in full public control. The IPEDS data include the zip codes of each school going back to 1980. We cross-walked those zip codes to identify the counties in which the schools resided. We then merged the OMB 1993 measure of rural-urban to each school, aggregated the number of rural and urban community colleges for each year, and weighted them by population. Single-year population data come from the BEA, which generates estimates using the Census Bureau's annual midyear (July 1) population estimates.[59]

Chapter 9

Chapter 9 includes discussion of uncontested seats in every congressional election from 1984 to 2020. Calculations were made as follows, using
data from the MIT Election Data and Science Lab and the Federal Election Commission.[60] We first found each election that included only one
major party candidate in the election-year seat contest, running as either
a Republican or Democrat. In New York, if a Democrat was not on the
ballot but a nominee of the Working Families Party was, we counted that
individual as a major candidate. With a team of research assistants, we
then cross-checked our designations with the Federal Election Committee official returns.[61] After doing so, we merged the rurality of each congressional member's district, using the measures described in more detail
above (see the section on chapter 6). We finally aggregated by party and
rurality of district.

Questions for Rural-Urban Interviews with Former and Present Local and State Party Officials and Organizational Leaders

1. Tell me about your own background.
   A. How long have you lived in _____? How long have you/
      did you work/hold the position as _____? (If applicable:)
      Where did you live previously and what brought you here?
   B. How did you get involved in the community/state and [in
      this organization/come to hold this position]? What were
      you doing previously? What led you to take on this role?
2. Has the county/state/rural areas of the state changed over
   time, say, since the 1990s [or since you've been involved]?
   If so, how?
   A. How about in terms of jobs, employment, living standards,
      presence of businesses?
   B. Population changes: Are people moving into the area? Who?
      What brings them? Are people leaving, and if so, who? Why?
      Do young people stay? If so, what do they do? If not, why?
   C. What are the biggest challenges faced by the local area?

3. Tell me about the Democratic/Republican Party in this county/state (especially rural areas).

   A. How strong is it? How does that compare to five years ago? Ten years ago? Twenty years ago? If things have changed, why? What do you attribute it to?

   B. How active/involved are local people in the party? What activities, candidates, or events have made them more/less involved?

   C. Sometimes an organization experiences a turning point, after which its development is different than what came before. Have you seen that happen here, whether it has made the party stronger, weaker, or simply different than it was before? If so, what was that turning point? How did it change things?

   D. What attracts people in this area to vote for Democratic/Republican candidates?

   E. Do you think particular policies have helped/hurt people in this county/rural areas of the state? Which one(s)? Why?

   F. What particularly excites/energizes Republicans/Democrats in this area? Particular issues, and if so, which ones (e.g., local school closings, local hospital closings, jobs, health care, social benefits, NAFTA/trade, abortion, immigration, Black Lives Matter, Defund the Police, gay rights, transgender issues, taxes, etc.)?

   G. Which organizing strategies have seemed more/less successful to you?

   H. To what extent do you feel that the local/state party is supported by the national party? Explain.

   I. Did the Tea Party/resistance movements help/hurt the local party? Explain.

   J. To what extent does the local party work together with other organizations (E.g., unions, churches, gun groups, etc.)? If other organizations are involved with the party, what role do they play? How important is their contribution to your overall efforts?

K. How excited/energized were local citizens by particular presidential candidates (e.g., Clinton/Trump, Biden/Trump)? Why?

L. What is the biggest challenge faced by the local/state party?

4. How do you see the future for residents of this area? Does it make you feel optimistic/pessimistic? Why?

5. I'd like to interview political and organizational leaders in the area, particularly those who were active in the late 1990s and early 2000s, whether or not they are still active. Can you suggest anyone whom you think I should interview?

6. Is there anything else about the state/county that you'd like me to know?

NOTES

Introduction

1. In order to protect the privacy of the county chairs we interviewed, we refer to them by pseudonym and refrain from using identifying information. We do not identify the counties in which they reside, noting instead only the region of the state.

2. Dankwart Rustow, "Transitions to Democracy: Toward a Dynamic Model," *Comparative Politics* 2 (1970): 337–63.

Chapter One: The Puzzle

1. This generalization is based on members' DW-NOMINATE scores, which are generated based on their voting record to produce a measure of how liberal (−1) or conservative (1) they are on a single-dimension scale. The last Democrat to serve the district, George "Buddy" Darden, was more conservative than most Democrats but more liberal than most Republicans, with a score of −0.16. Greene's score is 0.8, putting her among the ten most conservative members of the chamber. Estimates from Jeffrey B. Lewis, Keith Poole, Howard Rosenthal, Adam Boche, Aaron Rudkin, and Luke Sonnet, Voteview: Congressional Roll-Call Votes Database, 2025, https://voteview.com/.

2. In order to protect the anonymity of the county chair we interviewed, we do not specify the name of the local newspaper in which this article appeared.

3. We rely on this measure for two additional reasons. First, it is widely used in the rural sociology literature, allowing us to relate our findings to others and facilitate dialogue between scholars. (For example, see Brian C. Thiede, Jaclyn L. W. Butler, David L. Brown, and Leif Jensen, "Income Inequality Across the Rural-Urban Continuum in the United States, 1970–2016," *Rural Sociology* 85, no. 4 [2020]: 899–937; Daniel T. Lichter and Kenneth M. Johnson, "Urbanization and the Paradox of Rural Population Decline: Racial and Regional Variation," *Socius: Sociological Research for a Dynamic World* 9 [2023]: 1–21.) Second, it offers a relatively simple and parsimonious measure that makes much of our analysis more interpretable. See the appendixes for additional discussion. For an alternative view on the rural-urban continuum, see Zoe Nemerever and Melissa Rogers, "Measuring the Rural Continuum in Political Science," *Political Analysis* 29, no. 3 (2021): 267–286.

4. Elizabeth A. Dobis, Thomas P. Krumel Jr., John Cromartie, Kelsey L. Conley, Austin Sanders, and Ruben Ortiz, *Rural America at a Glance: 2021 Edition* (U.S. Department of Agriculture, Economic Research Service, 2021).

5. Owing to population growth, in each census, some counties that were formerly considered "rural" have been reclassified as "urban." As we will see, however, many rural counties have been subject to population stagnation.

6. According to both the U.S. Census Bureau and OMB's measures, all the states listed here rank in the top fifteen in terms of raw number of rural residents. The two measures differ some

but are highly correlated. Throughout the book, when discussing and/or analyzing states, we mostly rely on the Census Bureau's measure, and specify when we do.

7. M. V. Hood III and Seth C. McKee, *Rural Republican Realignment in the Modern South: The Untold Story* (Columbia: University of South Carolina Press, 2022).

8. How rural a state is depends in part on how one defines "rural," as we discuss in more detail in the appendixes. According to the Census Bureau, the median state in terms of rural population in 2020 was Kansas at 28 percent. According to the OMB, the median state in terms of rural population in 2020 was North Carolina at 21 percent.

9. Our analysis of these trends is discussed in more detail in the appendixes. See also Trevor E. Brown, Gisela Pedroza Jauregui, Suzanne Mettler, and Marissa Rivera, "A Rural-Urban Political Divide Among Whom? Race, Ethnicity, and Political Behavior Across Place," *Politics, Groups, and Identities* 13, no. 1 (2024): 229–242.

10. E.g., Lilliana Mason, *Uncivil Agreement: How Politics Became Our Identity* (Chicago: University of Chicago Press, 2018); Donald R. Kinder and Cindy D. Kam, *Us Against Them: Ethnocentric Foundations of American Opinion* (Chicago: University of Chicago Press, 2010); Ezra Klein, *Why We're Polarized* (New York: Avid Reader Press, 2020).

11. E.g., Doug McAdam and Karina Kloos, *Deeply Divided: Racial Politics and Social Movements in Postwar America* (New York: Oxford University Press, 2014); Nolan McCarty, Keith T. Poole, and Howard Rosenthal, *Polarized America: The Dance of Ideology and Unequal Riches* (Cambridge, MA: MIT Press, 2006); Christopher S. Parker and Matt A. Barreto, *Change They Can't Believe In: The Tea Party and Reactionary Politics in America* (Princeton, NJ: Princeton University Press, 2013); Angie Maxwell and Todd Shields, *The Long Southern Strategy: How Chasing White Voters in the South Changed American Politics* (New York: Oxford University Press, 2019).

12. In fact, recent research by Eric Schickler offers a persuasive corrective on the typical accounts that place the point of racial realignment by race in 1960, showing that "the New Deal coalition was being torn apart from within by about 1940." Eric Schickler, *Racial Realignment: The Transformation of American Liberalism, 1932–1965* (Princeton, NJ: Princeton University Press, 2016), 9. For an important exception, see Neil O'Brian, *The Roots of Polarization: From Racial Realignment to the Culture Wars* (Chicago: Chicago University Press, 2024). A related literature argues that "racial threat" has spurred political division more recently, whether in response to growing racial and ethnic diversity or to the election of the nation's first Black president, Barack Obama. In the pages that follow, we build on this research and test if racial and ethnic threats are particularly salient in rural areas. E.g., Michael Tesler, *Post-Racial or Most-Racial? Race and Politics in the Obama Era* (Chicago: University of Chicago Press, 2016); Parker and Barreto 2013; Ashley Jardina, *White Identity Politics* (New York: Cambridge University Press, 2019); John Sides, Michael Tesler, and Lynn Vavreck, *Identity Crisis: The 2016 Presidential Campaign and the Battle for the Meaning of America* (Princeton, NJ: Princeton University Press, 2018).

13. Nicolas Carnes and Noam Lupu, "The White Working Class and the 2016 Election," *Perspectives on Politics* 19, no. 1 (2021): 55–72; Herbert P. Kitschelt and Philipp Rehm, "Secular Partisan Realignment in the United States: The Socioeconomic Reconfiguration of White Partisan Support Since the New Deal Era," *Politics and Society* 47, no. 3 (2019): 425–479; Jeffrey M. Stonecash, "The Puzzle of Class in Presidential Voting," *The Forum* 15, no. 1 (2017): 29–49; Larry M. Bartels, *Unequal Democracy: The Political Economy of the New Gilded Age* (New York: Russell Sage/Princeton, 2008); Lainey Newman and Theda Skocpol, *Rust Belt Union Blues: Why Working Class Voters Are Turning Away from the Democratic Party* (New York: Columbia University Press, 2023); for a review, see Laura Bucci, "White Working Class Politics and the Consequences of Declining Unionization in the Age of Trump," review essay, *Politics, Groups, and Identities* 5, no. 2 (2017): 364–371.

14. James G. Gimpel, Nathan Lovin, Bryant Moy, and Andrew Reeves, "The Urban-Rural Gulf in American Political Behavior," *Political Behavior* 42 (2020): 1343–1368.

15. Katherine J. Cramer, *The Politics of Resentment: Rural Consciousness in Wisconsin and the Rise of Scott Walker* (Chicago: University of Chicago Press, 2016). Also see Robert Wuthnow, *The Left Behind: Decline and Rage in Rural America* (Princeton, NJ: Princeton University Press, 2018).

16. Dante J. Scala and Kenneth M. Johnson, "Political Polarization Along the Rural-Urban Continuum? The Geography of the Presidential Vote, 2000–2016," *Annals of the American Academy of Political and Social Science* 672 (2017): 162–184; Michael E. Shepherd, "Unhealthy Democracy: How Partisan Politics Is Killing Rural America," unpublished manuscript, 2021; Matthew D. Nelsen and Christopher D. Petsko, "Race and White Rural Consciousness," *Perspectives on Politics* 19, no. 4 (2021): 1205–1218; Gimpel et al. 2020. See Nicholas Jacobs and B. Kal Munis, "Place-Based Resentment in Contemporary U.S. Elections: The Individual Sources of America's Urban-Rural Divide," *Political Research Quarterly* 76, no. 3 (2022): 1102–1118; Kristin Lunz Trujillo, "Rural Identity as a Contributing Factor to Anti-Intellectualism in the U.S.," *Political Behavior* 44, no. 3 (2022): 1509–1532; Kristin Lunz Trujillo and Zack Crowley, "Symbolic Versus Material Concerns of Rural Consciousness in the United States," *Political Geography* 96 (2022): 102658; Jeffery Lyons and Stephen M. Utych, "You're Not from Here!: The Consequences of Urban and Rural Identities," *Political Behavior* 45 (2023): 75–101; B. Kal Munis, "Us over Here Versus Them over There . . . Literally: Measuring Place Resentment in American Politics," *Political Behavior* 44 (2020): 1057–1078.

17. For exceptions, see Jonathan A. Rodden, *Why Cities Lose* (New York: Basic Books, 2019), and Nicholas Jacobs and Daniel M. Shea, *The Rural Voter: The Politics of Place and the Disuniting of America* (New York: Columbia University Press, 2023).

18. Rodden 2019.

19. One important exception to the literature described above is Stephanie Ternullo's *How the Heartland Went Red: Why Local Forces Matter in an Age of Nationalized Politics* (Princeton, NJ: Princeton University Press, 2024). Ternullo offers insightful, in-depth analysis of how place has historically shaped and continues to shape partisan ties in three postindustrial small cities, with special attention given to the organizational makeup of such places.

20. As Paul Pierson and Eric Schickler, *Partisan Nation: The Dangerous New Logic of American Politics in a Polarized Era* (Chicago: University of Chicago Press, 2024), argue, when studying broad transformations—such as the rise of political polarization—there are good theoretical reasons to take a longer view of politics and to set one's sights on processes that unfold above the individual level. See also Paul Pierson, *Politics in Time: History, Institutions, and Social Analysis* (Princeton, NJ: Princeton University Press, 2004), and Schickler 2016.

21. A few scholars have considered public opinion differences in particular, but typically not with respect to policy issues. (For an important exception, see Jennifer Lin and Kristin Lunz Trujillo, "Are Rural Attitudes Just Republican?," *Political Science Research and Methods* 12, no. 3 [2023]: 1–10.) Instead, most focus on "in-group" or "out-group" attitudes such as resentment of urban dwellers, whether racial resentment (Matthew D. Nelsen and Christopher D. Petsko, "Race and White Rural Consciousness," *Perspectives on Politics* 19, no. 4 [2021]: 1205–1218), place-based resentment (Jacobs and Munis 2022), or other contributors to rural identity (Lunz Trujillo 2022). Consideration of policy issues has been more limited, for example, with study of how attitudes differ across the rural-urban continuum or in the South only, and in both instances at only one moment in time (e.g., Scala and Johnson 2017, 168–170; Hood and McKee 2022, 198–219).

22. Because we find that the rural-urban divide is mostly driven by non-Hispanic white Americans, most of our analysis here pertains to them. But policy differences among Black and Latino respondents are also negligible and in fact even smaller. See Brown et al. 2024.

23. These gaps mostly vanish when we account for other individual-level traits. Particularly noteworthy are the small differences when it comes to spending on "welfare," because social scientists have found that the term tends to elicit especially negative responses, conjuring racialized images of "welfare cheats" and unsympathetic poor people. Martin Gilens, *Why Americans Hate Welfare: Race, Media, and the Politics of Antipoverty Policy* (Chicago: University of Chicago Press, 1999).

24. Rodden 2019; David A. Hopkins, *Red Fighting Blue: How Geography and Electoral Rules Polarize American Politics* (New York: Cambridge University Press, 2017).

25. The importance of gun ownership to identity is examined by political scientist Matthew J. Lacombe in *Firepower: How the NRA Turned Gun Owners into a Political Force* (Princeton, NJ: Princeton University Press, 2021).

26. We combine several questions into an index, including whether "abortion should be made illegal in all circumstances"; whether policy should "prohibit abortions after the twentieth week of pregnancy"; and whether women should be able to "obtain an abortion as a matter of choice"; among others. Higher scores (scaled from 0 to 1) represent more conservative positions on abortion. See the appendixes for more details.

27. Using regression techniques to consider other characteristics of respondents, such as age, education level, and gender, we find that the differences are even smaller, at less than 5 percentage points. See the appendixes for more details.

28. Brown et al. 2024, 8.

29. We also looked at these trends over time, from roughly 2010 to 2020, and found that rural and urban white people tend to be moving in the same direction; that direction tends to be more liberal. See Brown et al. 2024.

30. The polarization literature underscores that issue positioning plays less of a role than group-based dynamics, as we discuss later. See Mason 2018. For additional evidence that "values" do not offer much explanatory value over the rural-urban political divide, see Kristin Lunz Trujillo and Jennifer Lin, "Real or Imagined? American Urban-Rural Differences in Political Values," *Political Research Quarterly*, Online First (2025), https://doi.org/10.1177/10659129251324464.

31. E.g., Elizabeth Sanders, *Roots of Reform: Farmers, Workers, and the American State, 1877–1917* (Chicago: University of Chicago Press, 1999); Laurence Goodwyn, *The Populist Moment: A Short History of the Agrarian Revolt in America* (New York: Oxford University Press, 1978).

32. Mary Summers, "From the Heartland to Seattle: The Family Farm Movement of the 1980s and the Legacy of Agrarian State Building," in *The Countryside in the Age of the Modern State*, ed. Catherine McNicol Stock and Robert D. Johnston (Ithaca, NY: Cornell University Press, 2001), 304–325.

33. A burgeoning literature has emerged examining the extent to which Americans have "sorted" into homogenous political communities. E.g., see Jacob R. Brown and Ryan D. Enos, "The Measurement of Partisan Sorting for 180 Million Voters," *Nature Human Behaviour* 5, no. 8 (2021): 998–1008. Yet as Gregory Martin and Steven Webster find, drawing on fine-grained publicly available voter registration data, "The estimated partisan bias in moving choices is on the order of five times too small to sustain the current geographic polarization of preferences." Gregory J. Martin and Steven W. Webster, "Does Residential Sorting Explain Geographic Polarization?," *Political Science Research and Methods* 8, no. 2 (2020): 215–231.

34. Christopher H. Achen and Larry M. Bartels, *Democracy for Realists: Whey Elections Do Not Produce Responsive Government* (Princeton, NJ: Princeton University Press, 2016), 4.

35. Achen and Bartels 2016, 18.

36. Kinder and Kam 2010, 8, 20.

37. Shanto Iyengar and Sean J. Westwood, "Fear and Loathing Across Party Lines: New Evidence on Group Polarization," *American Journal of Political Science* 59 (2015): 690–707; Donald Green, Bradley Palmquist, and Eric Schickler, *Partisan Hearts and Minds: Political Parties and the Social Identities of Voters* (New Haven, CT: Yale University Press, 2002); Christopher D. Johnston, Howard G. Lavine, and Christopher M. Federico, *Open Versus Closed: Personality, Identity, and the Politics of Identity* (New York: Cambridge University Press, 2017); Marc Hetherington and Jonathan Weiler, *Prius or Pickup?* (New York: HarperCollins, 2018); John R. Hibbing, Kevin B. Smith, and John R. Alford, *Predisposed: Liberals, Conservatives, and the Biology of Political Differences* (New York: Routledge, 2013).

38. Alan I. Abramovitz, *The Great Alignment: Race, Party Transformation, and the Rise of Donald Trump* (New Haven, CT: Yale University Press, 2018), 5–7.

39. Lilliana Mason, "'I Disrespectfully Agree': The Differential Effects of Partisan Sorting on Social and Issue Polarization," *American Journal of Political Science* 59 (2015): 128–145, esp. 129 and 130.

40. Estimates based on authors' calculations of the American National Election Studies (ANES) cumulative election file. See the appendixes for more details.

41. Richard Franklin Bensel, *The Political Economy of American Industrialization, 1877–1900* (New York: Cambridge University Press, 2000); Sanders 1999.

42. Seymour M. Lipset and Stein Rokkan, "Cleavage Structures, Party Systems, and Voter Alignments: An Introduction," in *Party Systems and Voter Alignments: Cross-National Perspectives*, ed. Seymour M. Lipset and Stein Rokkan (New York: Free Press, 1967), 1–65.

43. Seymour M. Lipset, "Some Social Requisites of Democracy: Economic Development and Political Legitimacy," *American Political Science Review* 53 (1959), 95–97.

44. Pierson and Schickler 2024, 17.

45. Jacob R. Brown and Ryan D. Enos, "The Measurement of Partisan Sorting for 180 Million Voters," *Nature Human Behavior* 5 (2021): 998–1008; Justin Frake, Reuben Hurst, and Max Kagan, "Partisan Segregation in the U.S. Workplace is Large and Rising" (February 7, 2024), http://dx.doi.org/10.2139/ssrn.4639165.

46. Lipset and Rokkan (1967, 10), call this a "functional" dimension, but we term it "political-economic," to highlight the interplay of policy change, political party development, and economic transformation.

47. Nicholas Short, "The Politics of the American Knowledge Economy," *Studies in American Political Development* 36, no. 1 (2022): 41–60; Judith Stein, *Pivotal Decade: How the United States Traded Factories for Finance in the Seventies* (New Haven, CT: Yale University Press, 2010); Sara Miles, *The Democrats and Silicon Valley: How to Hack a Party Line* (New York: Farrar, Straus and Giroux, 2001); Torben Iversen and David Soskice, *Democracy and Prosperity: Reinventing Capitalism Through a Turbulent Century* (Princeton, NJ: Princeton University Press, 2019).

48. Lipset and Rokkan (1967, 10, 12) term this a "territorial" dimension, which involves the "centralizing, standardizing, and 'rationalizing' machinery of the nation-state."

49. With respect to the latter, some scholars have suggested that the rising emphasis of so-called social issues in national politics might itself explain the rural-urban divide (e.g., Hopkins 2017; Rodden 2019), but we consider contestation over them to be only one manifestation of this broader phenomena of rural residents' perceptions of overbearing urban elites.

50. Tom Schaller and Paul Waldman, *White Rural Rage* (New York: Random House, 2024).

51. Suzanne Mettler and Robert C. Lieberman, *Four Threats: The Recurring Crises of American Democracy* (New York: St. Martin's, 2020).

52. For evidence of this argument, see Nelsen and Petsko 2021. Note that their analysis, however, rests on data from just recent years, raising the question of when anti-Black racism was activiated and why.

53. Jessica Trounstine, *Segregation by Design: Local Politics and Inequality in American Cities* (New York: Cambridge University Press, 2018); Richard Rothstein, *The Color of Law: A Forgotten History of How Our Government Segregated America* (New York: Norton, 2017).

54. We note that our analysis theoretically accords well with Stefano Bartolini and Peter Mair, *Identity, Competition, and Electoral Availability* (Cambridge, UK: Cambridge University Press, 1990), chapter 9, which emphasizes how cleavages can be forged by structural conditions (e.g., economic and population change), ideational factors (e.g., the development of rural consciousness or differentiation in worldviews by education), and organizational mobilization (e.g., evangelical churches).

55. The interview questionnaire appears at the end of the appendixes.

Chapter Two: Averting "Revolution in the Countryside"

1. Steven Ruggles, "The Decline of Intergenerational Coresidence in the United States, 1850 to 2000," *American Sociological Review* 72 no. 6 (2007): 964–989.

2. Kenneth S. Davis, *FDR: The New Deal Years, 1933–1937* (New York: Random House, 1979), 71.

3. Such instances may give the impression that today's rural-urban divide is nothing new. Certainly the late political scientist William Dean Burnham saw in such politics a manifestation of one of the major divides identified by Lipset and Rokkan, which he termed "the clash between 'community' and 'society,'" or a "local-cosmopolitan cleavage." He argues that "center-periphery conflict has been a major part of every realignment in the United States and was probably dominant in all but the last" in his book *Critical Elections and the Mainsprings of American Politics* (New York: Norton, 1970). See also Walter Dean Burnham, "Party Systems and the Political Process," in *American Party Systems*, ed. William N. Chambers and Walter Dean Burnham (New York: Oxford University Press, 1967), 283–285. Yet while those characterizations provide a helpful gloss for the ideas at stake in particular political conflicts, in fact rural and urban Americans were not neatly divided nationwide in their voting patterns. We distinguish who lives in rural and urban places by their actual voting patterns, and stand by our claim that never before has a national rural-urban cleavage divided Americans for several decades running, in voting in both presidential elections and now also congressional elections.

4. New Deal policies themselves varied in their visibility and traceability to government, which shaped their political effects. Brian T. Hamel, "Traceability and Mass Policy Feedback Effects," *American Political Science Review* (first view), published online August 1, 2024, https://doi.org/10.1017/S0003055424000704.

5. Paul Pierson and Eric Schickler, *Partisan Nation: The Dangerous New Logic of American Politics in a Polarized Era* (Chicago: University of Chicago Press, 2024).

6. Until recently, the winner-take-all, single-member districts facilitated the "big tent" nature of American political parties. Each party had to appeal to broad and diverse swaths of the country to win political power. Yet as several scholars have shown (see especially Jonathan A. Rodden, *Why Cities Lose: The Deep Roots of the Rural-Urban Political Divide* (New York: Basic Books, 2019), the recent nationalization of partisan politics has likely turned this logic on its head; the more centralized two-party system promotes polarization—including the rural-urban divide—by bundling issues and turning politics into an epic, winner-take-all battle, as opposed to the more consensual, multiparty proportional representation systems in Europe.

7. V. O. Key, *Politics, Parties, and Pressure Groups* (New York: Crowell, 1964), 315.

8. E. E. Schattschneider, *Party Government* (New Brunswick, NJ: Transaction Publishers, 2004 [1942]), 129–169.

9. Theodore J. Lowi, "Party, Policy, and Constitution in America," in Chambers and Burnham 1967, 253–254; Sidney M. Milkis, *Political Parties and Constitutional Government* (Baltimore: Johns Hopkins University Press, 1999), 14–15.

10. Pierson and Schickler 2024.

11. Burnham, "Party Systems and the Political Process," 282–283.

12. Elizabeth Sanders, *Roots of Reform: Farmers, Workers, and the American State, 1877–1917* (Chicago: University of Chicago Press, 1999), 101–111, 117–128; Gretchen Ritter, *Goldbugs and Greenbacks: The Antimonopoly Tradition and the Politics of Finance in America, 1865–1896* (New York: Cambridge University Press, 1997), 24, 47–49; James L. Sundquist, *Dynamics of the Party System: Alignment and Realignment of Political Parties in the United States*, rev. ed. (Washington, DC: Brookings Institution, 1983), 112–113.

13. Richard Valelly, "The Populist Scare of the 1890s—and the Aftermath That Changed American Populism," unpublished paper, 2017.

14. William Jennings Bryan, "A Cross of Gold," Democratic National Convention Address, American Rhetoric, July 8, 1898, www.americanrhetoric.com/speeches/williamjenningsbryan-1896dnc.htm.

15. Richard Franklin Bensel, *The Political Economy of American Industrialization, 1877–1900* (New York: Cambridge University Press, 2000), 285; United States Presidential Results by County (1896), Géographie Electorale, accessed March 1, 2025, http://geoelections.free.fr/USA/elec_comtes/1896.htm.

16. Burnham, "Party Systems and the Political Process," 285–286. Burnham refers to each of these, along with the "local-cosmopolitan" divide, as horizontal divisions, each distinct from class-based divides, which he terms "vertical" and which cut across these social or place-based ones.

17. Michael F. Holt, *Political Parties and American Political Development from the Age of Jackson to the Age of Lincoln* (Baton Rouge: Louisiana State University Press, 1992), 55–56.

18. U.S. Capitol History Society, "A Brief History of the Senate Committee on Agriculture, Nutrition, and Forestry," accessed March 1, 2025, https://capitolhistory.org/explore/historical-articles/a-brief-history-of-the-senate-committee-on-agriculture/; USDA, National Agricultural Library, "Celebrating 200 Years of the House Committee on Agriculture: 1820–2020," accessed March 1, 2025, www.nal.usda.gov/collections/exhibits/houseag200th/list.

19. Kenneth Finegold and Theda Skocpol, *State and Party in America's New Deal* (Madison: University of Wisconsin Press, 1995), 58.

20. Daniel P. Carpenter, *The Forging of Bureaucratic Autonomy: Reputations, Networks, and Policy Innovation in Executive Agencies, 1862–1928* (Princeton, NJ: Princeton University Press, 2001), 226–254.

21. Carpenter, *The Forging of Bureaucratic Autonomy*, 68–76, 123–143.

22. Elizabeth Sanders, *Roots of Reform: Farmers, Workers, and the American State 1877–1917* (Chicago: University of Chicago Press, 1999), 173–175.

23. U.S. Census, "Table 1. Urban and Rural Population: 1900 to 1990," October 1995, www2.census.gov/programs-surveys/decennial/tables/1990/1990-urban-pop/urpop0090.txt.

24. Iowa Data Center, "Urban and Rural Population for the U.S. and all States: 1900–2000," accessed March 1, 2025, www.iowadatacenter.org/datatables/UnitedStates/urusstpop19002000.pdf; Ruggles 2007.

25. Quote appears in Sundquist 1983, 187.

26. Sundquist 1983, 187–188; Richard Franklin Bensel, *Sectionalism and American Political Development: 1880–1980* (Madison: University of Wisconsin Press, 1984), 128–130, 137–146.

27. Sundquist 1983, 189.

28. Sarah T. Phillips, *This Land, This Nation: Conservation, Rural America, and the New Deal* (New York: Cambridge University Press, 2007), 23–24.

29. E.g., see Lizabeth Cohen, *Making A New Deal: Industrial Workers in Chicago* (New York: Cambridge University Press, 2008).

30. U.S. Census 1995, "Table 1."

31. Phillips 2007, 21, 63, 79, with quotations from Roosevelt on 21, 63; quotation from Phillips on 63.

32. Phillips 2007, 64, 65, 68–70.

33. David Darmofal, "The Political Geography of the New Deal Realignment," *American Politics Research* 36, no. 6, (2008): 943.

34. Phillips 2007, 76.

35. Phillips 2007, 79.

36. Phillips 2007, 78, 114, 116.

37. Wayne D. Rasmussen, "The New Deal Farm Programs: What They Were and Why They Survived," *American Journal of Agricultural Economics* 65, no. 5 (1983): 1159.

38. Phillips 2007, 126–127.

39. Paul H. Landis, "The New Deal and Rural Life," *American Sociological Review* 1, no. 4 (1963): 600.

40. Quote in William E. Leuchtenburg, *Franklin D. Roosevelt and the New Deal, 1932–1940* (New York: Harper and Row, 1963), 193.

41. Phillips 2007, 100, 23.

42. Leuchtenburg 1963, 157–158.

43. Quote in Leuchtenburg 1963, 158.

44. Leuchtenburg 1963, 60–61.

45. Robert Manduca, "Antitrust Enforcement as Federal Policy to Reduce Regional Economic Disparities," *Annals of the American Academy of Political and Social Science* 685, no. 1 (2019): 156–171; Ellis W. Hawley, *The New Deal and the Problem of Monopoly* (Princeton, NJ: Princeton University Press, 1966), 249–269.

46. Richard S. Kirkendall, *Social Scientists and Farm Politics in the Age of Roosevelt* (Ames: Iowa State University Press, 1966), 128–129.

47. Robert C. Lieberman, *Shifting the Color Line: Race and the American Welfare State* (Cambridge, MA: Harvard University Press, 1998); Suzanne Mettler, *Dividing Citizens: Gender and Federalism in New Deal Public Policy* (Ithaca, NY: Cornell University Press, 1998).

48. Phillips 2007, 195.

49. Mary Summers, "Recovering the Agricultural New Deal: Its Foundations, Legacies, and Losses," Nonsite.org, September 20, 2024, https://nonsite.org/recovering-the-agricultural-new -deal-its-foundations-legacies-and-losses/.

50. Rasmussen 1983, 1161.

51. Bensel 1984, 214–215.

52. Sidney Milkis, *The President and the Parties: The Transformation of the American Party System Since the New Deal* (New York: Oxford University Press, 1993), 56–57, 76.

53. Bensel 1984, 242–251.

54. John H. Fenton, *Midwest Politics* (New York: Holt, Rinehart, and Winston, 1957), 145.

55. M. V. Hood III and Seth C. McKee, *Rural Realignment in the Modern South: The Untold Story* (Columbia: University of South Carolina Press, 2022), 14.

56. Eric Schickler, *Racial Realignment: The Transformation of American Liberalism, 1932–1965* (Princeton, NJ: Princeton University Press, 2016), 253; Sundquist 1983, 225–227.

57. Sundquist 1983, 213.

58. Quotes in Bensel 1984, 194.

59. For evidence that the TVA in particular boosted political support for the Democratic Party, see Devin Caughey and Sara Chatfield, "Creating a Constituency for Liberalism: The Political Effects of the Tennessee Valley Authority," paper presented at the APSA Annual Meeting, Philadelphia, PA, September 1, 2016.

Chapter Three: Political-Economic Transformation

1. Katherine J. Cramer, *The Politics of Resentment: Rural Consciousness in Wisconsin and the Rise of Scott Walker* (Chicago: University of Chicago Press, 2016); Jennifer Sherman, *Dividing Paradise: Rural Inequality and the Diminishing American Dream* (Oakland: University of California Press, 2021). For a discussion of how economic inequality has grown in recent decades in rural counties, see Brian C. Thiede, Jaclyn L. W. Butler, David L. Brown, and Leif Jensen, "Income Inequality Across the Rural-Urban Continuum in the United States, 1970–2016," *Rural Sociology* 85, no. 4 (2020): 899–937.

2. We explore the prevalence and growth of public-sector jobs by place in chapter 8.

3. Robert Wuthnow, *The Left Behind: Decline and Rage in Rural America* (Princeton, NJ: Princeton University Press, 2018), 54.

4. For discussion of population loss from 2010 to 2020, see Kenneth M. Johnson, "Rural America Lost Population over the Past Decade for the First Time in History" (Carsey Research, National Issue Brief #160, Winter 2022), https://carsey.unh.edu/publication/rural-america-lost-population-over-past-decade-first-time-history.

5. Poverty estimates are generated using data from the Small Area Income and Poverty Estimates (SAIPE) Program. For more details, see the appendixes. We note, of course, that the official poverty rate does not account for the concentration of poverty that has happened in both rural and urban places. See Paul Jargowsky, "Concentration of Poverty in the New Millennium," Century Foundation, December 2013, https://tcf.org/content/report/concentration-of-poverty-in-the-new-millennium/; Tracey Farrigan and Timothy Parker, "The Concentration of Poverty Is a Growing Rural Problem," USDA, December 5, 2012, www.ers.usda.gov/amber-waves/2012/december/concentration-of-poverty/.

6. Per capita income estimates come from the Bureau of Economic Analysis (BEA). See the appendixes for more details. As we will see in chapter 8, rural incomes in recent decades have disproportionately been buoyed by public federal social transfers, meaning the difference in private income is likely greater.

7. In the case of policymakers we interviewed, we use their actual names if they gave us permission to do so, as is the case with Senator Bob Kerrey. Otherwise, we use pseudonyms or simply describe something about their role in public life.

8. Elizabeth A. Dobis and Jessica E. Todd, "The Most Rural Counties Have the Fewest Health Care Services Available," *Amber Waves*, USDA, 2020, www.ers.usda.gov/amber-waves/2022/august/the-most-rural-counties-have-the-fewest-health-care-services-available/; Michael E. Shepherd, "Unhealthy Democracy: How Partisan Politics is Killing Rural America," unpublished book manuscript, 2024.

9. Leah R. Abrams, Mikko Myrskyla, and Neil K Mehta, "The Growing Rural-Urban Divide in U.S. Life Expectancy," *International Journal of Epidemiology* 50, no. 6 (2021): 1970–1978.

10. Mara Casey Tieken, *Why Rural Schools Matter* (Chapel Hill: University of North Carolina Press, 2014), 158–159.

11. For a review, see Gerald Carlino and William R. Kerr, "Agglomeration and Innovation," in *Handbook of Regional and Urban Economics*, vol. 5, ed. Gilles Duranton, J. Vernon Henderson, and William C. Strange (New York: Elsevier, 2015), 349–404.

12. Enrico Moretti, *The New Geography of Jobs* (New York: Houghton Mifflin Harcourt, 2012).

13. Nicholas Short, "The Politics of the American Knowledge Economy," *Studies in American Political Development* 36, no. 1 (2022): 41–60.

14. Alfred Stepan and Juan J. Linz, "Comparative Perspectives on Inequality and the Quality of Democracy in the United States," *Perspectives on Politics* 9, no. 4 (2011): 841–856; Jacob S. Hacker, Alexander Hertel-Fernandez, Paul Pierson, and Kathleen Thelen, "The American Political Economy: A Framework and Agenda for Research," in *The American Political Economy: Politics, Markets, and Power*, ed. Jacob S. Hacker, Alexander Hertel-Fernandez, Paul Pierson, and Kathleen Thelen (Cambridge, UK: Cambridge University Press, 2021), 1–48.

15. Ganesh Sitaraman, Morgan Ricks, and Christopher Serkin, "Regulation and the Geography of Inequality," *Duke Law Journal* 70 (2021): 1763–1836; Philip Longman, "Bloom and Bust: Regional Inequality Is Out of Control," *Washington Monthly* November 8, 2015; Chase Foster and Kathleen Thelen, "Coordination Rights, Competition Law, and Varieties of Capitalism," *Comparative Political Studies* (2024), https://doi.org/10.1177/00104140241259461; Erik Peinert, "Monopoly Politics: Price Competition, Learning, and the Evolution of Policy Regimes," *World Politics* 75 no. 3 (2023): 566–607.

16. Sitaraman et al. 2021, 1786–1793; Andrew R. Goetz and Christopher J. Sutton, "The Geography of Deregulation in the US Airline Industry," *Annals of the Association of American Geographers* 87, no. 2 (1997): 238–263.

17. Quote appears in Sitaraman et al. 2021, 1783.

18. Richard Barton, "Upending the New Deal Regulatory Regime: Democratic Party Position Change on Financial Regulation," *Perspectives on Politics* 22 (2024): 391–408.

19. Christopher Witko, Jana Morgan, Nathan J. Kelly, and Peter K. Enns, *Hijacking the Agenda: Economic Power and Political Influence* (New York: Russell Sage, 2021); Anton Korinek and Jonathan Kreamer, "The Redistributive Effects of Financial Deregulation" (NBER Working Paper 19572, October 2013).

20. Richard Charles Barton, "Washington and Wall Street: The Democratic Party, Financial Deregulation, and the Remaking of the American Political Economy" (PhD diss., Cornell University, 2022), 70–71, 278–79.

21. Jodan Haedtler, "The 'Borking' of America," *Washington Monthly*, February 6, 2018.

22. Iowa PBS, "The Farm Crisis of the 1980s," accessed February 15, 2025, www.iowapbs.org /iowapathways/mypath/2422/farm-crisis-1980s.

23. Barry J. Barnett, "The U.S. Farm Financial Crisis of the 1980s," *Agricultural History* 74, no. 2 (2000): 366–380.

24. Estimates from the USDA. See Jerome M. Stam, Steven R. Koenig, Susan E. Bentley, and H. Frederick Gale Jr., *Farm Financial Stress, Farm Exits, and Public Sector Assistance to the Farm Sector in the 1980s* (USDA, Economic Research Service, 1991). See Mary Summers, "From the Heartland to Seattle: The Family Farm Movement of the 1980s and the Legacy of Agrarian State Building," in *The Countryside in the Age of the Modern State: Political Histories of Rural America*, ed. Catherine McNicol Stock and Robert D. Johnston (Ithaca, NY: Cornell University Press, 2001): 304–325.

25. James M. MacDonald, "Tracking the Consolidation of U.S. Agriculture," *Applied Economies Perspectives and Policy* 42, no. 3 (2020): 361–379.

26. James M. MacDonald and Robert A. Hoppe, "Examining Consolidation in U.S. Agriculture," *Amber Waves*, USDA, Economic Research Service, 2018, https://www.ers.usda.gov/amber -waves/2018/march/examining-consolidation-in-us-agriculture/.

27. David A. Domina and Robert C. Taylor, "The Debilitating Effects of Concentration in Markets Affecting Agriculture," *Drake Journal of Agriculture Law* 15 (2010): 81.

28. Cody McCracken, "Old MacDonald Had a Trust: How Market Consolidation in the Agricultural Industry, Spurred on by a Lack of Antitrust Law Enforcement, Is Destroying Small Agricultural Producers," *William and Mary Business Law Review* 13, no. 2 (2022), https://scholarship.law.wm.edu/cgi/viewcontent.cgi?article=1233&context=wmblr; Domina and Taylor 2010.

29. MacDonald and Hoppe 2018.

30. William A. Galston and Haren J. Baehler, *Rural Development in the United States: Connecting Theory, Practice, and Possibilities* (Washington, DC: Island Press, 1995), 93–94.

31. Carolyn Dimitri, Anne Effland, and Neilson Conklin, "The 20th Century Transformation of U.S. Agriculture and Farm Policy," USDA, Economic Research Service, 2005, https://www.ers.usda.gov/publications/pub-details/?pubid=44198.

32. Michael Stewart Foley, "'Everyone Was Pounding on Us': Front Porch Politics and the American Farm Crisis of the 1970s and 1980s," *Sociology Lens* 28, no. 1 (2014): 104–124; James N. Leiker, "Rage of the Rural Minority: The High Plains Farm Crisis and Farmer Activism in Colorado and Kansas," *Great Plains Quarterly* 39, no. 3 (2019): 265–289; Summers 2001.

33. Leiker 2019, 216–217; Jenny Barker Devine and David D. Vail, "Sustaining the Conversation: The Farm Crisis and the Midwest," *Middle West Review* 2, no. 1 (2015): 3.

34. E.g., see, Paul Lasley, ed., *Beyond the Amber Waves of Grain: An Examination of Social and Economic Restructuring in the Heartland* New York: Routledge, 1995); Pamela Riney-Kehrberg, "Children of the Crisis: Farm Youth in Troubled Times," *Middle West Review* 2, no. 1 (2015): 11–25; Pamela Riney-Kehrberg, *When a Dream Dies: Agriculture, Iowa, and the Farm Crisis of the 1980s* (Lawrence: University Press of Kansas, 2022).

35. Associated Press, "Farmer Suicide Rate Swells in 1980s, Study Says," *New York Times*, October 14, 1991, https://www.nytimes.com/1991/10/14/us/farmer-suicide-rate-swells-in-1980-s-study-says.html; Michael J. Belyea and Linda M. Lobao, "Psychosocial Consequences of Agricultural Transformation: The Farm Crisis and Depression," *Rural Sociology* 55, no. 1 (1990): 58–75; Suzanne T. Ortega, David R. Johnson, Peter G. Beeson, and Betty J. Craft, "The Farm Crisis and Mental Health: A Longitudinal Study of the 1980s," *Rural Sociology* 59, no. 4 (1994): 598–619.

36. Richard S. Krannich, Brian Gentry, Al E. Luloff, and Peter G. Robertson, "Resource Dependency in Rural America: Continuities and Change," in *Rural America in a Globalizing World*, ed. Connor Bailey, Leif Jensen, and Elizabeth Ransom (Morgantown: West Virginia University Press, 2014), 208–225.

37. William R. Freudenburg, "Addictive Economies: Extractive Industries and Vulnerable Localities in a Changing World Economy," *Rural Sociology* 57, no. 3 (1992): 305–332; J. Tom Mueller, "Natural Resource Dependence and Rural American Economic Prosperity from 2000 to 2015," *Economic Development Quarterly* 36, no. 3 (2022): 160–176; Robert Todd Perdue and Gregory Pavela, "Addictive Economies and Coal Dependency: Methods of Extraction and Socioeconomic Outcomes in West Virginia, 1997–2009," *Organization and Environment* 25, no. 4 (2012): 368–384.

38. Reed W. Walker, "Environmental Regulation and Labor Reallocation: Evidence from the Clean Air Act," *American Economic Review* 101, no. 3 (2011): 442–447; W. Reed Walker, "The Transitional Costs of Sectoral Reallocation: Evidence from the Clean Air Act and the Workforce," *Quarterly Journal of Economics* 128, no. 4 (2013): 1787–1835.

39. Marc A. C. Hafstead and Roberton C. Williams III, "Jobs and Environmental Regulation," *Environmental and Energy Policy and the Economy* 1 (2020): 192–240.

40. Arlie Russell Hochschild, *Strangers in Their Own Land: Anger and Morning on the American Right* (New York: New Press, 2016). It is worth noting that the first two decades of the

twenty-first century have seen a renaissance of sorts in rural extractive industries, particularly through a boom in domestic onshore oil and gas production. Yet growing research suggests that such industries produce limited growth at best, are limited to only a minor share of rural counties, and ultimately do not address the underlying structural constraints facing rural communities (Mueller 2022). See also Adam Mayer, Shawn K. Olson-Hazboun, and Stephanie Malin, "Fracking Fortunes: Economic Well-Being and Oil and Gas Development Along the Urban-Rural Continuum," *Rural Sociology* 83, no. 3 (2017): 532–567.

41. Sarah Low, "Manufacturing Is Relatively More Important to the Rural Economy than the Urban Economy," USDA, Economic Research Service, 2021, https://www.usda.gov/media/blog /2017/09/12/manufacturing-relatively-more-important-rural-economy-urban-economy.

42. It is well known that deindustrialization in major urban areas from the 1950s through the 1970s, and the resulting loss of jobs, was followed by greater poverty rates, unemployment, and even political demobilization, particularly among Black Americans. Thomas J. Sugrue, *The Origins of the Urban Crisis: Race and Inequality in Postwar Detroit* (Princeton, NJ: Princeton University Press, 1998); William Julius Wilson, *When Work Disappears: The World of the New Urban Poor* (New York: Knopf, 1996).

43. William A. Testa, "Trends and Prospects for Rural Manufacturing" (Regional Economic Issues Working Paper Series, no. 92-12, 1992), 21, fig. 4.

44. Nelson Lichtenstein and Judith Stein, *A Fabulous Failure: The Clinton Presidency and the Transformation of American Capitalism* (Princeton, NJ: Princeton University Press, 2023), 219.

45. Jiwon Choi, Ilyana Kuziemko, Ebonya Washington, and Gavin Wright, "Local Economic and Political Effects of Trade Deals: Evidence from NAFTA," *American Economic Review* 114, no. 6 (2024): 1540–1575; Gavin Wright, "Voting Rights, Deindustrialization, and Republican Ascendancy in the South" (Working Paper No. 135, Institute for New Economic Thinking, 2020), https://www.ineteconomics.org/uploads/papers/WP_135-Wright-VOTING-RIGHTS .pdf.

46. Quote in Lichtenstein and Stein 2023, 225.

47. James McCannan, *"Afta" NAFTA: The Free Trade Debate and Party Politics in the United States* (Instituto Technologico de Estudios Superiores de Monterrey, Mexico, 1999).

48. Rand Wilson, "Winning Lessons from the NAFTA Loss," *Labor Research Review* 1, no. 22 (1994): 29, 30–31; Kay Tamara and Rhonda Evans, *Trade Battles: Activism and the Politicization of International Trade Policy* (New York: Oxford University Press, 2018), 74, 102; Jennifer Merolla, Laura B. Stephenson, Carole J. Wilson, and Elizabeth J. Zechmeister, "Globalization, Globalizacion, Globalisation: Public Opinion and NAFTA," *Law and Business Review of the Americas* 11, nos. 3 and 4 (2005): 568.

49. McCannan 1999, 106.

50. Choi et al. 2024.

51. The fuller story of NAFTA's ratification appears in George W. Grayson, *The North American Free Trade Agreement: Regional Community and the New World Order* (New York: University Press of America, 1995), 195–221; Lichtenstein and Stein 2023, 219–240.

52. Our analysis is based on voting data from the website Voteview and the share of the rural population from each lawmakers' district as defined by the U.S. Census. See the appendixes for more details.

53. From 1994 to 2008, China accounted for over three-quarters of the growth in manufacturing value-added generated by low- and middle-income countries, as its share of manufacturing output within this group rose from 15 percent to 44 percent. Gordon H. Hanson, "The Rise of Middle Kingdoms: Emerging Economies in Global Trade," *Journal of Economic Perspectives* 26, no. 2 (2012): 41–64.

54. David H. Autor, David Dorn, and Gordon H. Hanson, "The China Shock: Learning from Labor-Market Adjustment to Large Changes in Trade," *Annual Review of Economics* 8, no. 1 (2016): 205–240.

55. Justin R. Pierce and Peter K. Schott, "Trade Liberalization and Mortality: Evidence from US Counties," *American Economic Review: Insights* 2, no. 1 (2020): 47–64.

56. Jong Hyung Lee, David C. Wheeler, Emily B. Zimmerman, Anika L. Hines, and Derek A. Chapman, "Urban–Rural Disparities in Deaths of Despair: A County-Level Analysis 2004–2016 in the US," *American Journal of Preventive Medicine* 64, no. 2 (2023): 149–156.

57. See Andrew M. Isserman and James Westervelt, "1.5 Million Missing Numbers: Overcoming Employment Suppression in County Business Patterns Data," *International Regional Science Review* 29, no. 3 (2006): 311–335.

58. Figure 3.3 relies on data from the U.S. Department of Labor and the BEA. See the appendixes for further details.

59. Wuthnow 2018.

60. Low 2021.

61. Adam Scavette, "The Role of Manufacturing in the Rural Fifth District," Federal Reserve Bank of Richmond, 2022, https://www.richmondfed.org/research/regional_economy/regional_matters/2022/rm_04_28_2022_manufacturing.

62. Amy Glasmeier and Priscilla Salant, "Low-Skill Workers in Rural America Face Permanent Job Loss" (Carsey Institute, Policy Brief No. 2, 2006), https://files.eric.ed.gov/fulltext/ED536116.pdf.

63. Gary P. Green, "Deindustrialization of Rural America: Economic Restructuring and the Rural Ghetto," *Local Development and Society* 1, no. 1 (2020): 15–25.

64. Nicholas Short, "Antitrust Deregulation and the Politics of the American Knowledge Economy," unpublished manuscript, 2022; Torben Iversen and David Soskice, *Democracy and Prosperity: Reinventing Capitalism Through a Turbulent Century* (Princeton, NJ: Princeton University Press, 2019).

65. Short, "Antitrust Deregulation," 2022.

66. Wuthnow 2018. To be sure, this is also a problem in postindustrial urban areas without thriving economies (Moretti 2012). But note that the pull is stronger from rural areas, where even fewer opportunities exist.

67. Moretti 2012.

68. Arne L. Kalleberg, *Good Jobs, Bad Jobs: The Rise of Polarized and Precarious Employment Systems in the United States, 1970s–2000s* (New York: Russell Sage Foundation, 2011); Amy K. Glasmeier and Marie Howland, *From Combines to Computers: Rural Services and Development in the Age of Information Technology* (Albany: State University of New York Press, 1995); Alexander C. Vias and Peter B. Nelson, "Changing Livelihoods in Rural America," in *Population Change and Rural Society*, ed. William A. Kandel and David L. Brown (Dordrecht: Springer, 2006), 75–102.

69. Galston and Baehler 1995.

70. Sherman 2021.

71. For work on NAFTA, see, e.g., Choi et al. 2024; Wright 2020. For research on the "China Shock," see David Autor, David Dorn, Gordon Hanson, and Kaveh Majlesi, "Importing Political Polarization? The Electoral Consequences of Rising Trade Exposure," *American Economic Review* 110, no. 10 (2020): 3139–3183. For research examining deindustrialization more broadly, see Leonardo Baccini and Stephen Weymouth, "Gone for Good: Deindustrialization, White Voter Backlash, and US Presidential Voting," *American Political Science Review* 115, no. 2 (2021): 550–567.

72. One important exception is Christian Cox, Derek A. Epp, and Michael E. Shepherd, "Access to Healthcare and Voting: The Case of Hospital Closures in Rural America," *American*

Political Science Review (2024), https://doi.org/10.1017/S0003055424001035. Note, however, that their analysis is restricted to rural areas, so it is unclear if hospital closures have a uniquely politicizing impact in rural areas relative to urban ones.

73. For a detailed discussion of our modeling strategy, see the appendixes.

74. Wuthnow 2018, 48, 54.

75. Rafaela Dancygier, Sirus H. Dehdari, David D. Laitin, Moritz Marbach, and Kare Vernby, "Emigration and Radical Right Populism," paper presented at the annual meeting of the American Political Science Association, Montreal, Canada, September 15–17, 2022; Paulina Patana, "Residential Constraints and the Politics Geography of the Populist Radical Right: Evidence from France," *Perspectives on Politics* 20, no. 3 (2022): 842–859.

76. For a discussion on inequality *between* metro areas, see Moretti 2012. For more on inequality *within* urban counties, see Thiede et al. 2020.

77. Justin Gest, *The New Minority: White Working Class Politics in an Age of Immigration and Inequality* (Oxford, UK: Oxford University Press, 2016).

78. Jonathan Rodden, "'Red America' Is an illusion: Postindustrial Towns Go for Democrats," *Washington Post*, Monkey Cage, February 14, 2017, https://www.washingtonpost.com/news/monkey-cage/wp/2017/02/14/red-america-is-an-illusion-postindustrial-towns-go-for-democrats-heres-the-data/.

79. Jacob S. Hacker, Amelia Malpas, Paul Pierson, and Sam Zacher, "Bridging the Blue Divide: The Democrats' New Metro Coalition and the Unexpected Prominence of Redistribution," *Perspectives on Politics* 22, no. 3 (2023): 609–629.

80. Ismail K. White and Chryl N. Laird, *Steadfast Democrats: How Social Forces Shape Black Political Behavior* (Princeton, NJ: Princeton University Press, 2020).

Chapter Four: Overbearing Elites and Rural Resistance

1. David Autor, "Skills, Education, and the Rise of Earnings Inequality Among the 'Other 99 Percent,'" *Science* 344, no. 6186 (May 2014): 843–851; Lisa Barrow and Cecilia Rouse, "Is College Still Worth It?," *The Economists' Voice* 2 no. 4 (2005); Christopher R. Tamborini, Chang-Hwan Kim, and Arthur Sakamoto, "Education and Lifetime Earnings in the United States," *Demography* 52 (2015): 1383–1407.

2. E.g., Sidney Verba, Kay Lehman Schlozman, and Henry Brady, *Voice and Equality: Civic Voluntarism in American Politics* (Cambridge, MA: Harvard University Press, 1995).

3. On the rising educational divide and how it relates to partisan voting, see Matthew Grossman and David A. Hopkins, *Polarized by Degrees: How the Diploma Divide and Culture War Are Dividing American Politics* (New York: Cambridge University Press, 2024); Herbert P. Kitschelt and Philipp Rehm, "Secular Partisan Realignment in the United States: The Socioeconomic Reconfiguration of White Partisan Support Since the New Deal Era," *Politics and Society* 47, no. 3 (2019): 425–479; Joshua Zingher "Diploma Divide: Educational Attainment and the Realignment of the American Electorate," *Political Research Quarterly* 75 no. 2 (2022): 263–277.

4. Our findings about the relationship between education and party support cohere with those of Grossman and Hopkins 2024 and Kitschelt and Rehm 2019; we, however, highlight the important role of place.

5. Lily Geismer, *Don't Blame Us: Suburban Liberals and the Transformation of the Democratic Party* (Princeton, NJ: Princeton University Press, 2015), 1–2.

6. Kitschelt and Rehm 2019; Sam Zacher, "Polarization of the Rich: The New Democratic Allegiance of Affluent Americans and the Politics of Redistribution," *Perspectives on Politics* 22 (2024): 338–356. Kitschelt and Rehm focus on white people only and examine the interaction

of income and education; Zacher focuses primarily on income and does not restrict his analysis to non-Hispanic whites.

7. On the growing competition between the parties, see Frances E. Lee, *Insecure Majorities: Congress and the Perpetual Campaign* (Chicago: University of Chicago Press, 2016).

8. Related arguments (some of which stress income) are made by Torben Iverson and David Soskice, *Democracy and Prosperity: Reinventing Capitalism Through a Turbulent Century* (Princeton, NJ: Princeton University Press, 2019), 225–226, and more generally, Ronald F. Inglehart, *Cultural Revolution* (New York: Cambridge University Press, 2018), 73–199.

9. Nicholas Short, "Antitrust Deregulation and the Politics of the American Knowledge Economy," unpublished paper, 2022, https://nick-short.com/research/#Antitrust-Project.

10. See Kitschelt and Rehm 2019.

11. Kitschelt and Rehm 2019. To be sure, important variation existed within each party, and social issues have always been part of American politics. There is also little reason to think these issues can be distinguished. For example, "Dixiecrats" and Blue Dog Democrats were racially and economically conservative yet remained in the Democratic Party for the better part of the twentieth century.

12. David A. Hopkins, *Red Fighting Blue: How Geography and Electoral Rules Polarize American Politics* (New York: Cambridge University Press, 2017), 114–127, 193–212; Jonathan A. Rodden, *Why Cities Lose: The Deep Roots of the Urban-Rural Political Divide* (New York: Basic Books, 2019), 84–90.

13. Michael E. Shepherd comes to a similar conclusion in "Unhealthy Democracy: How Partisan Politics Is Killing Rural America," unpublished book manuscript, 2024, chap. 4.

14. In a similar vein, Katherine Cramer has argued that such so-called social issues and distributive issues are often intertwined and can hardly be distinguished. Katherine Cramer, "Putting Inequality in Its Place: Rural Consciousness and the Power of Perspective," *American Political Science Review* 106, no. 3 (2012): 517–532.

15. Seymour M. Lipset and Stein Rokkan, "Cleavage Structures, Party Systems, and Voter Alignments: An Introduction," in *Party Systems and Voter Alignments: Cross-National Perspectives*, ed. Seymour M. Lipset and Stein Rokkan (New York: Free Press, 1967), 41, 23.

16. Robert Dahl, *How Democratic Is the American Constitution?* (New Haven, CT: Yale University Press, 2003), 43–44; Jonathan Rodden, "Comparative Federalism and Decentralization: On Meaning and Measurement," *Comparative Politics* 36, no. 4 (2004): 481–500. The Bill of Rights did not come to apply to citizens generally until it gradually became incorporated under the Fourteenth Amendment, through a series of Supreme Court decisions handed down from the 1890s through the 1960s.

17. Suzanne Mettler, *Dividing Citizens: Gender and Federalism in New Deal Public Policy* (New York: Cornell University Press, 1998); Robert C. Lieberman, *Shifting the Color Line: Race and the American Welfare State* (Cambridge, MA: Harvard University Press, 1998).

18. David Karol, *Red, Green, and Blue: The Partisan Divide on Environmental Issues* (New York: Cambridge University Press, 2019), 37; Grossman and Hopkins 2024, chap. 7.

19. While Democrats were more likely to indicate such issues to be important to them than were Republicans, nonetheless majorities of both parties, in both rural and urban areas, agreed. Robert Bonnie, Emily Pechar Diamond, and Elizabeth Rowe, *Understanding Rural Attitudes Toward the Environment and Conservation in America* (Nicholas Institute for Environmental Policy Solutions, Duke University, 2020).

20. Bonnie et al. 2020, 10.

21. Emily P. Diamond, "Understanding Rural Identities and Environmental Policy Attitudes in America," *Perspectives on Politics* 21, no. 2 (2023): 510.

22. Will Atwater, "NC Recognized as the Birthplace of the Environmental Justice Movement," NC Health News, August 26, 2022, www.northcarolinahealthnews.org/2022/08/26/nc-recognized-as-the-birthplace-of-the-environmental-justice-movement/; "3 Plead Guilty to Dumping PCBs in North Carolina," *New York Times*, June 5, 1979.

23. Northern Michigan Environmental Action Council, "Line 5," accessed March 4, 2025, www.nmeac.org/line_5.

24. Shi-Ling Hsu, "Scale Economies, Scale Externalities: Hog Farming and the Changing American Agricultural Industry," *Oregon Law Review* 94 (2015): 23–65.

25. Christiana Ochoa, Kacey Cook, and Hanna Weil, "Deals in the Heartland: Renewable Energy Projects, Local Resistance, and How Law Can Help," *Minnesota Law Review* 107, no. 3 (2023): 1067–1082.

26. These findings are derived from analysis of the Cooperative Election Study Policy Preferences dataset, similar to that conducted in chapter 1. They are consistent with Bonnie et al. 2020, 26, who find that a majority of rural dwellers consider it either "very important" or "pretty important" for "the United States to take action to reduce climate change," albeit with urban voters at a higher rate than rural ones, 69 percent compared to 54 percent.

27. Lawrence Susskind, Jungwoo Chun, Alexander Gant, Chelsea Hodgkins, Jessica Cohen, and Sarah Lohmar, "Sources of Opposition to Renewable Energy Projects in the United States," *Energy Policy* 165 (2022): 1–17. An inventory of opposed projects in all states appears in Hillary Aidun, Jacob Elkin, Radhika Goyal, et al., *Opposition to Renewable Energy Facilities in the United States: March 2022 Edition* (Sabin Center for Climate Change Law, Columbia University Law School, 2022), https://scholarship.law.columbia.edu/sabin_climate_change/186/.

28. Ochoa, Cook, and Weil 2023, 1063.

29. Maria A. Petrova, "NIMBYism Revisited: Public Acceptance of Wind Energy in the United States," *WIREs Climate Change* 4 (2013): 575–601.

30. Susskind et al. 2022, 5–12; Roberta Nilson and Richard C. Stedman, "Reacting to the Rural Burden: Understanding Opposition to Utility-Scale Solar Development in Upstate New York," *Rural Sociology* 88, no. 2 (2023): 1–28.

31. Nilson and Steadman 2023, 5.

32. Ochoa, Cook, and Weil (2023): 1095–1096, 1097, 1099.

33. Nilson and Steadman (2023): 17–18; Susskind, et al (2022): 9.

34. Susskind, et al. (2022): 9.

35. Ochoa, Cook, and Weil 2023, 1100; Nilson and Stedman 2023, 19; Roopali Phadke, "Public Deliberation and the Geographies of Wind Justice," *Science as Culture* 22, no. 2 (2013): 248.

36. Nilson and Stedman 2023, 19; Phadke 2013, 248.

37. Samantha Gross, *Renewables, Land Use, and Local Opposition in the United States* (Foreign Policy at Brookings, January 2020), www.brookings.edu/articles/renewables-land-use-and-local-opposition-in-the-united-states/. The transmission of renewable energy—to the mostly urban areas where concentrated population means demand will be highest—also presents greater challenges than the transport of fossil fuels.

38. Not all rural people oppose such developments; often production-oriented farmers are the most accepting of them, being accustomed to thinking about alternative ways to earn income so that they can maintain their land. Conservatives, too, offer less resistance, because they affirm the rights of private property owners to use their land as they wish. Douglas L. Bessette and Sarah B. Mills, "Farmers vs. Lakers: Agriculture, Amenity, and Community in Predicting Opposition to United States Wind Energy Development," *Energy Research and Social Science* 72 (2021): 1–11.

39. To be clear, these procedures are used fairly often by governors, especially with controversial legislation. Cuomo used such procedures twenty-nine times in 2011 and five times in 2012; his predecessors, both Democrats and Republicans, used such procedures far more often.

Robert J. Spitzer, "New York State and the New York SAFE Act: A Case Study in Strict Gun Laws," *Albany Law Review* 78, no. 2, (2014/2015): 751.

40. James B. Jacobs and Zoe Fuhr, *The Toughest Gun Control Law in the Nation: The Unfulfilled Promise of New York's SAFE Act* (New York: New York University Press, 2019), 9–15, 27, 32.

41. Jacobs and Fuhr 2019, 10, 17–20.

42. Spitzer 2014/2015, 763–765, 757.

43. Only a handful of states acted at the time, and most of them already had stronger-than-typical gun regulations. See Philip J. Cook and Kristin A. Goss, *The Gun Debate: What Everyone Needs to Know* (New York: Oxford University Press, 2014), 48, 108, 211.

44. Cook and Goss 2014, 169–171.

45. Rick Karlin, "SAFE Act Opponents Declare Victory," *Times Union* (Albany), November 5, 2014, https://blog.timesunion.com/capitol/archives/224071/safe-act-opponents-declare-victory/.

46. James A. Morone, *Hellfire Nation: The Politics of Sin in American History* (New Haven, CT: Yale University Press, 2003), 1–28.

47. V. O. Key, *Southern Politics in State and Nation* (New York: Knopf, 1949), 517–522, 649, 653.

48. Matthew D. Nelsen and Christopher Petsko, "Race and White Rural Consciousness," *Perspectives on Politics* 19, no. 4 (2021): 1205–1218, for example, find that those who identify as rural tend to associate urban dwellers not only with being elites, but also with stereotypically Black attributes, suggesting that "urban" itself is racialized. Also see Ryan Dawkins, Zoe Nemerever, Kal Munis, et al., "Place, Race, and the Geographic Politics of White Grievance," *Political Behavior* 46 (2024): 1813–1835; Nicholas F. Jacobs and Daniel M. Shea, *The Rural Voter: The Politics of Place and the Disuniting of America* (New York: Columbia University Press, 2023), chap. 8.

49. Katherine Schaeffer, "The Changing Face of Congress in 8 Charts," Pew Research Center, February 7, 2023, https://www.pewresearch.org/short-reads/2023/02/07/the-changing-face-of-congress.

50. Tali Mendelberg, *The Race Card: Campaign Strategy, Implicit Messages, and the Norm of Equality* (Princeton, NJ: Princeton University Press, 2001).

51. Christopher Parker and Matt Barreto, *Change They Can't Believe In: The Tea Party and Reactionary Politics in America* (Princeton, NJ: Princeton University Press, 2013).

52. E.g., see Adam M. Enders and Jamil S. Scott, "The Increasing Racialization of American Electoral Politics, 1988–2016," *American Politics Research* 47, no. 2 (2019), 275–303; Michael Tesler, *Post-Racial or Most-Racial? Race and Politics in the Obama Era* (Chicago: University of Chicago Press, 2016), 144–164.

53. Lilliana Mason and Nathan P. Kalmoe, "Roots, Risks, and Reward of Mass Polarization," in *Democratic Resilience: Can the United States Withstand Rising Polarization?*, ed. Robert C. Lieberman, Suzanne Mettler, and Kenneth M. Roberts (New York: Cambridge University Press, 2022), 190–193.

54. Mason and Kalmoe 2022, 190–193.

55. Diana C. Mutz, *Winners and Losers: The Psychology of Foreign Trade* (Princeton, NJ: Princeton University Press, 2021); Ashley Jardina, *White Identity Politics* (New York: Cambridge University Press, 2019); John Sides, Michael Tesler, and Lynn Vavreck, *Identity Crisis: The 2016 Presidential Campaign and the Battle for the Meaning of America* (Princeton, NJ: Princeton University Press, 2018); Justin Gest, *The New Minority: White Working Class Politics in an Age of Immigration and Inequality* (Oxford, UK: Oxford University Press, 2016).

56. American National Election Studies, *ANES Time Series Cumulative Data File: Codebook* (2022), 572, https://electionstudies.org/wp-content/uploads/2022/09/anes_timeseries_cdf_codebook_var_20220916.pdf.

57. Responses are also strongly correlated with the traditional racial resentment score ($r = .66$, $p = .001$).

58. We note that the roughly 9 percentage point gap amounts to rural respondents selecting, on average, an answer that is roughly one degree more conservative, on a scale of one to seven, than the average urban respondent.

59. Jacobs and Shea 2023, chap. 8; Nelson and Petsko 2021; Dawkins et al. 2023.

60. Arlie Russell Hochschild, *Strangers in Their Own Land: Anger and Mourning on the American Right* (New York: The New Press, 2016), 165.

61. Daniel T. Lichter, "Immigration and the New Racial Diversity in Rural America," *Rural Sociology* 77, no. 1 (2012): 3–35; Daniel T. Lichter, Domenico Parisi, Michael C. Taquino, and Steven Michael Grice, "Residential Segregation in New Hispanic Destinations: Cities, Suburbs, and Rural Communities Compared," *Social Science Research* 39 (2010): 215–230.

62. Percentages here are based on authors' calculation of data from the U.S. Census Bureau. See the appendixes for more details.

63. Jardina 2019, 100; Leonardo Baccini and Stephen Weymouth, "Gone for Good: Deindustrialization, White Voter Backlash, and US Presidential Voting," *American Political Science Review* 115, no. 2 (2021): 550–567.

Chapter Five: How Parties and Organizations Matter

1. This component, though not identified by Lipset and Rokkan, is included in the process of cleavage formation by Stefano Bartolini and Peter Mair, *Identity, Competition, and Electoral Responsibility, 1885–1985* (Lanham, MD: ECPR Press, 2007).

2. E.g., Alexander Hertel-Fernandez, *State Capture: How Conservative Activists, Big Businesses, and Wealthy Donors Reshaped the American States—and the Nation* (New York: Oxford University Press, 2019); Theda Skocpol and Vanessa Williamson, *The Tea Party and the Remaking of Republican Conservatism* (New York: Oxford University Press, 2012); Jake Rosenfeld, *What Unions No Longer Do* (Cambridge, MA: Harvard University Press, 2014); Matthew J. Lacombe, *Firepower: How the NRA Turned Gun Owners into a Political Force* (Princeton, NJ: Princeton University Press, 2021); Stephanie Ternullo, *How the Heartland Went Red: Why Local Forces Matter in an Age of Nationalized Politics* (Princeton, NJ: Princeton University Press, 2024).

3. Steven J. Rosenstone and John Mark Hansen, *Mobilization, Participation, and Democracy in America* (New York: Macmillan, 1993), 26–36, 177–188, 196–209.

4. V. O. Key Jr., *The Responsible Electorate: Rationality in Presidential Voting, 1936–1960* (Cambridge, MA: Harvard University Press, 1966), 2–3.

5. William A. Gamson and Andre Modigliani (1987) as quoted in Thomas E. Nelson and Donald R. Kinder, "Issue Frames and Group Centrism in American Public Opinion," *Journal of Politics* 58 (1996): 1055–1078, quote on 1057. In her study of three small Rust Belt cities, Stephanie Ternullo convincingly shows that local organizations—such as churches, nonprofits, and labor unions—can help define how citizens view similar problems in very different ways and, in turn, act on them divergently in the political arena, supporting Republicans in some instances and Democrats in others. Ternullo, *How the Heartland Went Red*.

6. John R. Zaller, *The Nature and Origins of Mass Opinion* (New York: Cambridge University Press, 1992).

7. Suzanne Mettler, *The Government-Citizen Disconnect* (New York: Russell-Sage, 2018), 134–135.

8. Frances E. Lee, *Insecure Majorities: Congress and the Perpetual Campaign* (Chicago: University of Chicago Press, 2016).

9. E.g., Matthew Levendusky, "How Does Local TV News Change Viewers' Attitudes? The Case of Sinclair Broadcasting," *Political Communication* 39, no. 1 (2022): 23–28; Elliott Ash, Sergio Galletta, Matteo Pinna, and Chris Warshaw, "From Viewers to Voters: Tracing Fox News' Impact on American Democracy," SSRN, October 31, 2024, http://dx.doi.org/10.2139/ssrn.5005797.

10. E.g., James Druckman, "Political Preference Formation: Competition, Deliberation, and the (Ir)relevance of Framing Effects," *American Political Science Review* 84 (2004): 671–686; M. Wojcieszak, S. de Leeuw, E. Menchen-Trevino, S. Lee, K. Huang-Isherwood, B. Weeks, "No Polarization from Partisan News: Over-Time Evidence from Trace Data," *International Journal of Press/Politics* 28 (2023): 601–626; Markus Prior, "Media and Political Polarization," *Annual Review of Political Science* 16 (2013): 101–127.

11. E.g., Markus Prior, *Post-Broadcast Democracy: How Media Choice Increases Inequality in Political Involvement and Polarizes Elections* (New York: Cambridge University Press, 2007); Danny Hayes and Jennifer L. Lawless, *News Hole: The Demise of Local Journalism and Political Engagement* (New York: Cambridge University Press, 2021), chap. 4.

12. Didi Kuo, *The Great Retreat: How Political Parties Should Behave—and Why They Don't* (New York: Oxford University Press, 2025).

13. Christopher H. Achen and Larry M. Bartels, *Democracy for Realists: Why Elections Do Not Produce Responsive Government* (Princeton, NJ: Princeton University Press, 2016).

14. Anthony Downes, *An Economic Theory of Democracy* (New York: Harper, 1957).

15. Daniel Schlozman, *When Movements Anchor Parties: Electoral Alignments in American History* (Princeton, NJ: Princeton University Press, 2015), chap. 2.

16. Bartolini and Mair, *Identity, Competition, and Electoral Availability*, 200.

17. Kuo 2025.

18. David R. Mayhew, *Placing Parties in American Politics: Organization, Electoral Settings, and Government Activity in the Twentieth Century* (Princeton, NJ: Princeton University Press, 1986), 1, 200; Paul Pierson and Eric Schickler, *Partisan Nation: The Dangerous New Logic of American Politics in a Polarized Era* (Chicago: University of Chicago Press, 2024), 93–94.

19. Robert Putnam, *Bowling Alone: The Collapse and Revival of American Community* (New York: Simon and Schuster, 2000); Theda Skocpol, *Diminished Democracy: From Membership to Management in American Civic Life* (Norman: University of Oklahoma Press, 2003).

20. Putnam 2000, 37–40.

21. Mayhew 1986, 7; Joel H. Sibley, "From 'Essential to the Existence of Our Institutions' to 'Rapacious Enemies of Honest and Responsible Government': The Rise and Fall of American Political Parties, 1790–2000," in *The Parties Respond*, 4th ed., ed. L. Sandy Maisel (Cambridge, MA: Westview, 2002), 1–18.

22. Daniel J. Galvin, *Presidential Party Building: Dwight D. Eisenhower to George W. Bush* (Princeton, NJ: Princeton University Press, 2010), 22.

23. Galvin 2010, 27; also see 23.

24. Schlozman 2015, 3–5.

25. David Greenstone, *Labor in American Politics* (New York: Alfred A Knopf, 1969); Taylor E. Dark, *The Unions and the Democrats: An Enduring Alliance* (Ithaca, NY: Cornell University Press, 1969).

26. E.g., Michele F. Margolis, "The Religious Sort: The Causes and Consequences of the Religiosity Gap in America," in *Democratic Resilience*, ed. Robert C. Lieberman, Suzanne Mettler, and Kenneth M. Roberts (New York: Cambridge University Press, 2022), 226–245; Mark J. Rozell and Clyde Wilcox, eds., *God at the Grassroots 2016: The Christian Right in American Politics* (New York: Rowman and Littlefield, 2018); Lacombe 2021; Michael Zoorab and Theda Skocpol, "The Overlooked Organizational Basis of Trump's 2016 Victory," in *Upending American Politics,*

ed. Theda Skocpol and Caroline Tervo (New York: Oxford University Press, 2020), 79–100; Hertel-Fernandez 2019; Theda Skocpol, "The Elite and Popular Roots of Contemporary Republican Extremism," in Skocpol and Tervo 2020.

27. Bartolini and Mair 2007, 212–249.

28. Lilliana Mason, "I Disrespectfully Agree: The Differential Effects of Partisan Sorting on Social and Issue Polarization," *American Journal of Political Science* 59, no. 1, (2015): 128–145.

29. Lawrence R. Jacobs, *Democracy Under Fire: Donald Trump and the Breaking of American History* (New York: Oxford University Press, 2022), 174–180; Schlozman 2015.

30. Paul Frymer and Jacob M. Grumbach, "Labor Unions and White Racial Politics," *American Journal of Political Science* 65 (2021): 225–240.

31. John H. Aldrich, *Why Parties? A Second Look* (Chicago: University of Chicago Press, 2011), 169–201; Kathleen Bawn, Martin Cohen, David Karol, Seth Masket, Hans Noel, and John Zaller, "A Theory of Political Parties: Groups, Policy Demands and Nominations in American Politics," *Perspectives on Politics* 10, no. 3 (2012): 571–597.

32. Michael Kazin, *What It Took to Win: A History of the Democratic Party* (New York: Farrar, Straus, and Giroux, 2022); Lily Geismer, *Left Behind: The Democrats' Failed Attempt to Solve Inequality* (New York: Public Affairs, 2022); Nelson Lichtenstein and Judith Stein, *A Fabulous Failure: The Clinton Presidency and the Transformation of American Capitalism* (Princeton, NJ: Princeton University Press, 2023).

33. Jacob S. Hacker, Amelia Malpas, Paul Pierson, and Sam Zacher, "Bridging the Blue Divide: The Democrats' New Metro Coalition and the Unexpected Prominence of Redistribution," *Perspectives on Politics* 22, no. 3 (2024): 609–629.

34. Richard B. Freeman and James L. Medoff, *What Do Unions Do?* (New York: Basic Books, 1985).

35. For a review, see Trevor E. Brown, "The New Politics (and Political Science) of Workers' Rights," *Political Science Quarterly* (2004), https://doi.org/10.1093/psquar/qqae055.

36. Lainey Newman and Theda Skocpol, *Rust Belt Union Blues: Why Working-Class Voters Are Turning Away from the Democratic Party* (New York: Columbia University Press, 2023), 50, 51–59.

37. Schlozman 2015, chaps. 3 and 6.

38. Alexander Hertel-Fernandez, "Collective Action, Law, and the Fragmented Development of the American Labor Movement," in *The American Political Economy: Politics, Markets, and Power*, ed. Jacob S. Hacker, Alexander Hertel-Fernandez, Paul Pierson, and Kathleen Thelen (New York: Cambridge University Press, 2022), 105.

39. Jake Rosenfeld, *What Unions No Longer Do* (Cambridge, MA: Harvard University Press, 2014).

40. Barry T. Hirsch, David A. Macpherson, and William E. Even, "Union Membership and Coverage Database from the CPS," UnionStats.com, 2024, www.unionstats.com.

41. David Macdonald, "Labor Unions and White Democratic Partisanship," *Political Behavior* 43 (2021): 859–879.

42. James Feigenbaum, Alexander Hertel-Fernandez, and Vanessa Williamson, "From the Bargaining Table to the Ballot Box: Political Effect of Right-to-Work Laws" (NBER Working Paper 24259, January 2018).

43. Bureau of Labor Statistics, U.S. Department of Labor, "Union Members—2024," news release, January 28, 2025, https://www.bls.gov/news.release/pdf/union2.pdf.

44. For an alternative view, see Nicholas F. Jacobs and Daniel M. Shea, *The Rural Voter: The Politics of Place and the Disuniting of America* (New York: Columbia University Press, 2023), chap. 3.

45. Lisa McGirr, *Suburban Warriors: The Origins of the New Right* (Princeton, NJ: Princeton University Press, 2001); Kevin M. Kruse, *White Flight: Atlanta and the Making of Modern Conservatism* (Princeton, NJ: Princeton University Press, 2005), 251–266.

46. Matt Grossman and David A. Hopkins, *Asymmetric Politics: Ideological Republicans and Group Interest Democrats* (New York: Oxford University Press, 2016), 285–292.

47. Alan Grant, "The Term Limitation Movement in the United States," *Parliamentary Affairs* 48, no. 3 (1995): 515–530.

48. Jennie Drage Bowser and Gary Moncrief, "Term Limits in State Legislatures," in *Institutional Change in American Politics: The Case of Term Limits*, ed. Karl T. Kurtz, Bruce E. Cain, and Richard G. Niemi (Ann Arbor: University of Michigan Press, 2007), 16–17.

49. Michael Harris, "Policy Termination: The Case of Term Limits in Michigan," *International Journal of Public Administration* 24 (2001): 331.

50. National Conference of State Legislatures, "The Term-Limited States," updated August 3, 2023, www.ncsl.org/about-state-legislatures/the-term-limited-states.

51. Andrew B. Hall, "Partisan Effects of Legislative Term Limits," *Legislative Studies Quarterly* 39, no. 3 (2014): 407. See also Scott R. Meinke and Edward B. Hasecke, "Term Limits, Professionalization, and Partisan Control in U.S. State Legislatures," *Journal of Politics* 65, no. 3 (2003): 898–908. Another study found that Republicans gained less than predicted from term limits: Richard J. Powell, "Minority Party Gains Under State Legislative Term Limits," *State Politics and Policy Quarterly* 8, no. 1 (2008): 32–47.

52. Some evidence also suggests that term limits led to an increase in polarization and undermined representation. See Susan M. Miller, Jill Nicholson-Crotty, and Sean Nicholson-Crotty, "Reexamining the Institutional Effects of Term Limits in US State Legislatures," *Legislative Studies Quarterly* 36, no. 1 (2011), 72–3, 90; Rick Farmer and Thomas Little, "Legislative Power in the Buckeye State: The Revenge of Term Limits," in *Legislating Without Experience*, ed. Rick Farmer, Christopher Z. Mooney, Richard J. Powell, and John C. Green (London: Lexington Books, 2007), 43–54; Michael P. Olson and Jon C. Rogowski, "Legislative Term Limits and Polarization," *Journal of Politics* 82, no. 2 (2020): 573.

53. Marjorie J. Spruill, *Divided We Stand: The Battle over Women's Rights and Family Values That Polarized American Politics* (New York: Bloomsbury, 2017), 75–83, 84–85.

54. Clyde Wilcox and Carin Robinson, *Onward Christian Soldiers? The Religious Right in American Politics* (Oxfordshire, UK: Taylor and Francis Group, 2010), 42–48; Schlozman 2015, 6; Spruill 2017, 299, 303.

55. Schlozman 2015, 90–94. When the *Roe v. Wade* decision was first handed down in 1973, evangelical leaders did not speak out against it. Only later in the decade would they recognize that it could serve as a powerful political issue that would unite them with many Catholics into a more powerful conservative political force. Schlozman 2015, 102–104. Also see Deal W. Hudson, *Onward, Christian Soldiers: The Growing Political Power of Catholics and Evangelicals in the United States* (New York: Threshold, 2008).

56. Schlozman 2015, 8.

57. Schlozman 2015, 199, 90.

58. Russell Shorto, "What's Their Real Problem with Gay Marriage? It's the Gay Part," *New York Times Magazine*, June 19, 2005.

59. David D. Kirkpatrick, "Conservatives Using Issue of Gay Unions as a Rallying Tool," *New York Times*, February 8, 2004.

60. David E. Campbell and J. Quin Monson, "The Religion Card: Gay Marriage and the 2004 Presidential Election," *Public Opinion Quarterly* 72, no. 3 (2008): 403.

61. Charles S. Bullock III, Susan A. MacManus, Jeremy D. Mayer, and Mark J. Rozell, *The South and the Transformation of US Politics* (New York: Oxford University Press, 2019), chap. 5; Wilcox

and Robinson 2010, 49–54; Schlozman 2015, 217–218 ; Sue O'Connell, "The Money Behind the 2004 Marriage Amendments," FollowTheMoney.org, January 27, 2006, www.followthemoney.org /research/institute-reports/the-money-behind-the-2004-marriage-amendments.

62. We use data from the U.S. Religious Census and the Association of Statisticians of American Religious Bodies (ASARB 2020). Specifically, we find that evangelical congregations in urban areas range from three per ten thousand people to roughly five over time, while they range from eleven to thirteen in rural counties.

63. A formal *suest*-based Wald test of difference of coefficients shows this development to be statistically significant.

64. It was originally called the National Right to Life Committee. Robert N. Karrer, "The National Right to Life Committee: Its Founding, Its History, and the Emergence of the Pro-Life Movement Prior to *Roe v. Wade*," *Catholic Historical Review* 97, no. 3 (2011): 538, 552.

65. National Right to Life, "History," accessed February 17, 2025, www.nrlc.org/about/history/.

66. Karrer 2011, 556.

67. Ideally, we would have access to nationwide data on such groups. Unfortunately, no such catalogue exists.

68. See the appendixes for further discussion of data collection and how we generated these estimates.

69. Ziad W. Munson, *The Making of Pro-Life Activists: How Social Movement Mobilization Works* (Chicago: University of Chicago Press, 2002), 20, 44.

70. Thomas M. Carsey and Geoffrey C. Layman, "Changing Sides or Changing Minds? Party Identification and Policy Preferences in the American Electorate," *American Journal of Political Science* 50, no. 2 (2006): 464–477.

71. Lacombe 2021, 4–6.

72. Robert J. Spitzer, *The Politics of Gun Control*, 7th ed. (New York: Routledge, 2018), 130–131.

73. Lacombe 2021, 12–13.

74. Lacombe 2021, 15–16.

75. Jennifer Carlson, *Citizen-Protectors: The Everyday Politics of Guns in an Age of Decline* (New York: Oxford University Press, 2015), 5, 21–22.

76. Philip J. Cook and Kristin A. Goss, *The Gun Debate: What Everyone Needs to Know* (New York: Oxford, 2014), 192–195.

77. Spitzer 2018, 130–131.

78. On how the NRA mobilized people to oppose gun control legislation, see Lacombe 2021, chap. 7.

79. Lacombe 2021.

80. Skocpol and Tervo 2020; Skocpol and Williamson 2012; Lacombe 2021.

81. Galvin 2010, 33.

Chapter Six: Polarizing Congress by Place

1. Sarah Binder, "The Dysfunctional Congress," *Annual Review of Political Science* 18 (2015): 85–101; Suzanne Mettler, "The Policyscape and the Challenges of Contemporary Politics to Policy Maintenance," *Perspectives on Politics* 14 (2016): 369–390. For a counterpoint, see David R. Mayhew, *Divided We Govern: Party Control, Lawmaking, and Investigations, 1946–2002*, 2nd ed. (New Haven, CT: Yale University Press, 2005).

2. Nolan McCarty, Keith T. Poole, and Howard Rosenthal, *Polarized America: The Dance of Ideology and Unequal Riches* (Cambridge, MA: MIT Press, 2006), 25–26; Frances E. Lee, *Beyond Ideology: Politics, Principles, and Partisanship in the US Senate* (Chicago: University of Chicago

Press, 2009); Frances E. Lee, *Insecure Majorities: Congress and the Perpetual Campaign* (Chicago: University of Chicago Press, 2016); Danielle M. Thomsen, *Opting Out of Congress: Partisan Polarization and the Decline of Moderate Candidates* (New York: Cambridge University Press, 2017). Others look at institutional change, e.g., the impact of greater party homogeneity on the tools provided to leadership, etc. John Aldrich, *Why Parties? A Second Look* (Chicago: University of Chicago Press, 2011); David W. Rohde, *Parties and Leaders in the Postreform House* (Chicago: University of Chicago Press, 1991); Barbara Sinclair, *Party Wars: Polarization and the Politics of National Policy Making* (Norman: University of Oklahoma Press, 2006); Sean M. Theriault, *Party Polarization in Congress* (New York: Cambridge University Press, 2008).

3. McCarty, Poole, and Rosenthal 2006, 44–54. The literature is vast, so we list only a few examples. Earl Black and Merle Black, *The Rise of Southern Republicans* (Cambridge, MA: Harvard University Press, 2002); Byron E. Shafer and Richard Johnston, *The End of Southern Exceptionalism: Class, Race, and Partisan Change in the Postwar South* (Cambridge, MA: Harvard University Press, 2006); Charles S. Bullock III, Donna R. Hoffman, and Ronald Keith Gaddie, "The Consolidation of the White Southern Congressional Vote," *Political Research Quarterly* 58, no. 2 (2005): 231–243; David Lublin, *The Republican South: Democratization and Partisan Change* (Princeton, NJ: Princeton University Press, 2004); Glenn Feldman, ed., *Painting Dixie Red: When, Where, Why, and How the South Became Republican* (Gainesville: University Press of Florida, 2011); Seth C. McKee, *Republican Ascendance in Southern US House Elections* (Boulder, CO: Westview Press, 2010); Charles S. Bullock III and Mark J. Rozell, eds., *The New Politics of the Old South*, 3rd ed. (Lanham, MD: Rowman and Littlefield, 2007).

4. M. V. Hood III and Seth C. McKee, *Rural Republican Realignment in the Modern South* (Columbia: University of South Carolina Press, 2022), chaps. 5 and 7.

5. One book that does explore this is David A. Hopkins, *Red Fighting Blue: How Geography and Electoral Rules Polarize American Politics* (New York: Cambridge University Press, 2017). See 193–212 on rural-urban dynamics.

6. The Americans with Disabilities Act passed the House on May 22, 1990, with only 20 members voting against it, including 3 Democrats and 17 Republicans. The Clean Air Act Amendments passed the House on May 23, 1990, with only 21 votes in opposition, including 5 Democrats and 16 Republicans. The Civil Rights Act of 1991 passed the House on November 7, 1991, with 251 Democrats in favor and only 5 opposed, and 127 Republicans in favor and only 33 opposed.

7. "Sweeping Law for Rights of Disabled," *CQ Almanac 1990*, 46th ed. (Washington, DC: Congressional Quarterly, 1991), 447–461. On final passage, in the Senate the vote was 91–6, and in the House 377–28.

8. Vote retrieved from the Voteview database, accessed March 8, 2025, https://voteview.com/.

9. Voteview, accessed March 8, 2025.

10. Voteview, accessed March 8, 2025.

11. Mettler 2016.

12. The White House, "The Clinton Presidency: Timeline of Major Actions," U.S. National Archives, accessed March 7, 2025, https://clintonwhitehouse5.archives.gov/WH/Accomplishments/eightyears-02.html.

13. "Special Report: 1993 Budget-Reconciliation Summary: The 1993 Reconciliation Act: How It Was Written," *CQ Weekly*, December 18, 1993, 5–21.

14. Ted Nordhaus, "Getting Real on Climate Change," *American Prospect*, November 22, 2008; Dawn Erlandson, "The BTU Tax Experience: What Happened and Why It Happened," *Pace Environmental Law Review* 12, no. 1 (1994), 178–184.

15. "Special Report: 1993 Budget-Reconciliation Summary."

16. David W. Brady, John F. Cogan, and Douglas Rivers, *How the Republicans Captured the House: An Assessment of the 1994 Midterm Elections* (Stanford, CA: Hoover Institution, Stanford

University, 1995); Gary C. Jacobson, "The 1994 House Elections in Perspective," in *Midterm: The Elections of 1994 in Context*, ed. Philip A. Klinkner (Boulder, CO: Westview Press, 1996), 12–16.

17. David Obey, *Raising Hell for Justice: The Washington Battles of a Heartland Progressive* (Madison: University of Wisconsin Press), 286.

18. Nordhaus 2008.

19. "Senate OKs Omnibus Anti-Crime Bill," *CQ Almanac 1993*, 49th ed. (Washington, DC: Congressional Quarterly, 1994), 293–300.

20. Robert J. Spitzer, *The Politics of Gun Control*, 7th ed. (New York: Routledge, 2018), 196.

21. William J. Eaton, "Assault Weapons Ban Clears House by Slim Margin," *Los Angeles Times*, May 6, 1994.

22. Spitzer 2018 196–199.

23. Jacobson 1996, 13–17.

24. John T. Woolley, "The 2022 Midterm Elections: What the Historical Data Suggest," American Presidency Project, August 30, 2022, www.presidency.ucsb.edu/analyses/the-2022 -midterm-elections-what-the-historical-data-suggest.

25. Richard L. Burke, "The 1994 Elections: The Overview GOP Wins Control of Senate and Makes Big Gains in House; Pataki Denies Cuomo 4th Term," *New York Times*, November 9, 1994.

26. Elaine C. Kamarck, "Assessing Howard Dean's Fifty State Strategy and the 2006 Midterm Elections," *The Forum* 4, no. 3 (2006), https://doi.org/10.2202/1540-8884.1141.

27. William Douglas and Kate Irby, "Shutdown, Health Care, Budget: How Moderate House Democrats Will Influence the Party," *McClatchyDC*, January 23, 2019.

28. Marianna Sotomayor, "Dwindling Blue Dog Democrats Look to Stage a Comeback for Moderates," *Washington Post*, August 8, 2023.

29. Jacob S. Hacker and Paul Pierson, *Off Center: The Republican Revolution and the Erosion of American Democracy* (New Haven, CT: Yale University Press, 2006); Larry M. Bartels, *Unequal Democracy: The Political Economy of the New Gilded Age* (New York: Russell Sage Foundation, 2008), chaps. 6–8; Jacob S. Hacker, Suzanne Mettler, and Dianne Pinderhughes, "Inequality and Public Policy," in *Inequality and American Democracy*, ed. Lawrence R. Jacobs and Theda Skocpol (New York: Russell Sage, 2005), 156–213.

30. This count includes two Independents who caucused with the Democrats. In fact, Democrats only had all sixty senators in place for three months, because the Minnesota election of Al Franken took eight months to resolve, and then after Democrat Ted Kennedy (MA) died, Republican Scott Brown won his seat in a special election in January 2010.

31. David Blumenthal and James A. Morone, *The Heart of Power: Health and Politics in the Oval Office* (Berkeley: University of California Press, 2009), 31–56.

32. Blumenthal and Morone 2009, 68–98.

33. Micah Hartman, Anne Martin, Olivia Nuccio, and Aaron Catlin, "Health Spending Growth at a Historic Low in 2008," *Health Affairs* 29, no. 1 (2010), https://doi.org/10.1377 /hlthaff.2009.0839; Robin A. Cohen and Michael E. Martinez, "Health Insurance Coverage: Early Release of Estimates from the National Health Interview Study, 2008," Centers for Disease Control and Prevention, last reviewed November 6, 2015, www.cdc.gov/nchs/data/nhis /earlyrelease/insur200906.htm#.

34. Suzanne Mettler, *The Submerged State* (Chicago: University of Chicago Press, 2011), 2.

35. Lawrence R. Jacobs and Theda Skocpol, *Health Care Reform and American Politics: What Everyone Needs to Know* (New York: Oxford University Press, 2010), 104; on timeline, 11–16.

36. Molly Ball, "How Nancy Pelosi Saved the Affordable Care Act," *Time*, May 6, 2020; Heather Caygle and John Bresnahan, "Pelosi Battles GOP to Save Obamacare—and Her Legacy," *Politico*, March 8, 2017.

37. Jacobs and Skocpol 2010, 56, 67–75.

38. John Nichols, "Refreshing Our Stupak Memory," National Public Radio, April 13, 2010.

39. Richard Simon, "Michigan Congressman Who Led Anti-Abortion Fight on Health Care Is Stepping Down," *Los Angeles Times*, April 10, 2010.

40. Jacobs and Skocpol 2010, 100, 118–119.

41. Simon 2010; Emily Wagster Pettus, "Hurled Bricks, Threats Surround Health Overhaul," Associated Press, March 25, 2010.

42. Carl Hulse and Jeff Zeleny, "In Blow to Democrats, Influential Congressman Will Retire After Four Decades," *New York Times*, May 5, 2010.

43. "Rep. David R. Obey (D)," in *CQ's Politics in America 2010 (the 111th Congress)*, ed. C. McCutcheon and C. L. Lyons (Washington, DC: CQ Press, 2009).

44. Obey's DW-Nominate score was −0.45. In the 111th Congress, he voted more liberally than 85 percent of the House and 74 percent of his Democratic peers. He was replaced by Republican Sean Duffy, who had a voting score of 0.51, more conservative than 77 percent of the House and 51 percent of his GOP peers in the 116th Congress. Republican Tom Tiffany succeeded Duffy, with a score of 0.64, more conservative than 88 percent of the House and 77 percent of his Republican peers.

45. Jennifer Tolbert, Patrick Drake, and Anthony Damico, "Key Facts About the Uninsured Population," Kaiser Family Foundation, December 28, 2023, www.kff.org/uninsured/issue-brief /key-facts-about-the-uninsured-population/.

46. David Blumenthal, Sara R. Collins, and Elizabeth Fowler, "The Affordable Care Act at 10 Years: What's the Effect on Health Care Coverage and Access?," Commonwealth Fund, February 26, 2020, www.commonwealthfund.org/publications/journal-article/2020/feb/aca-at -10-years-effect-health-care-coverage-access.

47. Suzanne Mettler, *Degrees of Inequality: How the Politics of Higher Education Sabotaged the American Dream* (New York: Basic Books, 2014), 145–158.

48. Daniel Carpenter, "The Contest of Lobbies and Disciplines: Financial Politics and Regulatory Reform," in *Reaching for a New Deal*, ed. Theda Skocpol and Lawrence R. Jacobs (New York: Russell Sage, 2011), 139–188; Christopher Witko, Jana Morgan, Nathan J. Kelly, and Peter K. Enns, *Hijacking the Agenda: Economic Power and Political Influence* (New York: Russell Sage, 2021), 176–217. Although the vote was not quite as close as the ACA and reconciliation votes, still it likely would not have passed without the support of rural Democrats. In the House, the first vote on Dodd-Frank in 2009 produced just 223 votes in favor (61 from the two most rural quintiles), and the 2010 vote on the conference report generated 232 votes (64 from the two most rural quintiles). In the Senate, Dodd-Frank had to withstand a filibuster. The final vote on July 15, 2010, was 60–39, with 2 Democrats voting against it.

49. Mettler 2011, 1–3.

50. Sarah Binder, "A Violent Mob Overran Congress. 3 Takeaways for the Weeks Ahead," *Washington Post*, January 11, 2021.

Chapter Seven: How the Rural-Urban Divide Shapes Political Power

1. Bowers gave numbers that differed slightly from the official ones; we have corrected them here.

2. Katherine J. Cramer, *The Politics of Resentment: Rural Consciousness in Wisconsin and the Rise of Scott Walker* (Chicago: University of Chicago Press, 2016); Nicholas Jacobs and B. Kal Munis, "Place-Based Resentment in Contemporary U.S. Elections: The Individual Sources of America's Urban-Rural Divide," *Political Research Quarterly* 76, no. 3 (2022): 1102–1118; B. Kal Munis, "Us over Here Versus Them over There . . . Literally: Measuring Place Resentment in American Politics," *Political Behavior* 44 (2020): 1057–1078.

3. Robert Dahl, *Who Governs? Democracy and Power in an American City* (New Haven, CT: Yale University Press, 1961); Harold Lasswell, *Politics: Who Gets What, When, How* (New York: Whittlesey House, McGraw-Hill, 1936).

4. Robert A. Dahl, *How Democratic Is the American Constitution?* (New Haven, CT: Yale University Press, 2003).

5. Some scholars and pundits who focus on rural politics have suggested the divide actually does not matter all that much for the distribution of power. Political scientists Nicholas K. Jacobs and Daniel Shea argue that "the overrepresentation of rural areas in the U.S. Senate and Electoral College is exaggerated. Or, simply put, rural areas' representation has not fundamentally changed, even as the evidence for a growing rural-urban divide has." What matters most, they contend, is the massive transformation in politics in rural areas: "The real power behind the rural vote is political, not institutional." See Nicholas Jacobs and Daniel M. Shea, *The Rural Voter: The Politics of Place and the Disuniting of America* (New York: Columbia University Press, 2023), 56–58. In a similar vein, journalist Sarah Melotte has argued that rural voters are not advantaged by the Senate and the Electoral College because most rural people do not live in states bolstered by the small-state bias (Sarah Melotte, "Analysis: Rural Voters Don't Wield Disproportionate Power in Senate, Electoral College," *Daily Yonder*, May 31, 2024, https://dailyyonder.com/analysis-rural-voters-dont-wield-disproportionate-power-in-senate-electoral-college/2024/05/31/). While it is true that the institutions themselves have not changed, the massive political changes underlying them have shifted their impact. And while it is the case that the majority of rural Americans live in highly populated, more urban states, such as New York, Texas, and California, elections for the U.S. president and Senate are not conducted via a national popular referendum of all citizens.

6. U.S. Census Bureau, "Population 1790 to 1990," accessed March 5, 2022, www2.census.gov/programs-surveys/decennial/1990/tables/cph-2/table-4.pdf.

7. U.S. Census Bureau, "United States Summary: 2010 Census of Population and Housing," table 12, 2012, https://www2.census.gov/library/publications/decennial/2010/cph-2/cph-2-1.pdf.

8. For further discussion of how the Census defines rural, see the appendixes.

9. Alfred Stepan and Juan J. Linz, "Comparative Perspectives on Inequality and the Quality of Democracy in the United States," *Perspectives on Politics* 9, no. 4 (2011): 841–856; Dahl 2003, 49.

10. Frances E. Lee and Bruce I. Oppenheimer, *Sizing Up the Senate: The Unequal Consequences of Equal Representation* (Chicago: University of Chicago Press, 1999).

11. Authors' analysis of the 2020 U.S. Census.

12. We find that the U.S. Census Bureau's measure for share of rural population and total population are correlated at about 0.5.

13. As of 1980, 26 percent of the entire U.S. population was rural, while the median state (Kansas) was 33 percent rural. As of 1990, 25 percent of the American population was considered rural, while the median state (Pennsylvania) was 31 percent rural. The 2000 census counted the American population as 21 percent rural, while the median state (Georgia) was 26 percent rural. The 2010 census considered 19 percent of the U.S. population to be rural, and the median state (Kansas) was 26 percent rural.

14. Neil Malhotra and Connor Raso, "Racial Representation and U.S. Senate Apportionment," *Social Science Quarterly* 88, no. 4 (2007): 1038–1048; John D Griffin, "Senate Apportionment as a Source of Political Inequality," *Legislative Studies Quarterly* 31, no. 3 (2006): 405–432.

15. Stepan and Linz 2011, 844–845.

16. The authors also show that the Senate currently underrepresents metropolitan or urban areas, Black Americans and Latinos, and union members. Richard Johnson and Lisa L. Miller,

"The Conservative Policy Bias of US Senate Malapportionment," *Political Science and Politics* 56, no. 1 (2023): 10–17, esp. table 1.

17. Joshua Holzer, "Most US States Don't Have a Filibuster—Nor Do Many Democratic Countries," The Conversation, March 2, 2021, https://theconversation.com/most-us-states -dont-have-a-filibuster-nor-do-many-democratic-countries-156093.

18. Roy Edroso, "Scott Brown Wins Mass. Race, Giving GOP 41–59 Majority in the Senate," *Village Voice*, January 20, 2010.

19. Authors' estimates of cloture motions from the U.S. Senate. See United States Senate, "Cloture Motions" (table), accessed February 19, 2025, www.senate.gov/legislative/cloture /clotureCounts.htm.

20. See Theda Skocpol and Lawrence R. Jacobs, *Reaching for a New Deal: Ambitious Governance, Economic Meltdown, and Polarized Politics in Obama's First Two Years* (New York: Russell Sage, 2011), particularly chaps. 7, 8, and 9.

21. Thomas Piketty, Emmanuel Saez, and Gabriel Zucman, "Distributional National Accounts: Methods and Estimates for the United States," *Quarterly Journal of Economics* 133, no. 2 (2018): 553–609.

22. Peter K. Enns, Nathan J. Kelly, Jana Morgan, Thomas Volscho, and Christopher Witko. "Conditional Status Quo Bias and Top Income Shares: How US Political Institutions Have Benefited the Rich," *Journal of Politics* 76, no. 2 (2014): 289–303.

23. Steven M. Teles, *The Rise of the Conservative Legal Movement: The Battle for Control of the Law* (Princeton, NJ: Princeton University Press, NJ, 2008).

24. David Montgomery, "Conquerors of the Courts," *Washington Post Magazine*, January 2, 2019.

25. K. Sabeel Rahman and Kathleen Thelen, "The Role of the Law in the American Political Economy," in *The American Political Economy*, ed. Jacob Hacker, Alex Hertel-Fernandez, Paul Pierson, and Kathleen Thelen (New York: Cambridge University Press, 2021), 78. See also Brian Highsmith, Maya Sen, and Kathleen Thelen, "Off-Balance: How US Courts Privilege Conservative Policy Outcomes," *Perspectives on Politics* (2025): 1–13.

26. Steven G Calabresi and James T. Lindgren, "Term Limits for the Supreme Court: Life Tenure Reconsidered," *Harvard Journal of Law and Public Policy* 29, no. 3 (2006): 769–877.

27. Nina Totenberg, "The Supreme Court is the Most Conservative in 90 Years," NPR, July 5, 2022, www.npr.org/2022/07/05/1109444617/the-supreme-court-conservative.

28. In 1962, in *Baker v. Carr*, the Supreme Court decided that redistricting qualifies as a justiciable question under the Fourteenth Amendment's equal protection clause. This set the stage for *Wesberry v. Sanders* and *Reynolds v. Simms* two years later, in which the court decided that state and House districts must be based on population densities that are roughly equivalent, institutionalizing the "one person, one vote," principle. Quote comes from Reynolds v. Simms, 377 U.S. 533 (1964).

29. Steven Ansolabehere and James N. Snyder, *The End of Inequality: One Person, One Vote and the Transformation of American Politics* (New York: Norton, 2008).

30. For a review of this vast literature, see Eric McGhee, "Partisan Gerrymandering and Political Science," *Annual Review of Political Science* 23 (2020): 171–185.

31. Sam Wang, "The Great Gerrymander of 2012," *New York Times*, February 2, 2013. For an example of such literature, see, e.g., Nicholas Stephanopoulos and Eric McGhee, "Partisan Gerrymandering and the Efficiency Gap," *University of Chicago Law Review* 82, no. 2 (2015): 831–900.

32. By constitution or statute, fifteen states consider keeping "communities of interest" whole when drawing state legislative districts; eleven states do the same for congressional districts.

33. Analysis of vote returns in this section comes from the MIT Election Data and Science Lab, "U.S. House 1976–2022," 2023, https://doi.org/10.7910/DVN/IG0UN2.

34. During the 2002–2010 election cycles, the median district in Michigan, in terms of rurality, was roughly 22 percent. The median district in the United States was 15 percent. See appendixes, figure A6.1.

35. See Stephanopoulos and McGhee 2015.

36. Unfortunately, with this and other measures, we lack the ability to disentangle the effects of gerrymandering from the prorural bias of winner-take-all districts in a highly polarized context. Nevertheless, examining the trends before the 2010 redistricting cycle are instructive, given that considerable gerrymandering occurred then.

37. On Michigan, see Mike Wilkinson, "Maps Show How Gerrymandering Benefitted Michigan Republicans," Bridge Michigan, September 25, 2018, www.bridgemi.com/michigan-government /maps-show-how-gerrymandering-benefitted-michigan-republicans; Beth LeBlanc, "GOP Emails: Let's 'Cram Dem Garbage' into Southeast Michigan Districts," Detroit News, July 26, 2018, www .detroitnews.com/story/news/politics/2018/07/26/gop-emails-dem-garbage-gerrymander -lawsuit/838694002/. On North Carolina, see Vann R. Newkirk II, "The Supreme Court Finds North Carolina's Racial Gerrymandering Unconstitutional," The Atlantic, May 22, 2017.

38. Jonathan A. Rodden, Why Cities Lose (New York: Basic Books, 2019), chap. 6.

39. Jowei Chen and Jonathan Rodden, "Unintentional Gerrymandering: Political Geography and Electoral Bias in Legislatures," Quarterly Journal of Political Science 8, no. 3 (2013): 239–269.

40. Indeed, we would not necessarily consider it a representative case study of the modern presidency in social scientific terms.

41. See Kaiser Family Foundation, "KFF Health Tracking Poll July 2019: The Future of the ACA and Possible Changes to the Current System, Preview of Priorities Heading into 2nd Democratic Debate," figure 13, accessed March 5, 2022, www.kff.org/affordable-care-act /poll-finding/kff-health-tracking-poll-july-2019/.

42. Kaiser Family Foundation, "KFF Health Tracking Poll: The Public's Views on the ACA," accessed March 5, 2022, www.kff.org/interactive/kff-health-tracking-poll-the-publics-views-on -the-aca/#?response=Favorable--Unfavorable&aRange=twoYear.

43. Maggie Haberman and Robert Pear, "Trump Tells Congress to Repeal and Replace Health Care Law 'Very Quickly,'" New York Times, January 10, 2017.

44. CBS News, "Which Executive Orders Did Trump Sign on Day One?," January 21, 2017, https://www.cbsnews.com/news/which-executive-orders-did-trump-sign-on-day-1/.

45. Congressional Budget Office Cost Estimate, "H.R. 1628 American Health Care Act of 2017," May 24, 2017, https://www.cbo.gov/system/files/115th-congress-2017-2018/costestimate /hr1628aspassed.pdf.

46. David Blumenthal, "ACA Repeal Would Devastate Already Struggling Rural Communities," Commonwealth Fund, June 27, 2017, www.commonwealthfund.org/blog/2017/aca-repeal -would-devastate-already-struggling-rural-communities.

47. Chris Warshaw (@cwarshaw), "My analysis showing the historic unpopularity of the GOP health care and tax bills is summarized in an op-ed by @mtomasky in today's @nytimes," Twitter (now X), December 15, 2017, https://x.com/cwarshaw/status/941693043756994560.

48. Frank Newport, "Americans Remain Negative on Tax Bill After Its Passage," Gallup, January 10, 2018, https://news.gallup.com/poll/225137/americans-remain-negative-tax-bill -passage.aspx.

49. Jess Bravin, "Supreme Court Pares Back Federal Regulatory Power," Wall Street Journal, June 28, 2024, https://www.nytimes.com/2024/06/28/us/supreme-court-chevron-ruling .html.

Chapter Eight: Does Public Policy Help Mend the Divide?

1. Suzanne Mettler and Joe Soss, "The Consequences of Public Policy for Democratic Citizenship: Bridging Policy Studies and Mass Politics," *Perspectives on Politics* 2, no. 1 (2004): 55–73; Anne Schneider and Helen Ingram, "Social Constructions of Target Populations: Implications for Politics and Policy," *American Political Science Review* 87 (1993): 334–347.

2. Paul Pierson, "When Effect Becomes Cause: Policy Feedback and Political Change," *World Politics* 45, no. 4 (1993): 595–628.

3. The literature on these dynamics is now vast. For an overview, see Suzanne Mettler and Mallory SoRelle, "Policy Feedback Theory," in *Theories of the Policy Process*, ed. Christopher J. Weible, 5th ed. (New York: Routledge, 2023).

4. Jamila Michener, *Fragmented Democracy: Medicaid, Federalism, and Unequal Politics* (New York: Cambridge University Press); Pamela Herd and Donald P. Moynihan, *Administrative Burden: Policymaking by Other Means* (New York: Russell Sage, 2018); Suzanne Mettler, *The Submerged State: How Invisible Government Policies Undermine American Democracy* (Chicago: University of Chicago Press, 2011).

5. Suzanne Mettler, *Government-Citizen Disconnect* (New York: Russell Sage, 2018).

6. Such policies may help to make up for the loss of income from employment in rural areas, in effect compensating those who have suffered from international trade. See Jiwon Choi, Ilyana Kuziemko, Ebonya Washington, and Gavin Wright, "Local Economic and Political Effects of Trade Deals: Evidence from NAFTA," *American Economic Review* 114, no. 6 (2024): 1540–1575. Our findings are in accord with those of other scholars, who find higher proportionate use of federal social transfers in rural areas than in urban ones, and relatively more rural people lifted out of poverty by such policies. See James P. Ziliak, "Economic Change and the Social Safety Net: Are Rural Americans Still Behind?" (working paper series, Washington Center for Economic Growth, 2019); Robert Wuthnow, *The Left Behind: Decline and Rage in Rural America* (Princeton, NJ: Princeton University Press, 2018), chap. 5.

7. Kaiser Family Foundation, "Health Insurance of the Total Population, Timeframe 2023," accessed March 9, 2025, www.kff.org/other/state-indicator/total-population/?currentTimeframe=0&sortModel=%7B%22colId%22:%22Location%22,%22sort%22:%22asc%22%7D.

8. Christopher J. Howard, *The Welfare State Nobody Knows* (Princeton, NJ: Princeton University Press, 2007), 96–98; Colleen Grogan and Eric Patashnik, "Between Welfare Medicine and Mainstream Entitlement: Medicaid at the Crossroads," *Journal of Health Policy, Politics, and Law* 28, no. 5 (2003): 829–833.

9. Kaiser Family Foundation, "Status of State Medicaid Expansion Decisions: Interactive Map," May 8, 2024, www.kff.org/affordable-care-act/issue-brief/status-of-state-medicaid-expansion-decisions-interactive-map/.

10. Judith N. Shklar, *American Citizenship: The Quest for Inclusion* (Cambridge, MA: Harvard University Press, 1998).

11. Wuthnow 2018, 95–115; Jennifer Sherman, *Dividing Paradise: Rural Inequality and the Diminishing American Dream* (Oakland: University of California Press, 2021), 175–189; Loka Ashwood, *For-Profit Democracy: Why the Government Is Losing the Trust of Rural America* (New Haven, CT: Yale University Press, 2018).

12. Katherine J. Cramer, *The Politics of Resentment: Rural Consciousness in Wisconsin and the Rise of Scott Walker* (Chicago: University of Chicago Press, 2016), 72–84, 127–138, 166.

13. Sherman 2021, 169–172.

14. E.g., see Joe Soss, *Unwanted Claims: The Politics of Participation in the U.S. Welfare System* (Ann Arbor: University of Michigan Press, 2000).

15. E.g., see Cramer 2016; Jennifer Sherman, *Those Who Work, Those Who Don't: Poverty, Morality, and Family in Rural America* (Minneapolis: University of Minnesota Press, 2009).

16. Estimates based on data from the U.S. Census Bureau. See appendixes for details.

17. R. Rush-Marlowe, *Strengthening Rural Community Colleges: Innovations and Opportunities* (Washington, DC: Association of Community College Trustees, 2021).

18. Andrew Crookston and Gregory Hooks, "Community Colleges, Budget Cuts, and Jobs: The Impact of Community Colleges on Employment Growth in Rural U.S. Counties, 1976–2004," *Sociology of Education* 85, no. 4 (2012): 365. Also see David E. Hardy and Stephen G. Katsinas, "Classifying Community Colleges: How Rural Community Colleges Fit," *New Directions for Community Colleges*, Spring 2007, 5–17.

19. Suzanne Mettler, *Degrees of Inequality: How the Politics of Education Sabotaged the American Dream* (New York: Basic Books, 2014), 111–131.

20. Crookston and Hooks 2012, 353.

21. Rush-Marlowe 2021, 2.

22. Jennifer Ma and Matea Pender, *Trends in College Pricing and Student Aid* (New York: College Board, 2023), 3.

23. Mettler 2014, 21–38.

24. Isabel M. Perera and Desmond King, "Racial Pay Parity in the Public Sector: The Overlooked Role of Employee Mobilization," *Politics and Society* 49, no. 2 (2021): 181–202; European Commission, *Employment in Europe, Annual Report* (2010), https://ec.europa.eu/employment_social/eie/index_en.html; Michael Dawson, *Behind the Mule: Race and Class in African American Politics* (Princeton, NJ: Princeton University Press, 1994), chap. 2; George Wilson, Vincent J. Roscigno, and Matt Huffman, "Racial Income Inequality and Public Sector Privatization," *Social Problems* 62, no. 2 (2015): 163–185.

25. Cramer 2016, 111–144.

26. John M. Eason, "Prisons as Panacea or Pariah? The Countervailing Consequences of the Prison Boom on the Political Economy of Rural Towns," *Social Sciences* 6, no. 1 (2017): 12.

27. Adam Dean and Jonathan Obert, "Shocked into Service: Free Trade and the American South's Military Burden," *International Interactions* 46, no. 1 (2019): 51–81; Adam Dean, "NAFTA's Army: Free Trade and US Military Enlistment," *International Studies Quarterly* 62 (2018): 845–856.

28. Douglas Kriner and Francis Shen, *The Casualty Gap: The Causes and Consequences of American Wartime Inequalities* (Oxford, UK: Oxford University Press, 2010).

29. Mettler 2018, 29–53.

30. While we know that rural counties increasingly rely on social transfers and public programs and increasingly support the Republican Party, examining these patterns at the county level can introduce what scholars describe as "ecological fallacy" problems. It could be the case, for example, that program recipients are simply not voting, or alternatively, perhaps they are voting for Democrats, but at lower rates than those who do not support such benefits.

31. Because our analysis of voting behavior in chaps. 3 through 5 is buttressed by individual-level data and qualitative interviews, we are less concerned about ecological fallacy issues there.

32. Daniel Beland, Phillip Rocco, and Alex Waddan, "Policy Feedback and the Politics of the Affordable Care Act," *Policy Studies Journal* 47, no. 2 (2018): 395–422; Daniel J. Galvin and Chloe N. Thurston, "The Democrats' Misplaced Faith in Policy Feedback," *The Forum* 15, no. 2 (2017), 333–343; Jonathan Oberlander and R. Kent Weaver, "Unraveling from Within: The Affordable Care Act and Self-Undermining Policy Feedbacks," *The Forum* 13, no 1 (2017): 37–62; Eric Patashnik and Julian Zelizer, "The Struggle to Remake Politics: Liberal Reform and the Limits of Policy Feedback in the Contemporary American State," *Perspectives on Politics* 11, no. 4 (2013): 1071–1087.

33. Michael E. Shepherd Jr., "Unhealthy Democracy: How Partisan Politics Is Killing Rural America" (PhD diss., Vanderbilt University, 2021), chap. 5, "Dying for the Donald? The Politics of the Rural Hospital Crisis."

34. Suzanne Mettler, Lawrence R. Jacobs, and Ling Zhu, "Policy Threat, Partisanship, and the Case of the Affordable Care Act," *American Political Science Review* 117, no. 1 (2023): 296–310.

35. For a review of this growing literature, see Kristin F. Butcher, "Assessing the Long-Run Benefits of Transfers to Low-Income Families" (Hutchins Center Working Paper #26, 2017), www.brookings.edu/wp-content/uploads/2017/01/wp26_butcher_transfers_final.pdf.

36. Tony F. Pipa and Zoe Swarzenski, "Regional Clusters and Rural Development: To What Extent Does EDA's Build Back Better Regional Challenge Include Rural Areas?," Brookings Institution, August 4, 2023, www.brookings.edu/articles/regional-clusters-and-rural-development-to-what-extent-does-edas-build-back-better-regional-challenge-include-rural-areas/; Mildred E. Warner and Austin M. Aldag, "Pandemic Relief Spending by New York Local Governments," *Journal of Rural Studies* 104 (2023), https://doi.org/10.1016/j.jrurstud.2023.103157.

37. Tony F. Pipa and Elise Pietro, "What's In It for Rural? Analyzing the Opportunities for Rural America in IIJA, CHIPS, and IRA," Brookings Institution, December 18, 2023, www.brookings.edu/articles/whats-in-it-for-rural-analyzing-the-opportunities-for-rural-america-in-iija-chips-and-ira-2/.

38. Joseph Parilla, Glencora Haskins, Lily Bermel, et al., "Strategic Sector Investments Are Poised to Benefit Distressed US Counties," Brookings Institution, February 13, 2024, www.brookings.edu/articles/strategic-sector-investments-are-poised-to-benefit-distressed-us-counties/. This report separates the categories of "micropolitan" (counties with "at least one urban area with a population between 10,000 and 50,000") and "rural," but both are included in the categorization of "rural" that we employ in our analysis. Figure 7 shows that 50 percent of funds go to micropolitan counties and 9 percent to the smaller category they define as "rural." We combine these two, indicating that 59 percent go to rural counties.

39. Chhaya Kapadia and Chris Sadler, "Commentary: Broadband Subsidy Enrollment Ends Today; Millions are at Risk of Losing Internet," *Daily Yonder*, February 7, 2024.

40. Tim DeStefano and John W. Mayo, *What Do the Early Data Indicate About the Affordable Connectivity Program?* (Georgetown University, McDonough School of Business, Center for Business and Public Policy, October 2023), https://cbpp.georgetown.edu/news/destefano-and-mayo-research-on-the-affordable-connectivity-program-shows-encouraging-signs-for-success/.

41. George W. Zuo, "Wired and Hired: Employment Effects of Subsidized Broadband Internet for Low-Income Americans," *American Economic Journal: Economic Policy* 13, no. 3 (2021): 447–482; Blair Levin, "The End of the Affordable Connectivity Program Is Almost Here, Threatening to Widen the Digital Divide," Brookings Institution, February 13, 2024, www.brookings.edu/articles/the-end-of-the-affordable-connectivity-program-is-almost-here-threatening-to-widen-the-digital-divide/.

42. Data permitting examination of these questions were not available before this book went to press.

Chapter Nine: A Path Forward

1. Six states that did ratify the ERA have since rescinded the decision, and all of them are among the nation's more rural states: Idaho, Kentucky, Nebraska, South Dakota, Tennessee—and, in 2021, North Dakota. A few other states have recently voted to ratify it, but long after the period for doing so expired, too late to make a difference.

2. Daniel J. Galvin, *Presidential Party Building: Dwight D. Eisenhower to George W. Bush* (Princeton, NJ: Princeton University Press, 2010), 3.

3. Neil Vigdor, Alexandra Berzon, and Nick Corasaniti, "Trump Meddler in Michigan, Matthew DePerno, Is Charged in Election Breach," *New York Times*, August 1, 2023.

4. Ali Swenson, "Fact Focus: Gaping Holes in the Claim of 2K Ballot 'Mules,'" Associated Press, May 3, 2022, https://apnews.com/article/2022-midterm-elections-covid-technology -health-arizona-e1b49d2311bf900f44fa5c6dac406762. In 2024, the producer issued an apology for the movie after learning that its contents were unfounded. "A Belated Apology for '2000 Mules,'" *Wall Street Journal*, June 6, 2024.

5. Website of the Grassroots Army, accessed March 2025, https://thegrassrootsarmy.com.

6. To be sure, being the minority party is challenging no matter which party one is in, as became evident in interviews with Republican leaders in rural counties dominated by Black Democrats. Said Hazel Lane, in eastern Georgia, "The biggest challenge is identifying Black people in the county who are conservative: They are so afraid. They won't come to our meetings. They don't want friends and neighbors to know they are conservative." In most rural counties, however, it is Democrats who are fearful of making their politics known.

7. He credited an organizer from New York who came to the county and trained canvassers, who used Vote Builder.

8. Kyle Ingram, "With Results Certified, Democrats Officially Break NC GOP's Supermajority—by One Seat," *News and Observer* (Raleigh), January 7, 2025; Alex Baltzegar, "NC Legislature Adds to Growing List of Overridden Cooper Vetoes: Elections, Energy, and Regulatory Reform," *Carolina Journal*, October 10, 2023.

9. Matt Bai, "The Inside Agitator," *New York Times*, October 1, 2006.

10. Galvin 2010, 1.

11. Senator Chuck Schumer, "User Clip: Every Blue Collar Democrat," C-SPAN, July 28, 2016, www.c-span.org/video/?c4632402/user-clip-blue-collar-democrat.

12. Jonathan Rodden, *Why Cities Lose: The Deep Roots of the Urban-Rural Political Divide* (New York: Basic Books, 2019).

13. Galvin 2010, 233–242.

14. Bai 2006.

15. Elaine C. Kamarck, "Assessing Howard Dean's Fifty State Strategy and the 2006 Midterm Elections," *The Forum* 4, no. 3 (2006): 1.

16. Bai 2006.

17. Galvin 2010, 243.

18. Kamarck 2006, 2.

19. Galvin 2010, 243.

20. Kamarck 2006, 4.

21. Kamarck 2006, 4.

22. Kamarck concedes that some of the thirty-nine districts benefited from financial contributions from the DCCC, yet when she assesses the dollar amounts given to the districts, she observes that organization made a significant difference even in those districts that received less than $10,000 from the DCCC.

23. Kamarck 2006, 6–7, quote on 6.

24. Galvin 2010, 259–260.

25. Ari Berman, "The Prophet," *The Nation*, December 17, 2008. Also see Mike Madden, "Obama's Debt to Howard Dean," *Salon*, November 12, 2008; Ari Berman, "The Dean Legacy," *The Nation*, February 28, 2008.

26. Barack Obama, "Remarks Appointing Tim Kaine as Chairman of the Democratic National Committee," American Presidency Project, January 8, 2009, www.presidency.ucsb.edu /documents/remarks-announcing-the-appointment-tim-kaine-chairman-the-democratic -national-committee.

27. Obama 2009.

28. Micah L. Sifry, "Obama's Lost Army," *New Republic*, February 9, 2017, https://newrepublic
.com/article/140245/obamas-lost-army-inside-fall-grassroots-machine.

29. Quoted in Peter Dreier and Marshall Ganz, "We Have Hope; Where's the Audacity?,"
Washington Post, August 30, 2009.

30. Galvin 2010, 261.

31. Sifry 2017, including quote.

32. Daniel Schlozman, "Beltway Blues," *Dissent*, Summer 2018, 16, 17.

Chapter Ten: Conclusion

1. Danny Hayes and Jennifer L. Lawless, *News Hole: The Demise of Local Journalism and
Political Engagement* (New York: Cambridge University Press, 2021).

2. B. Kal Munis and Robert P. Saldin, *Gone Country: Why Democrats Need to Play in Rural
America, and How They Can Do It Again* (Niskanen Center, March 2021).

3. Suzanne Mettler and Robert C. Lieberman, *Four Threats: The Recurring Crises of American
Democracy* (New York: St. Martin's Press, 2020).

4. Larry M. Bartels and Nicholas Carnes, "House Republicans Were Rewarded for Supporting Donald Trump's 'Stop the Steal' Efforts," *Proceedings of the National Academy of Sciences* 120,
no. 34 (2023), https://www.pnas.org/doi/10.1073/pnas.2309072120.

5. Jonathan Rodden, "Keeping Your Enemies Close: Electoral Rules and Partisan Polarization," in *Who Gets What?: The New Politics of Insecurity*, ed. Frances McCall Rosenbluth and
Margaret Weir (Cambridge, UK: Cambridge University Press, 2021), 129–160; Will Horne,
James Adams, and Noam Gidron, "The Way We Were: How Histories of Co-Governance Allevi-
ate Partisan Hostility," *Comparative Political Studies* 56, no. 3 (2023): 299–325.

6. Moving to a multiparty, proportional representation system would require that Congress
repeal the 1967 Uniform Congressional District Act, which bans a House district from electing
more than one representative.

7. To be sure, the same could be said about how Democrats craft policies in urban areas,
particular those that affect people marginalized by race and class.

Appendixes

1. For the OMB definition, see USDA, "What Is Rural?," 2024, www.ers.usda.gov/topics
/rural-economy-population/rural-classifications/what-is-rural/.

2. For a discussion of these changes, see USDA, "Background: Documentation of Rural,"
2024, https://www.ers.usda.gov/data-products/rural-urban-continuum-codes/documentation
/#background.

3. E.g., see Brian C. Thiede, Jaclyn L. W. Butler, David L. Brown, and Leif Jensen, "Income
Inequality Across the Rural-Urban Continuum in the United States, 1970–2016," *Rural Sociology*
85, no. 4 (2020): 899–937.

4. We would also note that several scholars have argued that political behavior can be placed
on a spectrum, most notably a nine-point scale that elaborates on the OMB's classification to
make it more granular. E.g., see Dante J. Scala and Kenneth Johnson, "Political Polarization
Along the Rural-Urban Continuum? The Geography of the Presidential Vote, 2000–2016," *Annals of the American Academy of Political and Social Science* 672, no. 1 (2017): 162–184. Yet as it
turns out, we do not lose much explanatory power if we collapse the spectrum. For an alternative view on the rural-urban continuum, see Zoe Nemerever and Melissa Rogers, "Measuring
the Rural Continuum in Political Science," *Political Analysis* 29, no. 3 (2021): 267–286.

5. See U.S. Census, "The Urban and Rural Classifications," accessed March 1, 2020, www2
.census.gov/geo/pdfs/reference/GARM/Ch12GARM.pdf.

6. David A. Bateman, Ira Katznelson, and John S. Lapinski, *Southern Nation: Congress and White Supremacy After Reconstruction* (Princeton, NJ: Princeton University Press, 2018).

7. David Leip's Atlas of U.S. Presidential Elections, "County-Level Election Returns," various years, https://uselectionatlas.org/BOTTOM/store_data.php.

8. See also Trevor E. Brown, Gisela Pedroza Jauregui, Suzanne Mettler, and Marissa Rivera, "A Rural-Urban Political Divide Among Whom? Race, Ethnicity, and Political Behavior Across Place," *Politics, Groups, and Identities* 13, no. 1 (2024): 229–242.

9. Angelo Dagonel, "Cumulative CES Policy Preferences," Harvard Dataverse, 2021, https://doi.org/10.7910/DVN/OSXDQO.

10. See supplementary material in Brown et al. 2024.

11. American National Election Studies (ANES), "Time Series Cumulative Data File, 1948–2020," 2021, https://electionstudies.org/data-center/anes-time-series-cumulative-data-file/.

12. Bureau of Economic Analysis, Various Economic, Employment, and Personal Income Data, by County, U.S. Department of Commerce, Regional Data Tables, 2022, https://apps.bea.gov/histdatacore/HistFileDetails.html?HistCateID=5&FileGroupID=294.

13. U.S. Census Bureau, "Decennial Census of Population and Housing Data," various years, www.census.gov/programs-surveys/decennial-census/data.html.

14. For a discussion, see Andrew M. Isserman and James Westervelt, "1.5 Million Missing Numbers: Overcoming Employment Suppression in County Business Patterns Data," *International Regional Science Review* 29, no. 3 (2006): 311–335.

15. Pamela Herd and Donald P. Moynihan, *Administrative Burden Policymaking by Other Means* (New York: Russell Sage Foundation, 2018).

16. Department of Labor, "TAA Overview," accessed March 22, 2022, www.dol.gov/agencies/eta/tradeact/data.

17. Bureau of Economic Analysis, *Local Area Personal Income and Employment: Concepts and Methods* (2024), 14, www.bea.gov/system/files/methodologies/BEA-Local-Area-Personal-Income-and-Employment-Concepts-and-Methods.pdf.

18. U.S. Census Bureau, "Small Area Income and Poverty Estimates: 2019," www.census.gov/library/publications/2020/demo/p30-08.html.

19. Bureau of Economic Analysis, "Regional Economic Accounts: Regional Definitions," accessed March 2, 2020, https://apps.bea.gov/regional/definitions.

20. Bureau of Economic Analysis 2022.

21. The one noteworthy deviation is that in period two (1992–2004), rural becomes significant with this dependent variable.

22. See discussion of evangelical churches.

23. For similar use of this, see Nathan J. Kelly and Christopher Witko, "Federalism and American Inequality," *Journal of Politics* 74, no. 2 (2012): 422, n. 7, https://doi.org/10.1017/S0022381611001678.

24. Nathaniel Beck, "Time-Series–Cross-Section Data: What Have We Learned in the Past Few Years?," *Annual Review of Political Science* 4, no. 1 (2001), https://doi.org/10.1146/annurev.polisci.4.1.271.

25. Margaret M. Weden, Christine E. Peterson, Jeremy N. Miles, and Regina A. Shih, "Evaluating Linearly Interpolated Intercensal Estimates of Demographic and Socioeconomic Characteristics of US Counties and Census Tracts 2001–2009," *Population Research and Policy Review* 34 (2015), https://doi.org/10.1007/s11113-015-9359-8.

26. U.S. Census Bureau, "Decennial Census of Population and Housing Data," various years, www.census.gov/programs-surveys/decennial-census/data.html.

27. American National Election Studies, *ANES Time Series Cumulative Data File: Codebook* (2022), 572, https://electionstudies.org/wp-content/uploads/2022/09/anes_timeseries_cdf_codebook_var_20220916.pdf.

28. Katherine Cramer, "Understanding the Role of Racism in Contemporary US Public Opinion," *Annual Review of Political Science* 23, no. 1 (2020), https://doi.org/10.1146/annurev-polisci-060418-042842.

29. For evidence of racial/ethnic threat affecting political behavior, see Ryan D. Enos, "What the Demolition of Public Housing Teaches Us About the Impact of Racial Threat on Political Behavior," *American Journal of Political Science* 60, no. 1 (2016), https://doi.org/10.1111/ajps.12156.

30. U.S. Census Bureau, "Decennial Census of Population and Housing Data," various years, www.census.gov/programs-surveys/decennial-census/data.html.

31. Data were retrieved from John-Paul Ferguson's personal website, accessed July 4, 2023, https://github.com/jpfergongithub.

32. C. Grammich, K. Hadaway, R. Houseal, et al., "Longitudinal Religious Congregations and Membership File (County Level)," Association of Religion Data Archives, November 29, 2018, www.thearda.com/data-archive?fid=RCMSMGCY.

33. National Rifle Association, "NRA Explore: Locate Clubs and Ranges Near You," accessed July 5, 2022, https://explore.nra.org/interests/clubs-and-associations/.

34. Bureau of Economic Analysis 2024, 14.

35. Right to Life Michigan, "Affiliates," accessed August 5, 2022, https://rtl.org/affiliates/.

36. Bureau of Economic Analysis 2024, 14.

37. District-level data on rurality come from various iterations of: U.S. Census Bureau, "Decennial Census of Population and Housing Data," various years, www.census.gov/programs-surveys/decennial-census/data.html.

38. Jeffrey B. Lewis, Keith Poole, Howard Rosenthal, Adam Boche, Aaron Rudkin, and Luke Sonnet, Congressional Roll-Call Votes Database, Voteview, 2025, https://voteview.com/.

39. District-level data on rurality, education, age, and racial demographics come from various iterations of: U.S. Census Bureau, "Decennial Census of Population and Housing Data," various years, www.census.gov/programs-surveys/decennial-census/data.html.

40. Bureau of Economic Analysis 2024, 14.

41. Bureau of Economic Analysis 2024, 14.

42. Jeffrey B. Lewis, Keith Poole, Howard Rosenthal, Adam Boche, Aaron Rudkin, and Luke Sonnet, Congressional Roll-Call Votes Database, Voteview, 2024, https://voteview.com/.

43. Bureau of Economic Analysis 2024, 14.

44. Nicholas O. Stephanopoulos and Eric M. McGhee. "Partisan Gerrymandering and the Efficiency Gap," *University of Chicago Law Review* 82 (2015), https://heinonline.org/HOL/P?h=hein.journals/uclr82&i=843.

45. MIT Election Data and Science Lab, "U.S. House 1976–2022," 2023, https://doi.org/10.7910/DVN/IG0UN2.

46. Bureau of Economic Analysis, "Regional Economic Accounts: Regional Definitions," accessed March 21, 2021, https://apps.bea.gov/regional/definitions/.

47. Bureau of Economic Analysis 2022.

48. Federal Reserve Bank of Minneapolis, "Consumer Price Index, 1913–," accessed March 21, 2021, www.minneapolisfed.org/about-us/monetary-policy/inflation-calculator/consumer-price-index-1913-.

49. Bureau of Economic Analysis 2024, 14.

50. Bureau of Economic Analysis 2022.

51. Federal Reserve Bank of Minneapolis, "Consumer Price Index, 1913–."

52. Bureau of Economic Analysis 2024, 14.

53. Bureau of Economic Analysis 2022.

54. Bureau of Economic Analysis 2024, 14.

55. See Jonathan Rodden, "The Great Recession and the Public Sector in Rural America," *Journal of Economic Geography* 24, no. 3 (2024), https://doi.org/10.1093/jeg/lbad015.

56. Department of Defense, Defense Casualty Analysis System, U.S. Military Casualties, accessed March 16, 2022, https://dcas.dmdc.osd.mil/dcas/app/home.

57. Bureau of Economic Analysis 2024, 14.

58. National Center for Education Statistics, various years, https://nces.ed.gov/ipeds/use-the-data.

59. Bureau of Economic Analysis 2024, 14.

60. MIT Election Data and Science Lab 2023.

61. Federal Election Commission, "Federal Election Results," various years, www.fec.gov/introduction-campaign-finance/election-results-and-voting-information/.

INDEX

Page numbers in *italics* refer to figures and tables

A NOTE ON THE TYPE

This book has been composed in Arno, an Old-style serif typeface in the classic Venetian tradition, designed by Robert Slimbach at Adobe.